THE GILL HISTORY OF IRELAND

General Editors: JAMES LYDON, PH.D.
MARGARET MACCURTAIN, PH.D.

Other titles in the series

Ireland before the Vikings   GEAROID MAC NIOCAILL
Ireland before the Normans   DONNCHA O CORRAIN
Anglo-Norman Ireland   MICHAEL DOLLEY
Gaelic and Gaelicised Ireland in the Middle Ages   KENNETH NICHOLLS
Ireland in the Later Middle Ages   JAMES LYDON
Tudor and Stuart Ireland   MARGARET MACCURTAIN
Ireland in the Eighteenth Century   EDITH MARY JOHNSTON
Ireland before the Famine, 1798–1848   GEAROID O TUATHAIGH
The Modernisation of Irish Society, 1848–1918   JOSEPH LEE
Ireland in the Twentieth Century   JOHN A. MURPHY

THE CHURCH IN MEDIEVAL IRELAND

John Watt

GILL AND MACMILLAN

Published by
Gill and Macmillan Ltd
2 Belvedere Place
Dublin 1
and in association with the
Macmillan
Group of Publishing Companies

Cover design by Cor Klaasen

Illustration: St Canice's Cathedral in Kilkenny
from James Graves and Prim: The History, Architecture
and Antiquities of the Cathedral Church of St Canice,
Kilkenny (National Library of Ireland)

7171 0562 8

Printed and bound in the Republic of Ireland by the
Richview Press Limited, Dublin

Contents

Foreword

Acknowledgements

1. THE REFORM OF THE CHURCH IN
   THE TWELFTH CENTURY   1

2. THE PAPACY, HENRY II AND THE
   IRISH CHURCH   28

3. THE RELIGIOUS ORDERS, 1127–1340   41
   Monks and Canons, 1127–1230   41
   Dominicans and Franciscans, 1224–1340   60
   Carmelites and Augustinians, 1272–1334   85

4. THE CHANGING EPISCOPATE IN
   THE THIRTEENTH CENTURY   87
   The Anglicisation of the Episcopate   87
   The Archbishops of Cashel, 1186–1316   110
   The Archbishops of Dublin, 1181–1306   116

5. THE RULE OF LAW 130
   Ireland and the Papacy 130
   Provincial legislation 150
   Courts ecclesiastical and civil 171

6. THE CENTURY BEFORE THE
   REFORMATION 181
   The Church in decline 181
   The Friars and reform 193
   The Laity 202

Conclusion 215

Glossary 218

Bibliography 221

References 226

Index 229

MAPS
1. Diocesan centres established at the Council of
   Rathbreasail (1111) and modified at the
   Council of Kells (1152) 25
2. Cistercian Houses in 1228 55
3. Dominican Houses, 1224–1305 63
4. Franciscan Houses, 1229–1336 72
5. Diocesan structure in the thirteenth century 93

TABLES
1. The Growth of the Friars, 1220–1340 61
2. Anglicisation of dioceses, 1178–1333 88

Foreword

THE study of Irish history has changed greatly in recent decades as more evidence becomes available and new insights are provided by the growing number of historians. It is natural, too, that with each generation new questions should be asked about our past. The time has come for a new large-scale history. It is the aim of the Gill History of Ireland to provide this. This series of studies of Irish history, each written by a specialist, is arranged chronologically. But each volume is intended to stand on its own and no attempt has been made to present a uniform history. Diversity of analysis and interpretation is the aim; a group of young historians have tried to express the view of their generation on our past. It is the hope of the editors that the series will help the reader to appreciate in a new way the rich heritage of Ireland's history.

JAMES LYDON, PH.D.
MARGARET MACCURTAIN, PH.D.

Acknowledgements

I should like to record my deep sense of personal debt to Fr Aubrey Gwynn, S.J., *doyen* of Irish medieval ecclesiastical studies, without whose work, even to attempt a book like this would have been impossible. I am very grateful to Dr E. F. D. Roberts of the National Library of Scotland, Mr K. W. Nicholls and Mr A. P. Wells who very kindly allowed me a preview of their important forthcoming publications. Rev. Dr M. B. Crowe was of great assistance to me in supplying me with periodical literature which I found difficult to locate. So too were Miss Susan Appleton and Mrs Sheena Haines for typing and secretarial services. Mr Derek Waite of the Hull University Library Drawing Service prepared material for the maps and chronological charts. I am very grateful, too, to my wife Marianne who has helped considerably at every stage in the writing of this book.

J. A. WATT

1 The Reform of the Church in the Twelfth Century

A FRESH spirit of renewal breathed through the Irish Church in the century before the Anglo-French Invasion. Historians might disagree slightly as to the precise point when the 'reformation and revolution' began.[1] For one, it might be the series of royal pilgrimages to Rome in the years 1028–64, the first overt symptom of a break-out from that isolation from the rest of the universal Church which had become a feature of the Irish Church in the Dark Ages. For another, it might well be the year 1074 when the clergy and people of Dublin asked Lanfranc, archbishop of Canterbury to consecrate their bishop-elect, Patrick, and thereby initiated (if indeed it had not begun earlier) a connexion between Canterbury and the Norse-Irish sees which lasted over half a century. For another again, it might be with the letter of uncertain date which Gregory VII (1073–85) addressed to Turlough O Brien, king of Munster, when the official voice of the Church broke a silence towards Ireland which had lasted, apparently, since the year 640. All historians would take seriously the view that the council of Cashel of 1101, the first of the reforming councils which brought great changes in the canon law and ecclesiastical structure of the Irish Church, marked the formal beginning of the twelfth-century *aggiornamento*.

Whichever date or event or document or personality is chosen is not perhaps of great consequence. The important point for the historian to record is that in the last quarter of the eleventh century, different parts of the Irish

Church were receptive towards outside influences in the cause of reform. As the twelfth century progressed, other parts of Ireland and other outside influences became involved. A wide variety of churchmen and zealous laity in Ireland sought to turn to constructive use a multiplicity of foreign influences.

Chronologically the first of these influences for which any substantial documentation has survived was the product of the link between Dublin and Canterbury. The beginnings of this connexion remain obscure. In 1074 the Dubliners assured Archbishop Lanfranc that they had always submitted happily to the jurisdiction of his predecessors, 'from whom we are mindful we received ecclesiastical rule'. Lanfranc in reply agreed that in consecrating Patrick as bishop of Dublin he was acting according to the custom of his predecessors. But no other evidence of any previous custom has survived. The establishment of the diocese seems to have owed something to the initiative of Sitric, Norse king of Dublin (d.1042), possibly a consequence of his pilgrimage to Rome in 1028. The suggestion that the first bishop of Dublin, Dunan or Donatus, was consecrated at Canterbury may mean that the origin of the see owed something too to Anglo-Scandinavian influences. It was almost certainly tension between the Irish and the 'foreigners of Dublin', as the contemporary Irish annals describe them, which made the Dubliners look outside Ireland for assistance in establishing their new diocese. There may well have been also a canonical reason for going outside Ireland in that there is some evidence (contained in the letter of Lanfranc given later in this chapter) that at this time the Irish practice of episcopal consecration was at variance with the practice of the universal Church.

Whatever the factors which forged the link between Dublin and Canterbury, it is certain that the consecration of Bishop Patrick by Lanfranc in 1074 began a connexion between the Norse-Irish episcopate and England of some force in the winds of change which were to blow through the Irish Church in the twelfth century. Four, probably five, bishops-elect of Dublin, one of Waterford and one of Limerick were canonically examined and consecrated by archbishops of Canterbury and swore canonical obedience to them. Four of these were formerly monks in the Canterbury province. Bishop Patrick of Dublin was a monk of Worcester, trained in the school of the great St Wulfstan. Donngus, his successor in Dublin (1085–95) was a monk under Lanfranc at Canterbury. Bishop Samuel (1096–1121) was a monk of St Alban's. The first bishop of Waterford, Malchus (1096–1135), was a monk of Winchester.

It was not only that these prelates had close personal links with Canterbury. There was a formal, canonical bond. These Norse-Irish bishops swore canonical submission to Canterbury and that in a form which acknowledged Canterbury's primacy over Ireland. The canonical oath in its standardised form is typified by that sworn in 1096:[2]

> I, Samuel, having been chosen for the rule of the Church of Dublin which is situated in Ireland and being about to be consecrated by you, reverend father Anselm, archbishop of the holy Church of Canterbury and primate of all Britain [*totius Britanniae primas*: to be read possibly as inclusive of Ireland], do promise that I shall keep canonical obedience in all things to you and to all your successors.

It is of more consequence to examine the practical consequences of this bond for Ireland rather than the claim to primacy itself. But something must be said, partly because of its intrinsic interest and partly because it may have had some influence in the preliminaries to the Invasion.

The claim that Canterbury held primacy over Ireland was first ventilated in Lanfranc's justification of Canterbury's primacy over York. In 1072, after Pope Alexander II had ordered an examination of the ancient traditions of the English Church, Lanfranc informed the Pope that historical investigation demonstrated that 'from the time of the blessed Augustine, first archbishop of Canterbury to the time of Bede . . . my predecessors exercised primacy over the church of York, over the whole of the island called Britain, as well as over Ireland'. It was in 1074 when Bishop Patrick was making his submission that Lanfranc called himself for the first time *Britanniarum primas* (primate of the Britains), in a formula designed to express the whole of the primatial claim he had put to the pope. His justification of the claim was purely historical and rested on an optimistic interpretation of Bede's *Ecclesiastical History of the English People* 2.4:

> In short, he [Laurence, Augustine's successor] not only took care of the new church formed among the English, but endeavoured also to employ his pastoral solicitude among the ancient inhabitants of Britain, as also the Scots, who inhabit the island of Ireland, which is next to Britain.

Lanfranc was able to exploit the Dublin connexion as the contemporary practical implementation of this claim and he and the champions of his successors (such as Eadmer claiming to voice the view of St Anselm) continued to assert against York the principle that Canterbury was primate of all England, Scotland, Ireland and the adjoining islands. Ireland entered into the English primatial dispute as an incidental to the main issue. We may surmise that it was mentioned at all not so much because archbishops of Canterbury thought it of any great urgency to vindicate claims over that country as because it helped to buttress the argument against York. The more geographically extensive Canterbury's primacy, the more impressive its solidity.

Historians sometimes speak of Dublin and the other Norse-Irish sees as suffragans of the Canterbury province and there is some contemporary evidence to justify this description. But these dioceses were not a constituent part of the province. Bishops of these sees are not to be discovered playing any role in councils or judicial proceedings. Save for an occasional appearance at consecrations they did not participate in the life of Canterbury. The archbishops of Canterbury for their part gave help in the form of consecrating bishops, gifts of books and church ornaments, training of monks. Little is known in detail of this assistance. Rather more is known of another sort of help – the instruction, advice and occasionally rebuke which was proferred from time to time. There survive five letters which Lanfranc sent to different people in Ireland and eight written by St Anselm. They are for the most part admonitory and their general tone and substance are well illustrated in this letter written in 1074 by Lanfranc to Turlough O Brien:

Lanfranc, sinner and unworthy archbishop of the holy church of Canterbury to Terdelvacus, magnificent king of Ireland, blessing with service and prayers.

God grants no greater mercy to a land than when he raises to the government of souls and bodies those who love peace and justice, and most especially when he entrusts the kingdoms of this world to the rule of good kings. For hence comes peace, strife is calmed and (to include everything in brief) observance of the Christian religion is made firm. The intelligent observer understands that God conferred this gift on the peoples of Ireland when he granted the right of royal power over this land to your excellency. For our brother and fellow-bishop Patrick had told us so many and so great qualities of your highness, your gentleness and kindness towards the good, your strict severity towards the evil, your most careful justice towards all human kind, that though we have never seen you, yet we love you as though we had and desire to counsel you profitably and to help you most sincerely as though we had seen you and knew you well.

To speak truth, however, among many pleasing things, some things have been reported to us which are not pleasing. It is reported that in your kingdom a man will abandon his lawfully wedded wife at his own will, without any canonical process taking place and with a temerity deserving of punishment, takes to himself some other wife who may be of his own kin or of the kindred of the wife whom he has abandoned, or whom another has abandoned with similar wickedness, according to a law of marriage which is rather a law of fornication; that bishops are consecrated by one bishop only; that many bishops are ordained in towns and cities; that at baptism children are baptized without consecrated chrism; that holy orders are conferred by bishops for money.

All these practices and any others like them are contrary to the authority of the Gospels and the Apostles, contrary to prohibitions of the holy canons, contrary to the teaching of all the orthodox Fathers who have gone before us: as is well known to all who have even a little theological knowledge. The more these practices are detestable in the sight of God and his saints, the more earnestly must you forbid them by your orders without any delay, and if what you have forbidden is not corrected, you must punish the offenders by the strict severity of your wrath. For you can offer no greater nor more acceptable gift to God than your zeal to rule both divine and human affairs by binding laws.

Being mindful, therefore, of the divine judgment at

which you must render account to God of the kingdom he has entrusted to you, command the bishops and religious to come together in unity, show your own presence with your nobles to this holy assembly and strive to rid your kingdom of all these evil customs and all others contrary to the laws of the Church, so that the king of kings and lord of lords, seeing your royal majesty obedient in all respects to his commandments, that you are clement to his servants and his faithful for fear and love of him and that you are a zealous opponent of the enemies of his divine religion, may hear in mercy your prayers and the prayers of your loyal subjects who cry to him, crush your enemies and grant you lasting peace in this world and life everlasting in the world to come.

This letter shows Lanfranc urging the king of Munster and his clergy to extirpate certain evils – a defective marriage law and sexual ethic, maladministration of the sacraments, excessive multiplication of bishops, simony. Here was the adumbration of much of the reformers' programme. Here too was the suggestion of the chief means of initiating reform – in a council of senior clergy with lay participation. It is possible that Turlough's Dublin council of 1084 (of which nothing is known in detail) was one of the consequences of Lanfranc's advice. St Anselm was to press similar views on Turlough's son Murtagh, not long before the first major reform council which met at Cashel in 1101. As made even more clear in a second letter, Anselm was especially concerned with two faults: marriage practices ('It is said that men exchange their wives as freely and publicly as a man might change his horse') and the consecration of bishops without their having a defined diocesan area allocated to their pastoral care.

It will not have escaped notice that though the formal

7

connexion was between Canterbury and Dublin, there were informal contacts between Lanfranc and Anselm and the kings of Munster. The name O Brien indeed occurs in all contexts of the reform movements in its opening stages: Donnchad was on pilgrimage to Rome in 1064; it was to Turlough that Lanfranc wrote in 1074 and Pope Gregory VII sometime afterwards; Murtagh corresponded with St Anselm and with his brother Dermot, was associated with the request to Canterbury in 1096 for consecration of Waterford's first bishop; when Limerick received its first bishop, 1106–7, it had recently become Murtagh's principal city. It is clear that the primary impulse for reform came from Munster. The great symbol of this leadership came in 1101. The council held at Cashel in that year is notable for three things. Firstly, the dramatic Rock of Cashel, a royal seat and fortress since prehistoric times, was solemnly handed over to the Church by Murtagh free of any lay encumbrance. Its career as the seat of the metropolitans of the Munster province began with this grant, though as yet the title 'archbishop of Cashel' was not known to canon law. Secondly, a programme of reform by conciliar decree was initiated. Thirdly, Maol Muire O Doonan 'chief bishop of Munster', presided over this council not merely in his capacity as 'chief bishop' but as 'chief legate . . . with authority from the pope himself'. Thus began a formal link with the papacy through papal legates which associated the reform movement directly with Rome and lasted down to the times of Innocent III and Honorius III when the Anglo-French colony was already in being.

The decrees of the council of Cashel have come to us in terse and sometimes ambiguous form. Their brevity and occasional obscurity should not, however, be allowed to mask the importance of the issues involved: simony, the quality of the clergy, freedom of the Church, clerical celibacy, clerical privilege, matrimonial law. These were the characteristic issues of reform programmes throughout Christendom in this period. Yet the three decrees making reference to erenaghs which in the context must be read as meaning abbots give this legislation its distinctively Irish note. The decrees have survived in an Irish version but not in Latin.[3] There is some discussion among the experts about the rendering of certain words; the reader must be referred to Fr Gwynn's lucid exposition of this technically complex problem.[4]

There were old and new elements in these canons. In certain respects the legislation was an attempt to consolidate and extend earlier legislation, notably the provisions freeing churches from subjection to lay lords and the correction of abuse of sanctuary. On the other hand, the decree on marriage marked the first step in a projected revolution, constituting a root and branch attack on the bases of Irish familial society. But it would not in itself have met all the criticisms held about Irish customary matrimonial law made by a Lanfranc or a St Anselm. In this context, the reformers had an uphill task. There was to be criticism of Irish marriage and sexual practices by the papacy later in the century and by others in the later middle ages. If English observers are to be believed, some serious defects had not been eradicated even by the sixteenth century. Also new, though consonant with the traditions of the early Irish Church, was the legislation insisting that abbots should be celibate priests. This principle was to win more immediate acceptance. It was put into practice within a few years of the council and that in Armagh itself.

From 996, the *comarba* (heirs, successors) of St Patrick in Armagh had been selected from the ranks of Clann Sinaich. They were married men and unordained. They held the position of abbot of the unreformed monastery of Armagh, having custody of the staff of Jesus and other Patrician relics, administering the lands of the abbey and levying, where possible, the tribute traditionally due throughout the country to Patrick's heirs. In 1105 the family's monopoly of the office was continued with the succession of Celsus (Cellach). But he became a priest and the following year, while on circuit in Munster collecting tribute, was ordained 'eminent bishop', possibly by Bishop O Doonan, leader of the reformers of that province and papal legate. This consecration marked the reception of Armagh into the fold of the reformers and an important step forward in the progress of their cause.

Very shortly after this significant event, the reformers received another accession of strength in the person of Gilbert (Gilla Espuic), first to be consecrated bishop of Limerick. The establishment of a see in the chief town of the O Briens in part continued the Norse-Irish and O Brien link with Canterbury. For Gilbert, though not consecrated at Canterbury (his successor was to be) was a friend of St Anselm and maintained contact with Canterbury both by letter and by personal visit. Gilbert of Limerick has a double claim to fame in the story of the twelfth-century reform. He was to be papal legate for some twenty eight years and in that capacity presided over the council of Rathbreasail (1111) which began the all-important process of restructuring the Irish episcopal system. He was also to be the only known theorist of reform in Ireland with his treatise *De statu ecclesiae* (Concerning Church Order), written after he had been appointed papal legate.

The basic flaw in the constitutional structure of the Irish Church in the early twelfth century was that there were too many bishops and their powers were too weak. Lanfranc had complained that numerous bishops were consecrated for single towns and cities. When the council of Rathbreasail assembled there is reason to believe that more than fifty bishops were present and it is likely there were other bishops in Ireland who were not at the council.

This superabundance of prelates is far from being evidence of overgovernment of the Church. It is on the contrary, evidence of its loose and archaic structure, a symptom of organisational weakness. The Irish Church was not organised on territorial diocesan lines. The focal points of ecclesiastical organisation had for long been the monasteries, Armagh, Derry, Clonard, Kells, Clonmacnois, Cong, Emly, Lismore, Glendaloch and the rest. Almost all jurisdictional authority had come into the hands of the abbots of these houses who might or might not be bishops. The status of a bishop was thus non-jurisdictional and the connexion between the episcopate and the power of jurisdiction (ecclesiastical government) as well as the power of order (to ordain) which the rest of the Church considered essential was often lost sight of. The multiplication of bishops was one consequence of this state of affairs. There were worse consequences for sound ecclesiastical government when the abbots were, as so frequently in this period, laymen.

The *De statu ecclesiae* of Bishop Gilbert of Limerick was a simple instruction for 'the bishops and priests of all Ireland' in those norms of hierarchy which all in Christendom save the Irish Church took for granted. Their implications for Ireland were revolutionary. Bishop Gilbert conveyed his message about the gradations, orderings and interconnexions of the Christian world by way of a commentary on a diagrammatic representation of the hierarchical pyramid. The diagram with its overlapping arches is somewhat tortuous in its detail but its main outline is clear enough. At the apex sits Christ whilst beneath him are his vicar the Pope, flanked by Noah, Christ's Old Testament prefiguration and the emperor, head of the hierarchy of the lay world. Down the scale goes the narrative from Christ through the different ranks of prelate and orders of the clergy to the bedrock division of society into those who pray, those who plough and those who fight. The spiritual and temporal hierarchies are equivalated: pope with emperor, king with primate, and so on. The treatise is homiletic, each grade being instructed in its duties. The general tone of the treatise sounds of an earlier age than the more developed legal treatises that the Gregorian reform had called into production elsewhere and the mention of Amalarius of Metz (died c.850) suggests that Gilbert looked more to Frankish sources than Gregorian ones. But if the treatise sounds old-fashioned for its date it had a revolutionary message for defenders of the old order in the Irish Church. What made its impact forceful in the Irish context was the clear separation of diocese and monastery. Abbots are put firmly back in the cloister, though it is postulated that they should be priests. The purpose of monks is to abandon all worldly pursuits and serve God alone in prayer. It is certainly not to minister to the laity unless a bishop should order them to do so. It is the bishop who sits firmly at the apex of the one pyramid which rises from the parish and from the other, rising from the monastery. He, not an abbot, is ecclesiastical government. Further, dioceses are expected to be territorial, fixed in number and the episcopate itself firmly subject to the Pope.

It is difficult to determine whether Gilbert wrote this treatise to prepare the way for the council of Rathbreasail or to propagate its message. But it was this council which began the total displacement of the traditional anachronistic monastery-based constitution of the Irish Church.

The council which assembled in 1111 on the plain of Tipperary under the presidency of the papal legate Gilbert and the leadership of Malchus of Cashel (formerly a monk of Winchester), possibly Bishop O Doonan, Celsus of Armagh, along with King Murtagh and a miscellaneous host of clergy and laity, had two main objectives. One was to carry further the reforming work started ten years earlier at the council of Cashel: 'to enjoin rule and good conduct upon all, both laity and clergy', as the Annals of Ulster put it. Of the legislation which sought to put this aim into practice, we have no specific knowledge except the information that 'it was at this synod that the churches of Ireland were given up entirely to the bishops free for ever from the authority and rent of the lay princes'. This was in line with c.2 of the council of Cashel and in the spirit of Murtagh's grant of Cashel to the Church. The second aim was unprecedented: the establishment of a territorial diocesan system. [Map 1]

On this issue, the reformers had two main principles in mind. The first was a division of the country according to the traditional division of *Leath Cuinn* (Northern Half) and *Leath Mogha* (Southern Half). It was entirely logical for Armagh and Cashel to assume the headship of what became two ecclesiastical provinces. Then each province was to be divided into twelve dioceses. The choice of this number apparently derived from Bede's *Ecclesiastical History* with its account of how Augustine of Canterbury had been instructed by Pope Gregory I to set up two provinces each with twelve bishops. This papal ruling for sixth-century England was to serve as model for twelfth-century Ireland according to the writer of the now lost *Annals of Clonenagh*.

If Bede was in fact the source of the reformers' scheme, it proved rather more successful than might be expected. Seventeen of the specified dioceses were to keep their identity: Armagh, Connor, Down, Derry, Clogher, Tuam, Killala, Clonfert, Cashel, Killaloe, Limerick, Emly, Lismore, Cork, Leighlin, Kilkenny, Ferns. The framers of the new constitution did not think they had come up with all the answers. The clergy of Connacht were left free to change the boundaries, though not the number of the five dioceses allocated to this region. On the other hand the elevation of Clonmacnois to diocesan status by political pressure, outside the council, from local interests in the kingdom of Meath was probably the sort of situation the reformers most wanted to avoid.

Perhaps the most surprising feature of the whole project was the omission of any reference to Dublin, the first territorial diocese to be established in Ireland, now in being for over half a century. That there was tension between what may now be properly called the Irish hierarchy and especially Armagh and Dublin, appears in a letter written from Dublin in 1121 to Ralph d'Escures, archbishop of Canterbury, asking for the consecration of Gregory, their bishop-elect. The Archbishop was told: 'the bishops of Ireland are very jealous of us and especially that bishop who lives in Armagh, because we are unwilling to be subject to their rule but wish always to be under your authority'. Gregory was duly consecrated but was unable to obtain possession of the see, for Celsus had taken his place. Whether the archbishop of Armagh ruled Dublin personally and for how long this unusual state of affairs continued, remain impossible to know. Gregory did however secure possession of his see later, to become the first archbishop of Dublin. The Canterbury-Dublin connexion came to an end with him.

It is not until the council of Rathbreasail that there is any indication that the reform movement had influenced Connacht. As elsewhere, the attitude adopted by lay rulers to ecclesiastical affairs was of great importance. In the West the spread of reform was caught up with the rise of the O Connors. The symbol of this dynasty's interest in the Church in this period is the magnificent processional cross which was also a reliquary for a fragment of the True Cross, now known as the Cross of Cong, commissioned by Turlough O Connor c.1122. The cross is also evidence of a different sort. While the organisation of the Connacht dioceses in this period remains most obscure, there is some indication of the state of ecclesiastical government contained in the second of the inscriptions which the Cross bears. This refers to Donal Mac Flannacan O Duffy as bishop of Connacht (Elphin?) and at the same time abbot of Roscommon and abbot of Clonmacnois. The third inscription conveys the information that he was succeeded in his see by another member of his family. Coarbial families were to persist longer in the West than elsewhere.

It was not to be expected, however, that the traditional ecclesiastical dynasties would give place readily anywhere in Ireland. This became clear in Armagh when Celsus died in 1129. Clann Sinaich, in the customary way, produced a candidate to fill the vacancy. But Celsus had anticipated this development. On his deathbed in Ardpatrick, he had designated one of his protégés as his successor and 'by the authority of Patrick' had commanded Conor O Brien, king of Thomond and Cormac Mac Carthy, king of Desmond and all the nobles of Ireland to put his wish into effect. The protégé was Maol Maodoc Ua Morgair (Malachy), destined to be the veritable personification of the whole reform movement.

Malachy was an Armagh man by origin. His father had been a teacher in the Armagh schools and it was in the primatial city that Malachy received his first training as a religious under the ascetic Imar O Hagan and his ordination to the priesthood in 1119 at the hands of Celsus. In the ten years which preceded his designation to Armagh, Malachy had become an experienced religious and prelate, highly regarded in reforming circles in both Armagh and Cashel provinces. In an early spell of diocesan administration (1119–21) as Celsus' vicar in Armagh, he had shown himself a vigorous reformer. St Bernard in his invaluable *Life of Malachy* was to give a vivid and precise picture of Malachy's reforming activity in this period:

In all churches he ordained the apostolic sanctions and the decrees of the holy fathers, and especially the customs of the holy Roman Church. Hence it is to this day that there is chanting and psalmody in them at the canonical hours after the fashion of the whole world: for there was no such thing before, not even in the city [of Armagh]. He, however, had himself learnt to sing in his youth, and soon he introduced song into his monastery while as yet no one in the city, nor in the whole diocese, either could or would sing. Then Malachy instituted anew the most wholesome usage of confession, the sacrament of confirmation, the contract of marriage: all of which were either unknown to the people or neglected by them.

Throughout his life Malachy's personal preference was for the cloister and his career was to be as much connected with monasticism as with the episcopate. The next two years (1122–4) he was to spend at the monastery of Lismore, then, under Malchus, monk of Winchester, first bishop of Waterford, archbishop of Cashel, a major centre of reform. In 1124, however, he was recalled to the north by Celsus to become coarb of St Comgall at Bangor and bishop of Connor joined with Down. He reconstituted the monastery at Bangor with the help of religious from Imar's monastery of SS Peter and Paul at Armagh. It is possible, indeed likely, that this monastery had already adopted the rule of the canons of St Augustine, thereby becoming the first of the many houses of that order which were to come into existence as part of the twelfth-century reform. It was an order with which Malachy was to have an especial connexion. There is another possible link between Malachy and the monasticism of the universal Church dating from this period, though his role in making it remains unknown. In 1127 there was established at Erenagh (Carrig) in his diocese of Down a daughter house of Savigny of the order of Tiron. The foundation was by Niall Mac Dunlevy and it originated from Furness in Lancashire. The Benedictine Savigniac houses were to become Cistercian in 1147. But by then Malachy had already very strong connexions with the Cistercians. As to his activities as bishop in this period of his life, there is some typically eloquent testimony from St Bernard. The great Cistercian had no high opinion of Malachy's new subjects:

When he began to administer his office, the man of God understood that he had been sent not to men, but to beasts. Never before had he known the like, in whatever depth of barbarism: never had he found men so shameless in their morals, so wild in their rites, so impious in their faith, so barbarous in their laws, so stubborn in discipline, so unclean in their life. They were Christians in name, in fact they were pagans. They did not give first-fruits or tithes; they did not enter on lawful marriage; they made no confessions; nowhere was there to be found any who might either seek or impose penance. Ministers of the altar were few indeed: but what need was there of more when even the few lived idle lives among the laity? They had no prospect of fruitful work in their office among so wicked a people. In the churches was heard neither the voice of a preacher nor of a singer.

The very blackness of Bernard's picture off-set the success of Malachy's intensive pastoral activity:

Barbarous laws disappeared, Roman laws were introduced: everywhere ecclesiastical customs were received and the contrary rejected: churches were rebuilt and a clergy appointed to them: the sacraments were duly solemnised, and confessions were made: the people came to the church, and those who were living in concubinage were united in lawful wedlock. In short all things were so changed that the word of the Lord may today be applied to this people: *Which before was not my people, now is my people.*

In 1127, however, Malachy was driven out of Bangor by Conor O Loughlin and once again betook himself, with his community, to Malchus at Lismore. Here he formed a friendship with Cormac Mac Carthy who had been expelled from his kingdom of Desmond by Turlough O Connor and had also taken refuge at Lismore. Cormac managed to regain his throne and proved himself a loyal supporter of the reformers. He was the patron of Malachy's new monastery at *Ibracense* (Ui Braccain, near Cashel?), built new churches at Lismore, founded Gill Abbey at Cork and is commemorated especially by the famous chapel on the Rock of Cashel, consecrated in 1134, which bears his name. He was not to shirk the responsibility which Celsus had laid on him to assist in securing the succession of Malachy to Armagh.

Hereditary succession to Armagh did not end without Clann Sinaich putting up a fight. It speedily found a successor for Celsus in Murtagh, son of Donal, Celsus' predecessor in the Armagh abbacy. For some three years, despite Celsus' known wish, Malachy refused to challenge Murtagh until Malchus and Gilbert of Limerick (whose career as papal legate after Rathbreasail otherwise remains unknown) 'called together the bishops and princes of the land and came to Malachy with one accord prepared to use force', as St Bernard records it. Malachy pleaded the impossibility of his making any headway against a family 'which now for almost two hundred years had held as by hereditary right the sanctuary of God'. Finally, however, he consented: 'You are leading me to death but I obey in the hope of martyrdom'. The event was not to be quite so drastic, but it was to prove difficult and dangerous enough.

Malachy's acceptance was conditional. Should he succeed in accomplishing the freedom of the Church of

Armagh, he would be allowed to return to the cloister. At first, he was not able to live in the city itself and it was Murtagh who secured the tribute due to the coarb of Patrick. In 1134, however, Murtagh died and his Sinaich successor, Niall, who was Celsus' brother, was less well-established. He was driven out, probably by Donal O Carroll, king of Oriel, taking with him the symbols of Patrician authority: the Staff of Jesus, the Bell of St Patrick and the Book of Armagh. Malachy was to recover these and gain undisputed possession of Armagh. With the death of Niall in 1139 the days of Ui Sinaich monopoly of Armagh were over.

By that date, however, Malachy had already redeemed the promise made to him that he might withdraw from Armagh when circumstances permitted. To Armagh in 1137 from the abbacy of Derry came Gelasius (Gille Mac Liag) who was still to have charge of the province at the time of the Anglo-French Invasion. He had ruled the *familia S. Columbae* (the family of St Columba) from 1121 and Derry was to continue for some decades after he had left to be a centre of restored monastic fervour. That Malachy had a connexion with Gelasius is certain since he chose him as his successor. Derry monasticism was almost certainly still of the traditional Irish type. It is likely enough Malachy fostered that type also, though no evidence has survived of his attitude to the older forms of the monastic vocation. Much more is known about his relationship with the great monastic movement which was sweeping Christendom in the twelfth century and which was to transform monasticism in Ireland.

It has already been mentioned that a Savigniac Benedictine monastery had been established from Lancashire in the Down diocese in 1127. Some historians have thought it probable that Malachy had visited northern England in the years before this foundation and that his first contact with monasticism outside Ireland dates from this period of his life. There is no proof, however, that Malachy had ever left Ireland before 1139, in which year he began the first of his two visits to Rome. Malachy set out with a twofold aim. Generally, he wished for apostolic sanction for the radical changes the reformers were bringing about. More specifically, he sought confirmation of the metropolitan sees of Armagh and Cashel and the grant to their incumbents of palls, symbols of archiepiscopal office, without the papal grant of which, in strict canon law, an archbishop should not exercise his function. But though the primary reason for his journey was episcopal rather than monastic, some very important consequences were to follow from it for the future of monasticism in Ireland.

In the spring of 1140, Malachy visited the Cistercian monastery of Clairvaux and began his close personal friendship with St Bernard. Malachy's attachment was not, however, merely personal; he became a devoted admirer of the Cistercian interpretation of the rule of St Benedict. When he arrived in Rome he petitioned Pope Innocent II, unsuccessfully, for permission to resign his see to join the Order. Returning home by way of Clairvaux, he left four of his companions with St Bernard to be trained as Cistercians in order to introduce the Order into Ireland. Among them was Christian O Conarchy who was to be first abbot of Mellifont, the first Irish Cistercian house, as well as first of the numerous Cistercian bishops in Ireland and papal legate. Back home in Ireland, Malachy sent other novices to Clairvaux and sought out a suitable site for a Cistercian monastery. This he obtained from that Donal O Carroll, king of Oriel, who may have been his ally in the Armagh succession crisis in 1134. If the usual Cistercian custom of sending thirteen monks to a new foundation, in commemoration of Christ and the Apostles, was followed, the first Mellifont community was very likely one quarter Irish and three quarters French. St Bernard's letters to Malachy make it clear that friction developed between the two nations and the French went back to Clairvaux. Nevertheless Mellifont (1142) prospered and Cistercianism took solid root in Ireland. There were probably eight monasteries of the Mellifont filiation well established before the Anglo-French Invasion: Bective, co. Meath (1147); Inishlounaght, co. Tipperary (1147–8); Baltinglass, co. Wicklow (1148); Monasteranenagh, co. Limerick (1148); Kilbeggan, co. Westmeath (1150); Newry, co. Down (1153); Abbeydorney, co. Kerry (1154): a daughter of Monasteranenagh; Boyle, co. Roscommon (1161, after temporary foundations elsewhere). In addition, two Savigniac houses, Erenagh and St Mary's, Dublin became Cistercian in 1147–8.

The progress in Ireland of the rule of the Augustinian canons in the same period was even more rapid. But the spread is much less well-documented and it is difficult to make firm judgements about Malachy's individual contribution to it. There were some sixty-three houses of canons already established before the Invasion, some forty-one at the time of Malachy's death in 1148. It is known that as well as visiting Clairvaux on his first visit to Rome, Malachy visited the canons at Arrouaise, near Arras, who followed the rule of St Augustine with observances borrowed from the Cistercians as advised by St Bernard. Abbot Gualtier writing nearly forty years after Malachy's visit recorded in the Cartulary of Arrouaise:[5]

Malachy of holy memory, archbishop of the Irish, breaking his journey with us, examined and approved our customs, had copies taken of our books and the use of our church and took them with him to Ireland, and ordered almost all the clergy in episcopal sees and in many other places in Ireland to accept and observe our order and habit and especially the divine office in church.

Whether Malachy did make such an order cannot be known nor indeed whether it was his intention to establish Arroasian cathedral chapters at all. The only cathedral chapter to adopt that rule was Holy Trinity, Dublin, where it was introduced by St Laurence O Toole after Malachy's death. Evidence unambiguously associating Malachy with the 'many other places in Ireland' where Augustinian houses were founded is sparse. Nor is it easy to determine precisely how many of these houses followed the Arroasian observance. It might be borne in mind also that St Bernard recorded that Malachy had a longstanding connexion and admiration for the Augustinians of Guisborough in Yorkshire and that he had met the abbot of another Yorkshire Augustinian house, that of Kirkham. Neither of these houses was Arroasian. Thus it is by no means certain that Malachy, always eclectic in his monastic tastes, confined himself to the Arroasian type. But it is reasonably clear that his was the important influence in the introduction of canons in such northern houses as Saul, Down, Bangor and Knock. The introduction of the canons was a widespread phenomenon and it would be unwise to attribute it to a single source or a single pattern. But however much historians might differ about Malachy's precise role in the introduction of canons, their remarkable spread is outstanding evidence of the reform movement gathering momentum throughout Ireland.

Mention must also be made of the development of the religious life for women which, too, was a feature of this period and with which Malachy was also connected. Here again it is difficult to determine the precise degree of his influence. It is known that he established houses of nuns in 1144. St Mary's, Clonard, was to be head house of the Augustinian canonesses of the Arroasian congregation down to 1223–4. It may have had as many as thirteen dependencies by 1195. Some of these were possibly 'double' (as was Arrouaise itself) i.e. monasteries with houses of both canons and canonesses separate but adjacent and sharing the same church.

Tantalisingly fragmentary though our information is, it is clear that a great wave of monastic expansion was beginning to swell in Ireland in the thirties and forties of the twelfth century and that the personal influence of Malachy was an important feature of a movement which did more than anything else to change the face of the Irish Church.

There was, however, another aspect of Malachy's work which also introduced radical change. This concerned a further instalment of the reconstruction of the diocesan system. St Bernard gives precise information of what Malachy wanted from Innocent II and of the Pope's reaction:

> Malachy prayed that the constitution of the new metropolis [Cashel] be confirmed, and that palls be given for both sees [Armagh and Cashel]. The privilege of confirmation was given at once; but as for the palls the supreme pontiff told him that more formal action must be taken. 'You must call together the bishops and clerks and magnates of the land, and hold a general council; and so with the assent and common desire of all you shall then demand the palls by persons of good repute, and your request will be granted'.

Malachy returned to Ireland as papal legate but the projected council did not meet until 1148, when fifteen bishops with supporting clergy met on Inis Pádraig. Malachy was reluctant to undertake a second journey to Rome but was prevailed on to go as the spokesman of the Irish Church's request for palls. On the night of 1-2 November 1148, however, he died at Clairvaux on the outward part of his journey. When Bernard died in 1153 he was buried alongside Malachy before the high altar of Clairvaux.

Sometime after Malachy's death 'the kings of Ireland and the Irish Church', according to the report of John of Salisbury, asked, probably more than once, for a papal legate to be sent to them. Cardinal John Paparo finally arrived in Ireland in 1151 and in 1152 in his legatine capacity presided over a council of the Irish Church whose work was to complement and complete that of Rathbreasail.

There is some confusion in the sources as to where Cardinal Paparo's council took place: it seems most probable that some of its sessions were held at Kells and others at Mellifont. There is rather less ambiguity about the nature of its work. By apostolic authority it legislated against simony and usury, against robbery, sexual irregularity and the defective marriage law. It also commanded the prompt payment of tithe. But its main business was with the diocesan system.

One major innovation in this context was not accepted without protest, particularly from Armagh. Instead of just the two provinces of Armagh and Cashel, there were four; Tuam and Dublin were the additions. It was emphasised however, that Armagh held the primacy.

The structure established at Kells–Mellifont was very nearly that which held good for the remainder of the middle ages. [Map 1]

Armagh province was to comprise eleven dioceses: Armagh itself, Connor, Down, Louth (later Clogher), Clonard, Kells, Ardagh, Raphoe, Maghera (later Derry), Duleek, Dair-Inis (later Kilmore). Cardinal Paparo ruled that on the deaths of certain present incumbents smaller and poorer sees should be suppressed and absorbed into the larger. Under this provision (and for various political reasons), in 1216, Bishop Simon Rochfort was to consolidate Clonard, Kells and Duleek into the diocese of Meath, centred on Trim. The diocese of Dromore was a creation of the later twelfth century.

Dublin was allocated five suffragan sees: Glendaloch,

- ● Common centres
- ○ Kells only
- ▲ Rathbreasail only

Metropolitan centres established
in 1152 in caps., (**TUAM**)

Derry ●

Raphoe ○

Ardstraw ▲

Connor ●

Clogher ▲

ARMAGH ●

Down ●

Killala ●

Achonry ○

Ardcarn ▲

Dair-Inis ○

Louth ○

Mayo ○

Roscommon ○

Ardagh ○

Kells ○

Duleek ●

Cong ▲

TUAM ●

Clonard ●

Clonfert ●

DUBLIN ○

Kilmacduagh ○

Kildare ○

Glendaloch ●

Kilfenora ○

Roscrea ○

Killaloe ●

Leighlin ●

Scattery ○

Limerick ●

Kilkenny ●

Ferns ●

Mungret ○

Emly ●

CASHEL ●

Ardfert ○

Ratass ▲

Waterford ○

Lismore ●

Cork ●

Ardmore ○

Cloyne ○

Ross ○

Provincial boundaries ⁓

Diocesan centres established at the Council of Rathbreasail (1111) and
modified at the Council of Kells (1152).

25

Ferns, Kilkenny, Leighlin, Kildare. Innocent III confirmed the union of Dublin and Glendaloch in February 1216.

Cashel province was the most divided: Killaloe, Limerick, Iniscathaig (Scattery Island), Kilfenora, Emly, Roscrea, Waterford, Lismore, Cloyne, Cork, Ross, Ardfert. In addition, Ardmore and Mungret laid claim to diocesan status, but their claims did not mature. Roscrea and Iniscathaig were to be restored to Killaloe from which they had become detached since Rathbreasail.

Tuam was to comprise: Mayo, Killala, Roscommon (later Elphin), Clonfert, Achonry, Kilmacduagh. Annaghdown came into existence in the later twelfth century. Mayo, somewhat protractedly, was united to Tuam by the papacy, 1202–40.

Some of these arrangements were to lead to conflict later but, on the whole, the system was established with remarkable facility. The constitutional modernisation of the Irish Church, at provincial and diocesan level, was virtually completed by the work of this council. The integration of the Norse-Irish sees with the Irish was a notable achievement. The new-found unity of the Irish hierarchy is symbolised in the election to Dublin in 1162 of St Laurence O Toole, abbot of Glendaloch, scion of a Leinster royal house, a prelate in the Malachian mould.

The impression of a certain slackening of the momentum of reform after the death of Malachy and the council of Kells-Mellifont is largely due to the absence of source material as useful to the historian as St Bernard's *Life of Malachy* or the *Annals of Clonenagh*. In this period we must look to evidence of another sort: the establishment of monasteries and convents and the building of churches. As has been seen, new Cistercian and Augustinian houses continued to be founded in the third quarter of the century. The same period was also one of importance in church construction. Cormac's Chapel at Cashel, consecrated in

1134, had introduced Ireland to a new style of church building. Like the reform movement itself, the Chapel drew its inspiration from a variety of sources, English, Continental, Irish, to make it 'one of the most surprising anthologies of Romanesque art'.[6] Its influence, at least in church decoration if not in architecture, was immediate and widespread. Its influence can be traced primarily in the South West, in the Mac Carthy and O Brien kingdoms. It was, however, in the sixties and seventies that the typical Hiberno-Romanesque style churches were being built across the midlands, many of them, as might be expected, in the new diocesan centres. That Clonfert and Tuam had especially important examples of the new style is important evidence that the western province did not stand aloof from the general trend.

Appraising the reform movement on the eve of the Anglo-French invasion, it is clear that very much had been attempted and much had been achieved: a new constitutional framework for the better functioning of the pastoral mission; a great surge of monastic fervour; the adoption of the principles of the Gregorian reform in the attack of simony, lay control and clerical marriage and specially, in adherence to Roman canon law; religious leaders of acknowledged sanctity, backed by lay rulers; and the launching of an attack on unchristian elements in marriage practices. No doubt, much remained to be reformed. Hereditary ecclesiastical offices had not been completely abolished, matrimonial laxities persisted, Irish political society continued turbulent, ignorance and superstition were still prevalent. Nevertheless it is impossible to believe that Ireland was incapable of continuing self-reform. But the papacy came to the conclusion that the religious prosperity of Ireland demanded its political subjection to the kings of England.

2 The Papacy, Henry II and the Irish Church

THERE was apparently more enthusiasm for the papacy from the reformers' side than for the reformers from the papacy. At any rate Pope Adrian IV, in 1155, 'granted and donated Ireland' to Henry II to be held by him 'in hereditary right'. John of Salisbury, the Pope's intimate friend recorded this extraordinary decision in his *Metalogicon*:

> In response to my petition the pope granted and donated Ireland to the illustrious English king, Henry II, to be held by him and his successors, as his letters still testify. He did this by that right of longstanding from the Donation of Constantine whereby all islands are said to belong to the Roman Church. Through me the pope sent a gold ring set with a magnificent emerald as a sign that he had invested the king with the right to rule Ireland; it was later ordered that this ring be kept in the public treasury.

Such a concession could hardly have been because of any lack of reverence towards the apostolic see. The reformers deserved well of the papacy. *Ut Christiani ita et Romani sitis* ('As you are children of Christ so be you children of Rome') was a dictum of St Patrick himself. But it serves as the motto of the reformers. The turning of Irish wills and hearts to Rome is one of the most striking features of the reform movement. Rome was a pilgrimage centre for Irish and Norse-Irish alike in the eleventh century, contact had been established between Pope

Gregory VII and the Munster reformers and an Irish monastery was established there before the end of that century. The councils of Cashel and Rathbreasail were presided over by Irish bishops acting as papal legates. Gilbert of Limerick's treatise of reform theory insisted repeatedly on Roman primacy and the subordination of the episcopate to the Pope and proposed that the archbishops in the new diocesan structure should either be consecrated at Rome by the Pope or have palls conferred on them by him. Imar O Hagan, Malachy's earliest spiritual director, died at Rome whilst on pilgrimage. For Malachy, too, Rome was a shrine of devotion. For him, Roman canon law and liturgical use supplied the norms for the Irish Church. It was as spokesman of the Irish hierarchy that he sought the conferment of the pallia, thereby acknowledging the rule of the papacy. The council of Kells–Mellifont, meeting under a papal legate, by its acts proclaimed its obedience to the apostolic see. St Malachy, St Laurence O Toole, and Christian O.Cist., bishop of Lismore, preserved the virtual continuity of *legati nati* from the beginning of the century down to, and even after, the Invasion.

It has been said in Ireland, off and on, since the early fourteenth century that Adrian's motive was simply to accommodate the expansionist ambitions of his fellow countryman Henry II. It was about the same time as John of Salisbury's petition to the Pope that Henry II's Council meeting at Winchester was agreeing to the desirability of conquering Ireland on behalf of the King's brother, William. But it would be inconsistent with everything we know of the thoughts and actions of that outstanding Pope to accept he was motivated by anything quite so crudely self-interested. More specifically, however, it has been argued that the initiative for the petition came from Canterbury. The Council of Kells–Mellifont deprived Canterbury of such relics of primatial pretensions as it still nurtured. Canterbury now pressed the claims of Henry II on the Pope, it is argued, in order to gain her lost right. John of Salisbury, secretary to Archbishop Baldwin of Canterbury and personal friend of the Pope was thus, it is suggested, an eminently suitable agent to forward these ambitions.

Yet it is a difficult case to substantiate. It is true that at the time of Kells-Mellifont, one chronicler, Robert of Torigny recorded that the grant of the four palls to the Irish archbishops was 'against the custom of the ancients and the dignity of the church of Canterbury from whom the bishops of Ireland were wont to seek and accept the blessing of consecration'. But there is no evidence that either at that time or in 1155 or after Henry II's successful vindication of his lordship that Canterbury sought to assert or recover any allegedly traditional jurisdictional claim, primatial or otherwise, either over the Irish Church as a whole or over individual dioceses in Ireland.

Evidence of Pope Adrian's thinking is offered us by Giraldus Cambrensis. Writing in his *Conquest of Ireland* (1188–89), he recorded that some years after he had left Ireland, though much occupied in war, Henry II was sufficiently mindful of what needed attention there, that he sent to Pope Alexander III asking for authorisation of his lordship and approval of his scheme to evangelise the Irish people in accordance with the laws and customs of the Church of England. The papal privilege successfully procured, it was solemnly read and assented to, in a council of bishops held at Waterford (1173–4: nothing further is known of this council). The King's envoys had brought also the text of a privilege which he had procured from Alexander's predecessor, Pope Adrian, having sent John of Salisbury, later bishop of Chartres, to Rome to obtain it. It was by this same John, Giraldus continued, that the Pope had sent a gold ring as a symbol of investiture which was immediately deposited with the privilege in the royal archives at Winchester. The link between this privilege, the celebrated *Laudabiliter,* and John of Salisbury's account of his request to Adrian IV as related in his *Metalogicon* is obvious.

There is nothing very ambiguous about what *Laudabiliter* says. In the conventional manner of papal letters which are replies to petitions or requests, it begins with a résumé of the petition itself. Henry II had declared his intention of boosting his chances of worldly glory and eternal salvation by extending the Church, spreading the Faith and rooting out evils. He had acknowledged that the apostolic see had special rights over all Christian islands and therefore it was to the apostolic see that he had recourse for 'counsel and favour' about entering the island of Ireland in order to bring its people to the observance of law and to eradicate the weeds of vices there. He had expressed himself willing to pay an annual tribute to St Peter of one penny per house. The Pope listened favourably to this request, agreed that Henry should enter Ireland for these purposes, adjured him to respect the freedom of the Church and do all in his power to promote the glory of God and the salvation of souls. As far as Henry's political authority in Ireland was concerned, the key phrase ran: '. . . et illius terrae populus honorifice te recipiat et sicut dominum veneretur' ('. . . and the people of that land should receive you honourably and reverence you as lord').

On the evidence of this letter, it is manifest that Adrian IV had allowed himself to be persuaded that it was 'the ardour of faith and the love of religion' which impelled Henry II to the conquest of Ireland and that the best interests of the Irish Church would be forwarded by Henry's assumption of the lordship of the country. But have we here a genuine letter of Adrian IV?

The authenticity of *Laudabiliter* has been often, perhaps too often, debated. Let it be said at once that there can be no conclusive proof of its authenticity. The only one hundred per cent proof of the authenticity of a papal letter is its presence in the papal registers or on some retrospective authentification of the letter by later popes. Papal registers for this pontificate, as for the twelfth century generally, have not survived intact. *Laudabiliter,* then, must be assessed according to the same sort of tests to be applied to the hundreds of other twelfth-century documents which look like papal letters.

In the days of defective editions of John of Salisbury's *Metalogicon* it was perhaps just about possible to argue that his testimony about a papal grant of Ireland to Henry II was 'nothing more than a clumsy interpolation which was probably not inserted in his work till many years after the first Anglo-Norman invasion of our island'.[1] The proper appraisal of the manuscript tradition of the book has demonstrated conclusively that this is an untenable view. Modern historians are equally agreed that John of Salisbury, one of the century's outstanding churchmen, had neither the character nor the motive to falsify his evidence and that, in the context in which he was writing, he would not be mistaken in any fact of significance. The premise, then, of any discussion of the authenticity of *Laudabiliter,* is acceptance of the fact that Pope Adrian did grant lordship of Ireland to the kings of England and that he committed this to writing.

That the text which Giraldus Cambrensis published as Adrian's privilege as petitioned for by John of Salisbury is an authentic papal letter is now generally believed by historians both in Ireland and abroad. That its format conforms in general terms to the known style and conventions of the papal chancery of the period has been established. That the papacy should be asked to authorise changes in lordship over different regions and itself claim to have authority to do so has numerous precedents, not least in the history of Norman conquest in Sicily and England. The specific claim of papal sovereignty over all islands ('omni-insular doctrine')[2] mentioned by both John of Salisbury and *Laudabiliter* had precedents. especially in letters of Pope Urban II.

On the other hand, there are puzzling, even suspicious circumstances attending the context within which Giraldus Cambrensis included the text of *Laudabiliter*. Giraldus stated that Henry II caused the privilege to be read at a council held at Waterford some years after the Invasion. This statement prompts the question why, if he had had the privilege since 1155, he had not used it earlier, for instance at the council of Cashel when its impact must have been greater. And why was the existence of such a crucial privilege apparently unknown to Irish churchmen for so long? Further, Giraldus went on to add an alleged letter of Alexander III's *Quoniam ea,* also, he stated, read at the Waterford council, ratifying and confirming Adrian's 'concession concerning the lordship of the kingdom of Ireland'. There is little doubt that *Quoniam ea* fails to satisfy any of the standard authenticity tests and historians have unanimously agreed to reject it. But if Giraldus can adduce an unauthentic confirmation might not the adduced privilege itself be suspect?

We should not, however, exaggerate the importance of *Laudabiliter*. Whatever the precise degree of the short-comings of Giraldus Cambrensis's narrative and its supporting documentation, it remains true, on John of Salisbury's evidence, that Adrian IV, before the event, did authorise Henry II to enter Ireland and assume its lordship. It remains true too, on the evidence of papal letters which Giraldus did not cite but which are unquestionably authentic, that Alexander III took a similar line after the event. And popes after him continued to recognise the validity of the Irish lordship of the kings of England. Further, after 1213, when King John finally came to terms with Pope Innocent III, the kings of England held Ireland as a papal fief at an annual rent of three hundred marks sterling. The papacy thus had a formal definition of the status of Ireland; *Laudabiliter*, or cognate documents, had nothing to contribute to the definition of that status. Though *Laudabiliter* was often to be brought to its notice in the middle ages, it never specifically acknowledged it as a papal document.

To the papacy, Henry II presented himself as entering Ireland for his own and Ireland's religious advancement. Observers in England were apparently less impressed with his religious zeal and found more mundane (and more convincing) reasons for his action. Gervase of Canterbury would seem to have the right of it:

> There are two reasons why the king went to Ireland: the call of the Irish to be defended against Richard [de Clare: Strongbow] and the call of Richard made to prevent their being protected against him. But the third, and in my opinion the one which was the principal and especial reason, was that if sentence of interdict should be inflicted [as result of the murder of Archbishop Thomas Becket, 29 December 1170], he might the easier avoid it or the more secretly observe it[3]

Though Henry II went to Ireland, then, primarily for political and possibly for personal reasons, there was to be an important ecclesiastical dimension to his Irish policies. Its most striking manifestation came towards the end of 1171 when he summoned the whole Irish hierarchy along with abbots and numerous other clergy to a council at Cashel. Christian O Conarchy, one of the first Mellifont community and later bishop of Lismore, presided in his capacity as papal legate, Henry II being represented principally by Ralph, abbot of the Cistercian house of Buildwas in Shropshire and Ralph, archdeacon of Llandaff. The council proceeded to a general public enquiry into the misdeeds of the Irish people. The results of this discussion and investigation were carefully recorded under the seal of the legate. Though this document does not survive, the constitutions of the council based on it, do.

Since they emerged from a debate among Irish reforming bishops, it is not surprising to find that the eight decrees of the second council of Cashel are of the same type as those promulgated in pre-Invasion reform councils. Legislation was enacted about marriage and lay testamentary dispositions to safeguard the position of the widow and children, payment of tithe, proper administration of the sacraments and the liturgy, freedom of the Church from lay control, clerical privilege. The outstanding novelty is a principle which is to have far reaching consequences. For the future, the Irish Church was to be brought in all respects (*modis omnibus*) into conformity with the English Church. This principle was to provide English kings for the future with a ready-made and simple ecclesiastical policy for Ireland. It meant, in particular, that the system of Church-State relations obtaining in England should obtain equally in Ireland. Methods of ecclesiastical appointment, the jurisdiction of the ecclesiastical courts, clerical privilege and the rest were to be regulated by that particular accommodation of ecclesiastical and lay interests which had already evolved in England or was to do so in the future. The *libertas ecclesiae* (liberty of the Church) was to be that particular brand of freedom of the Church which the common law of England defined.

We have looked at the attitudes towards the Invasion of the papacy and of Henry II. It is time to examine the viewpoint of the most interested party of all, the Irish Church.

The whole hierarchy had met to consider the situation with which it was confronted by foreign invasion, even before the arrival of Henry II. At a council held in Armagh in 1170, there were long and anxious debates, about which, however, we are unfortunately uninformed. But it did decide unanimously, Giraldus recorded, that invasion had been visited on the Irish people by God as a punishment for their sins and especially for their long-established practice of buying English people for slaves. To assuage God's wrath, it was ordered that all the English in slavery throughout Ireland should be given their freedom. The information that the Irish clergy thought God had loosed the English on the Irish people to chastise them for their sins, a characteristic enough medieval sentiment in the face of disaster (the feeling was still there in Elizabethan Ireland), does not take us very far into the minds of the Irish churchmen. They submitted speedily enough to Henry II, accepting him as their lord and king, swearing fidelity to him and his heirs for ever and solemnising this declaration with charters bearing their seals. These submissions were sent to Pope Alexander III. Also to the Pope from the Irish bishops went a pessimistic account of the religious shortcomings of the Irish people. Alexander's reaction is clear from his reply to the Irish bishops:

> Your letters, and the trustworthy reports of others frequently brought to the attention of the apostolic see, have informed us how great are the enormities of vice with which the Irish people is contaminated and how they have put aside the fear of God and the faith of the Christian religion to put their salvation in jeopardy. We have further learnt from your letters that our dearest son in Christ Henry noble king of the English, prompted by God, has with his assembled forces subjected to his rule that barbarous and uncivilised people ignorant of divine law, and that what was being unlawfully practised in your country is already with God's help beginning to decrease, and we are overjoyed. . .

It seems equally clear from this text that the Irish hierarchy had accepted Henry II not merely, fatalistically, as a punishment for sin, but, positively, as a precaution against its future recurrence. The reformers in Ireland had decided that Henry II was an acquisition to their cause and had told the Pope this. Alexander III could, then, write to the bishops, to the princes of Ireland who had sworn fealty to Henry II 'of your own free will', and to the King himself, apparently secure in the belief that the acceptance of Henry's lordship was agreeable to the invader and invaded alike. The Pope made his own position abundantly clear, and incidentally throws light on the position of the Irish bishops, in his *Celebri fama* to Henry II, a letter of considerably more historical significance than *Laudabiliter*. The full text reads:[4]

Alexander, bishop, servant of the servants of God, to his dearest son in Christ, Henry, noble king of the English, greeting and apostolic blessing.

With gladness of heart we have learned much by way of common talk and truthful report of how as a pious prince and magnificent king you have with God's help and at his inspiration as we unquestioningly believe you have extended your majesty's power and wonderfully and magnificently triumphed over the disordered and indisciplined Irish, a people, we have heard, the Roman rulers, conquerors of the world in their time left unapproached, a people unmindful of the fear of God which as if unbridled indiscriminately turns aside from the straight road for the depths of vice, throws off the religion of Christian faith and virtue and destroys itself in internecine slaughter. We refrain from mentioning at the present time the other enormities and vices to which this same people, neglecting the practice of the Christian religion, so irreverently devotes itself, about which our venerable brothers Christian, bishop of Lismore, legate of the apostolic see and the archbishops and bishops of the country have informed us in their letters, and our dear son R[alph] archdeacon of Llandaff a prudent and discreet person and bound to your royal majesty with a chain of especial devotion, who has examined this state of affairs with the eye of faith, has discreetly and carefully revealed to us orally: this people, as perhaps has come to the attention of your majesty more fully, openly cohabit with their stepmothers and do not blush to bear children by them; a man will misuse his brother's wife while his brother is still alive; a man will live in concubinage with two sisters and many have intercourse with daughters of mothers they have deserted. All eat meat throughout Lent; they do not pay tithe neither do they respect as they ought God's holy churches and ecclesiastical persons. Hence, with a great land and sea force mobilised, as we have learned from the communication of the archbishops and bishops and more fully and specifically from the account of the aforesaid archdeacon, you having made the decision, on the prompting of the divine compassion, to subject this people to your lordship to eradicate the filth of such great abomination, we show as we should our gratitude and approval in every way, while giving credit for the working of grace to him from whom all good proceeds and who is pleased to favour in the way of salvation the pious acts and intentions of the faithful, beseeching with votive prayers that just as the forbidden things which are done in that country are already beginning to stop and the seeds of virtue to sprout instead of those of vice through the power of your majesty, so with God's help this people will accept through you the full discipline of the Christian religion, and, the defilement of sin rejected, gain for you an unfading crown of imperishable glory and achieve salvation for themselves. We ask your royal excellency, warning and exhorting you in the Lord, imposing a burden on you for the remission of sins, that in the matter you have so praise-worthily begun, you will readily confirm and strengthen your resolve and recall and maintain that people through your power to practice of the Christian faith, so that just as you have started the great work in regard to that people, we believe, for the remission of your sins, so you may be worthy to receive an eternal crown for bringing it to salvation. And because, as your excellency knows, the Roman Church has a different right over an island than over mainland, we, hoping and confiding that in the fervour of your devotion you would wish not only to preserve the rights of this Church but even to increase them and where it has no right, to confer it, ask your majesty and earnestly admonish him to take care studiously to uphold for us the rights of St Peter in that land and if indeed nothing is held there, your majesty will constitute and assign due right to that Church, so that then we may be beholden to you and you may be seen to offer the first-fruits of your glory and triumph to God.

In accordance with the logic of this letter, the Irish lay rulers were commanded to remain submissive to Henry II and to keep their oaths of fealty unbroken. The Irish bishops were instructed to excommunicate, after admonition, all those who did not. The papacy could not have made its political position more plain. But lest any ambiguity should remain there was in 1177 a cardinal-legate to reinforce the message:

While Vivian was papal legate in Ireland he summoned a council of bishops to Dublin at which he made formal public declaration of the right of the king of the English in Ireland and the papal confirmation of it, strictly commanding and charging both clergy and laity under pain of excommunication not to dare to forsake their allegiance in any rash venture.[5]

Pope Alexander III's successors continued to underwrite the English lordship. In 1182, Lucius III consecrated John Cumin, virtually nominated to the archbishopric of

Dublin by Henry II. In 1186, the same Pope sent a crown to England and a legate to put it on the head of Prince John, to make him king of Ireland. The plan came to nothing but the political attitude that informed it is obvious. The papal position in relation to Ireland was established in the reign of Henry II. It was to be confirmed in 1213 with Innocent III's acceptance of Ireland from King John as a papal fief. Though from time to time thereafter the kings of England were to be admonished for wrongs committed in Ireland, the papacy was never before the Reformation seriously to reconsider its authorisation of the English claim to sovereignty over Ireland. English kings of course never hesitated to put this authorisation to their political and ecclesiastical service as seemed to them appropriate. But whether the Irish Church would continue to be so acquiescent to English lordship, was to be another question altogether. The examination of this problem, fundamental to the whole understanding of the development of the medieval Irish Church, must be pursued through the history of the religious orders, of the episcopate and of the legal framework within which churchmen sought to fulfil their spiritual mission.

3   The Religious Orders, 1127–1340

Monks and Canons, 1127–1230

It has been estimated, though the margin of uncertainty is broad, that some two hundred monasteries (including convents of nuns) had survived the period of monastic decadence caused by the Norse invasions and were still functioning in the eleventh century. It is known that in the twelfth century some at least of these centres knew a renewed stirring of life along the lines of traditional Irish monastic rules. Derry was the most conspicuous example of this revival. There is indeed a little evidence, of Dublin provenance and possibly relating to Glendaloch, that monasticism of the ancient indigenous type was still alive in the fourteenth century. But the future of monasticism in Ireland did not lie with ancient traditions either Celtic or Benedictine, but with the new turn given to the perennial principles of the religious life by the dynamic orders and congregations whose growth in eleventh and twelfth-century Christendom constitutes such striking evidence of the deepening and extending influence of the Gregorian reform movement. By 1171 it is impossible to say with certainty that any monasteries were following any customary Irish rule. Many had become Augustinian or had been eclipsed in the immense attraction exercised by the Cistercians.

Our knowledge of the momentous change in the Irish monastic scene is very superficial and partial in that the evidence allows no glimpse into the internal regimen of individual monasteries, except when things were going wrong, and rarely permits assessment of monastic personalities. It is true that some lives of saints afford an occasional touch of humanity. St Bernard's vivid and rhetorical life of Malachy is the classic of medieval Irish hagiography. The Canon of Eu's life of Laurence O Toole, despite its conventional hagiographical approach, does give some impression of the saintly archbishop. But no writings from any Irish monastic pen have survived which would illumine the scene as do, for example, the works of the great Cistercian Ailred of Rievaulx and the biography of him by his pupil, Walter Daniel.

Twelfth-century Irish monasticism can at least, however, be measured with a fair degree of accuracy, thanks in large part to the labours of Dr Neville Hadcock and Fr Aubrey Gwynn.

All the evidence suggests that there were no Benedictine monasteries in Ireland in the early eleventh century. There were, however, some Irish Benedictine communities in southern Germany (*Schottenklöster*) already established at this time, of which the most important was St James, Ratisbon. The third abbot of this house, Christian by name, was a relation of the Mac Carthy, king of Desmond, whose name has been immortalised in Cormac's chapel at Cashel. Abbot Christian founded a second abbey of St James at Würzburg. In the early 1130s monks left Würzburg to establish a monastery at Cashel. By 1148 there was another Würzburg foundation, at Rosscarbery in co. Cork. Dependencies of other Continental Benedictine houses were established elsewhere in Ireland: from Savigny, Erenagh (1127) and St Mary's, Dublin (1139); from Cluny, Athlone (*c.*1150?). Six Cistercian houses may have begun their careers as black monk communities: Holy Cross, Kilcooly, Jerpoint, Killenny, Monasterevin and Newry. But we know little of the beginnings of these houses.

In marked contrast, we are relatively well-informed about the introduction of the Cistercians into Ireland. St Malachy's part in this has already been noticed in an earlier chapter. It was of course Mellifont which took pride of place in the establishment of Cistercians. The abbey church was completed and consecrated with great ceremony in 1157, before an assembly of reformers commensurate with the importance of the occasion. *The Annals of the Four Masters* chronicled the event:

> A synod was convened by the clergy of Ireland and some of the kings, at the monastery of Droicheat-átha (Drogheda), the church of the monks. There were present seventeen bishops, together with the Legate and the successor of Patrick; and the number of persons of every other degree was countless. Among the kings were Muircheartach Ua Lochlainn, Tighernan Ua Ruairc, Ua hEochadha and Ua Cearbhaill. After the consecration of the church by the successor of Patrick, Donnchadh Macleachlainn was excommunicated by the clergy of Ireland and banished by the kings from the kingdom of Meath; and his brother Diarmaid was made king in his place. Muircheartach Ua Lochlainn presented seven score cows, and three score ounces of gold, to God and to the clergy, as an offering for the health of his soul. He granted them also a town-land at Droicheat-átha, i.e. Finnabhair-na-ninghean (Fennor). Ua Cearbhaill also gave them three score ounces of gold; and the wife of Ua Ruairc, the daughter of Ua Macleachlainn, gave as much more, and a chalice of gold on the altar of Mary, and cloth for each of the nine other altars that were in that church.

The Legate mentioned was Christian O Conarchy, trained at Clairvaux under the eye of St Bernard himself, first abbot of Mellifont, now bishop of Lismore. The *coarb* of Patrick was the saintly reformer, Gelasius. The O Carroll mentioned was Donnchadh, king of Oriel and the founder of Mellifont.

The abbey itself, An Mhainistir Mhór – antonomastically, 'The Great Monastery' to the Irish people – was a phenomenon in Irish ecclesiastical life. Its church was the largest yet seen in Ireland. In being built of stone, it marked a change in Irish church building conventions. In embodying in its plan the latest development of coenobitic monasticism, it marked a major turning-point in the long Irish tradition.

As is well known, Cistercian monasteries throughout Christendom were built to a standard pattern, modified only in details as particular local circumstances might dictate. Many Irish exemplars are still to be seen. What determined the whole construction was the fundamental distinction between the two classes housed in a Cistercian abbey: the *conversi* or laybrothers, whose work lay in the fields and the *monachi* or choir monks following the tripartite life enjoined by St Benedict, community prayer, work and spiritual reading. The two classes were accommodated in separate choirs in church which gave a Cistercian church a distinctive plan. They were also housed separately, with their accommodation divided by the cloister which, to catch the sun, lay to the south of the church. The west range was the brothers' and with the monks on the east range there were naturally to be found such important rooms as the chapter house, library and *scriptorium* or writing room for these were for activities in which the brothers had no part. The south range was reserved for domestic rooms, in particular for kitchens and refectories (separate for monks and brothers). The fine unusual, octagonal Mellifont Lavabo, dating from *c.*1200, standing in the cloister outside the monks' refectory has become one of the best-known constructions of Irish medieval ecclasiastical architecture.

By 1171 Mellifont had seven daughter houses which in

turn produced four more foundations. The Invasion did not stop growth. By 1200 the Mellifont filiation numbered twenty-one which included at least two foundations in each of the provinces.

Much the most numerous of the new foundations, however, were those for canons regular following the rule of St Augustine: about sixty five of them at the time of the Invasion. Some were new foundations. Some, perhaps most, were conversions of ancient foundations and many of the most venerable names in Irish monasticism took on a new lease of life from this time.

The rule of St Augustine is a statement of the general principles which should govern communal religious life in poverty, rather than a set of precise, detailed regulations. As such, it has the great merit of flexibility and after the eleventh century was increasingly adapted to accommodate many different religious purposes. Looked at from one point of view, the canons regular 'played the part of Martha in the Church',[1] turning their hands to a great variety of apostolic tasks in parishes, hospitals and schools. But they might also follow a way of life far removed from active involvement in the world. Some congregations, falling under the spell of St Bernard were scarcely distinguishable from Cistercians, abstaining from meat, keeping perpetual silence and full choir observance of the canonical hours, enlisting lay brothers and organising themselves under the authority of an annual general chapter. St Malachy had been in intimate contact with both these broad types of regular canon. The first type, the pastoral in outlook, had been especially successful in northern England under the encouragement of the archbishops of York, who found them valuable evangelists in barbarous Yorkshire. It was at Guisborough in that county that Malachy made his earliest and probably his most enduring contact with Augustinian canons. The second type, the more purely monastic, was represented by the congregation of Arrouaise, visited by Malachy in 1140 and a copy of whose constitutions and observances he carried into Ireland. Unfortunately we have no evidence to allow us to detail the particular nuance of individual houses. It is clear, however, that there was general recognition among the religious leaders of twelfth-century Ireland that the rule of St Augustine was peculiarly adaptable for the reform of monasticism. The flexibility of the rule and its appropriateness for pastoral work made the canons an admirable instrument for the general restoration of religious discipline where there had been severe break-down.

The name of Malachy and after him, of Laurence O Toole, must inevitably occupy the fore-front of any account of the introduction of the canons regular. Nevertheless, the role of the laity was important and must not pass unremarked, for it was their benefactions and support that made possible the introduction and spread of the canons. Unfortunately, the earliest beginnings of most of these houses cannot be known and many a patron's generosity has not been recorded for us. But certain names stand out. Murtagh O Loughlin, claimant of the High Kingship, benefactor of Mellifont, founded the nuns' house at Clonard and the men's at Durrow. Donnchadh O Carroll, king of Oriel and founder of Mellifont was associated also with the establishment of Augustinian houses at Knock, Louth and Termonfeckin. The king of Connacht, Turlough O Connor was perhaps the most assiduous promoter of all of the Augustinian canons. His patronage embraced houses at Annaghdown, Clonfert, Roscommon, Cong, Tuam, Clonmacnois and Cloon-tuskert (co. Roscommon).

Two turning points in the history of Irish monasticism may be deduced from any survey of this period. In 1127, Niall Mac Dunlevy founded a monastery for Benedictine monks of the congregation of Savigny and probably stemming from Tulketh (Lancs.) at Erenagh in Down, a diocese then under the jurisdiction of St Malachy. This was almost certainly the very first of the new wave of monastic foundations which was to bring Ireland in due course into touch with all the recent developments of monasticism in the Latin west. These developments were associated particularly with the Augustinians and Cistercians. A second new wave was to begin with the arrival in Ireland of the friars, the Dominicans in 1224, the Franciscans in 1234. In the century or so that lies between these dates and the arrival of the first foreign monks at Erenagh in 1127, some one hundred religious houses (not including those for nuns, which present complex problems of origins) had been founded or refounded under native Irish auspices. About twenty of these foundations, ten Augustinian and ten Cistercian, date from after the Invasion.

The new foreign aristocracy showed itself to be a generous patron of monks and canons and the spread of religious houses in the areas it controlled was hardly less impressive than progress in Irish Ireland. It is not necessary to detail every benefaction though, generally speaking, the surviving evidence makes this easier to do for Anglo-French than for Irish foundations. A few examples must suffice to illustrate the process. John de Courcy transformed the monastic scene in east Ulster. To his chief town of Downpatrick were brought Benedictines from Chester, Augustinian canons from Carlisle and the Order of the Holy Cross (*Fratres Cruciferi*). From Dryburgh in Scotland came Premonstratensian canons to Carrickfergus; from Stogursey (Stoke Courcy), Benedictines to St Andrew-in-Ards ('Black Abbey'); from Furness in Lancashire, Cistercians came to Iniscourcy (Inch) to replace the monastery at Erenagh which he had destroyed. William Marshal made a comparable impact in Leinster. His foundations were: Cistercian abbeys at Duiske and Tintern; *Fratres Cruciferi* in New Ross; Augustinian canons and the Order of St

Thomas of Acon in Kilkenny; Knights Hospitallers in Wexford. Occasionally a powerful baron might retard the cause of monasticism as much as he advanced it. William de Burgh founded the important Augustinian house of Athassel and it was very likely he who was responsible for the founding of the Premonstratensian abbey of Tuam. But elsewhere his influence was less happy. The Annals record that in 1204 he plundered the monasteries of Clonfert, Meelick and Clonmacnois and in 1203 the Cistercian monastery of Abbeyknockmoy. But most of this new class of Irish landowner seem to have founded more religious houses than they ravaged. By 1230, some eighty new monasteries and priories had been set up under Anglo-French patronage.

Easily the biggest group among these was the twenty six houses for Augustinian canons. The very first Anglo-French foundation was Augustinian: the abbey of St Thomas the Martyr (Thomascourt) in Dublin founded on the instructions of Henry II in 1177. In the early 1190s it became an abbey of the congregation of St Victor in Paris and there followed five more priories of this congregation, one not hitherto represented in Ireland.

Also new to Ireland was the second largest group of Anglo-French houses, the fifteen priory-hospitals of the *Fratres Cruciferi*. These 'Crossbearing Brothers' (the name derived from their practice of carrying a staff surmounted by a cross) were also regular canons following the rule of St Augustine. There is an element of mystery as to how they became so prominent in Ireland. They were not at this date established in England nor did they ever become very strong there. It is not possible either to establish any link between Ireland and congregations on the Continent north of the Alps. It seems the Irish houses were modelled on the pattern of the Italian congregation, but the specific points of connexion between Ireland and Italy remain unknown.

Also followers of the rule of St Augustine, were the Knights Hospitallers of St John of Jerusalem whose strength in Ireland by 1230 stood at thirteen houses. Care of the sick was one aspect of the Hospitallers but in Ireland it was the military activity of the Knights which seemed the more stressed. Kilmainham became the headquarters of the Hospitallers and its prior was usually a leading figure in the political and, often, the military life of the colony. The Order, like the Knights Templars (six houses by 1230), was primarily an instrument for policing the country, though it is known that some Templar detachments (possibly including native Irishmen) at least left Ireland for the Holy Land. The Order of St Thomas the Martyr of Acon (Acre) was also composed of knights and infirmarians following the rule of St Augustine. It was of English origin and while its general intent was no doubt military, the priories at Carrick-on-Suir and Kilkenny were hospitals. Also founded as a hospital, with the brethren following the Augustinian rule, was the Trinitarian house at Adare.

The last group to be mentioned under the heading 'Augustinian' sought a way of life under the rule, very different from that of monk-nurses and monk-soldiers. The canons of Prémontré (the Premonstratensians) were new to Ireland. Like the congregations of Arrouaise, already well-established here, this order had come under the influence of St Bernard and its observance and constitution reflected Cistercian principles. It was not, however, destined to flourish in Anglo-Ireland. It survived most vigorously in Connacht.

The invaders did something to improve the standing of the black monks in Ireland with five new foundations. They did even more for the white monks. Nine foundations: Dunbrody (1184: from Dublin which had become Cistercian with the other Savigniac houses in 1147), Inch (1187: from Furness), Grey Abbey (1193 from Holmcultram), Comber (1200: from Whitland in Wales), Duiske (1204:

from Stanley), Abington (1206: from Furness), Abbeylara (1214: from Dublin), Tracton (1225: from Whitland. Its monks were Welsh-speaking, at least in its earliest years). These abbeys, with ten founded by Irishmen since the Invasion, brought the total number of Cistercian houses in Ireland to thirty-one. This was almost half the number of those in England and about three times the number in each of Scotland and Wales.

By 1230 the number of religious houses for men, of all orders, in Ireland was about two hundred of which one hundred and twenty were of Irish foundation and eighty, Anglo-French. Comparable figures for Scotland and Wales were forty-six and thirty-three respectively. The comparison no doubt reflects differences in respective sizes of population. But it certainly indicates how substantial had been the progress of the reform movement in Ireland.

Our knowledge of the relationship between Irish abbeys and priories with their mother houses on the Continent is sketchy. The constitution of the congregation of Arrouaise laid down that heads of houses should attend the general chapter held annually at Arrouaise itself. We have no information about Irish participation in any of these meetings. But a letter of Pope Innocent III, written in 1200, instructed prelates in Ireland to ensure that Irish abbots did attend the General Chapter. The enlisting of papal authority suggests that absenteeism was of long standing. Nothing is known of the result of this instruction.

Only one document seems to have survived to throw light on the connexion between the Irish white canons and their mother house of Prémontré. In 1215–16, Richard de Burgo made an endowment for the abbey at Tuam and obtained a safe-conduct for four canons to visit Prémontré to learn at first hand of the best observance of the Order's way of life. A letter bearing on this mission has survived and is worth reproducing in full for the light it throws on the poverty of Prémontré itself and the problems of the Tuam community:

Gervase, by the patience of God called abbot of Prémontré, to the venerable brother in Christ, W. abbot of Vicoigne, sincere salutations in the love of Our Lord. The bearer of this letter, Isaac, canon of the church of the Holy Trinity in the suburbs of the metropolis of Tuam, which professes to be the only place of our order in Ireland, recently came from the furthest boundaries to Prémontré, sent by his abbot to France to learn the French language and to live under the discipline and rigour of our order, which in his own church, on account of the fewness of the brethren living in those barbarous parts, he was not acquainted with.

Though greatly pleased with his intention, we would have been better pleased if he had come properly clad so as not to be a burden to us. For last year when the weather was severe, there came to us from the same premonstratensian church, three brethren, each with a single habit, age worn and thin in texture; they came in order to take back to their monastery ecclesiastical books of our order containing the observances. We had therefore to see them properly clothed and helped them in their requirements.

When, however, earlier this year, we were burdened by these three and also by another seven strangers for whom we had to provide clothing, there will not be enough fleece for us to clothe all who come and we are unable to bear alone the burden of our order.

We send Isaac to you, requesting and instructing you to keep him for a time, supplying him with just enough clothing out of the stock of your brethren, and consoling him as a man not accustomed to the cloistral customs and rigours of our order.[2]

The letter points to some of the hazards involved in

transplanting French monasticism into Gaelic Ireland. There were problems of distance, of language, of conservatism and suspicion of foreigners. These problems were felt from the very introduction of the Cistercians into Ireland, with whom there was early experience of the pitfalls that lay in the path of monastic reformers. Even in its earliest days, some of the monks of Mellifont did not take readily to the full Cistercian observance and there was tension between Irish and French monks. The evidence comes in a letter (1144) of St Bernard to St Malachy:

> But because there is still need for vigilance in a new country among a people little accustomed to the monastic life and unfamiliar with it, I beg you in the Lord not to remove your care from them until the work you have so well begun has been perfectly finished. Concerning the brethren [French monks] who have returned I would have been well content for them to remain with you. But perhaps those natives of your country who are little disciplined and who found it hard to obey observances that were strange to them, may have been in some measure the occasion of their return.[3]

St Bernard was exhorting St Malachy to vigilance. The ordinary established constitutional body exercising vigilance was the General Chapter of abbots held annually in mid-September at Cîteaux, whose abbot presided. The Cistercian constitution attached particular importance to attendance at this meeting of the supreme authority. Attendance was compulsory and absence without leave was severely punished. In 1190 Irish abbots were dispensed from annual attendance and allowed to go once in four years; the abbot of Mellifont was charged with the responsibility of ensuring that some abbots came each year and that obligations should be fulfilled. In 1195 this rule was amended: three abbots were to come annually, selected by the abbot of Mellifont. But absenteeism remained a problem and the General Chapter was frequently calling attention to the gravity of this matter and using the sanctions of the Order to try to remedy it.

Absenteeism from the General Chapter escalated into revolt against it by the abbeys of the Mellifont filiation. The bare outline of the main events of what the General Chapter came to call the *conspiratio Mellifontis* (the Mellifont rebellion) is to be recovered from that body's statutes, which contain the official record of the decisions taken to suppress it. This record is terse, eschewing all detail of information or explanation. But it makes all too clear that this was a storm which was shaking to pieces the whole structure of Cistercianism among the Irish.

The first real suggestion of trouble comes in the statutes for 1202 when the abbot of Clairvaux was instructed to discipline Maigue and its daughter houses concerning whom many complaints had been put forward. Nothing more is heard of this, however. But in 1216 the abbot of Clairvaux was instructed to take steps to have Mellifont reformed in head and members because of the *multa enormia* that had grown up there. Visitors were appointed, charged with this mission and despatched to Ireland. The statutes for 1217 tell how the abbot of Mellifont refused them admission, barring the abbey gate with a crowd of lay brothers. There was trouble too at Jerpoint where on the third day of visitation the abbot successfully called on the community to rise in revolt against the visitors. Four other abbots, of Baltinglass, Killenny, Kilbeggan and Bective, supported this action. The revolt was obviously of alarming dimensions.

The canker showed no signs of yielding easily to the treatment prescribed by the central authority. The statutes for 1219, 1220 and 1221 make it clear, though only in the most general terms, that 'enormia' and 'excessus' in the houses of the Mellifont filiation were still causing the General Chapter the most serious concern. The abbot of

Cîteaux was later to tell Pope Gregory IX that Visitors were sent annually to Ireland to correct abuses. They were deliberately chosen from many different nations to avoid suspicion of national partialities. All brought back the same story of 'destruction, wasting of properties, conspiracies, rebellions and frequent plottings of death'. The Pope was also told that 'in the abbeys of Ireland the severity of Cistercian discipline and order is observed in scarcely anything except the wearing of the habit, in that there is neither observance of choir service nor of silence in the cloister nor of the discipline of the chapter meeting nor use of the common table in the refectory nor of monastic quiet in the dormitory according to the manner of our order'.

Inevitably the General Chapter resorted to drastic measures. In the visitation of 1227, conducted by the abbots of the French abbeys of Froidmont and Trois Fontaines, the abbots of Assaroe, Boyle, Fermoy, Abbeydorney and Newry were deposed. That these houses had become involved shows that the whole Mellifont filiation had become affected. Steps were taken against other abbeys. In order to ensure proper visitation, which ordinarily was the responsibility of the abbot of the parent house, three Irish houses were reallocated. Maigue was removed from Mellifont and placed under Margam in Monmouthshire; Baltinglass from Mellifont to be made subject to Fountains in Yorkshire and Suir from Maigue's jurisdiction to that of Furness in Lancashire. The portents for the success of this tough policy were not good however. When the Visitors replaced the Irish abbot of Baltinglass with an Englishman the new abbot was forcibly ejected by the community.

We are unusually well-informed about the visitation which followed in 1228, thanks to the fortuitous survival of the letter-book of the abbot who conducted it. [Map 2] This was Stephen of Lexington, abbot of Stanley in Wiltshire. Stephen, a graduate of both Oxford and Paris,

Houses of the Mellifont filiation in *italics*

Cistercian houses at the time of Stephen of Lexington's visitation (1228).

55

had been well on the way to a comfortable career in the diocesan church in England when, about the year 1221, under the influence of St Edmund Rich, he opted for a more spiritual life. He was to become abbot of Clairvaux in 1243 and show himself to be one of the outstanding figures in thirteenth-century Cistercian history. The charge laid on him at the General Chapter of 1227 to correct Mellifont and its offspring, his first major work for the Order, was to test to the utmost his spiritual and intellectual calibre as well as his qualities of human understanding.

The rebel Cistercians gave the Visitor a warm reception. His life was threatened, his representatives assaulted, his party harassed. At the three key houses of Mellifont, Suir and Maigue he found monasteries transformed into castles prepared for siege, with armed monks and brothers barring his entry. But he was brave, persistent and zealous for the good of the Order. The reconciliation to the authority of the Order of these three communities in arms was a signal achievement.

Abbot Stephen attempted to be statesmanlike and to provide a final solution for a problem that had been too serious for far too long. For the most part, the basic principles of his solution were already laid down for him either in the ordinary Cistercian rules, or in the decisions of earlier visitors, which had been confirmed by the General Chapter. He had some resources to call upon. One was his carefully collected 'team' of assistants. Another was that he was empowered to enlist the aid of the secular arm to meet force with force. This he did on a number of occasions; he did not hesitate to enlist the political powers of both nations to back up the authority of the General Chapter. A third, and this was the fundamental one, that throughout the crisis, there remained a basic core of Irish monks who either had remained obedient to the Order or could be persuaded, under the paternal solicitude which Cistercian visitation procedure enjoined on a visitor, to be led back into the fold. These monks made it possible for Stephen of Lexington to envisage the rebuilding of the Cistercian province in Ireland. Otherwise, such had been the degree of departure from the Cistercian rule, the involvement of monks in lay society and the prevalence of moral irregularities, that a strict Cistercian might have thrown up his hands in despair at a situation beyond control.

Stephen had a very clear idea of what needed to be done by way of reconstruction. First, the individual communities must be put on a sound basis. Those considered guilty of rebellion against the Order and whose continued presence was considered dangerous were transferred to other houses (this was standard Cistercian practice in cases of *conspiratio*) abroad. In certain houses, communities were to be limited in numbers (this applied probably to Mellifont and Jerpoint). Only those with some rudiments of education should be admitted as novices. In particular, knowledge of French and Latin was required. It was decreed:

> No one shall be admitted to be a monk, no matter what his nationality, unless he can confess his faults in French or Latin, in order that when the visitors and correctors of the order come he can understand them and be understood by them.

Or again, put in fuller form:

> By the authority vested in us, we forbid you under pain of deposition or expulsion to admit anyone as a monk unless he can confess his guilt in French or Latin. By this statute we do not intend to exclude any nation, English, Scots, Welsh or Irish but only those who are useless to the order and completely unproductive. For how can a man love the order or how will he bear the burden of silence or the discipline of the enclosure, who is totally ignorant of how to find solace in scripture and cannot meditate even a little by night and day on the law of God?

Irish postulants, he thought, should be encouraged to study abroad, at Oxford or Paris or at some other suitable centre of learning. But the fundamental training of monks must take place in the home monastery. To promote this, Stephen continued the policy already tried (not with very much success so far) of introducing an experienced spiritual leader as abbot with other experienced and trustworthy monks to support him. The big snag about this was that the newcomers were inevitably English or French or were not generally welcomed. A decree such as the following left Stephen open to the charge of national discrimination:

> As punishment for the revolts which have arisen gener-
> ally throughout the Irish houses, it is strictly forbidden
> for any monk of that people to be appointed abbot, in
> order that obedience to the order be fully proved and
> that having first learned how to be pupils, they may in
> due time be more capable masters.[4]

In practice Stephen exempted several abbeys from this rule and Boyle, Corcomroe, Newry and Abbeyshrule remained under Irish abbots and visitation was entrusted to Irish monks.

For the remainder of the Mellifont filiation there was a further step in the reduction of Irish monks to purely pupil status. The principle of reallocating Irish houses to different mother-houses outside Ireland had already been intro-duced. Stephen of Lexington took it to its logical con-clusion. Fourteen houses were placed under the jurisdiction of one or other of Clairvaux, Margam, Furness or Foun-tains. The abbots of these houses would for the future be responsible for the visitation of their Irish daughters and for the maintenance of discipline in them. Stephen of Lexington saw these new liaisons as an essential part of the re-education of Irish monks and urged the abbots to under-take their duties with the utmost conscientiousness.

Abbot Stephen left behind him instructions and advice in plenty. There were very detailed regulations issued, after visitation, to individual houses. The Jerpoint community, for example, was presented with a list of no less than ninety-seven decrees (though the document as it stands in the edited version of Stephen's *Register* may be a conflation of one set of rules for Jerpoint with a second set issued for Mellifont). Then there were the thirteen articles issued to all the Cistercian monasteries in Ireland, of which a copy was to be kept in every abbey to be read by the abbot to the community once a month for a year. Finally, since Stephen had been promoted to the abbacy of Savigny and was unable to undertake visitation a second year as the General Chapter had originally intended, there was the lengthy advisory brief he left for his successors to implement.

Stephen's instructions and admonitions covered a very wide variety of topics. They were intended to put an end to abuses, restore the full observance of the Cistercian way of life, safeguard monastic properties, initiate a regime of benign paternalism to train a new generation of religious, isolate trouble-makers and institute an effective visitation system. In breadth and depth, they constituted a radical reform programme.

The visitation did not, however, put an immediate end to disaffection within the Order and there was renewed violence in the years after Stephen's departure. But the position improved in the course of the thirteenth century and by 1274 the General Chapter felt able to withdraw the restrictions it had imposed on the pre-eminence of Mellifont among the Irish Cistercian houses. The *status quo* was restored and the former system of visitation was reintroduced. The Irish province, however, never wholly succeeded in throwing off the malaise that had led to the visitation of Stephen of Lexington and remained a source of serious concern to the General Chapter.

Dominicans and Franciscans (1224–1340)

THE set-back to the progress of the religious life caused by the severe crisis of the 'Mellifont Rebellion' was counterbalanced by the extraordinarily rapid advance of all four Orders of Friars. By *c.*1340 when, for the time being, the first surge of enthusiasm was spent, there were some eighty five houses of Friars: thirty-three Franciscan, twenty-five Dominican, sixteen Carmelite and eleven Augustinian. In each of the Orders, the first mendicants to come to Ireland were English, the first houses were established in the colonial towns – Dublin and Drogheda had houses of all four Orders, Cork of three of them, seven other towns of two of them. No Anglo-Irish centre of any significance was without at least one house of one of the Orders – and each remained constitutionally linked in one way or another to the parent English province. But the Irish-speaking world was also caught up in this great tide of religious fervour and played its part too in the spread of all four Orders. The two nations intermingled in these new international religious militias. As the Cistercians lost their way down paths of conservative insularity and in tangles of national animosities, the Friars reopened Ireland to the most revolutionary developments in the religious life of thirteenth-century Christendom, mitigated the bitterness of national strife and brought a fresh approach to the evangelisation of the people at large. Unfortunately, in their turn, sections of the Friars were to be overtaken by the plague of medieval Ireland: the clash of the two nations. But for over half a century after 1224 and even later, though somewhat more intermittently, the seed of the Friars' apostolate fructified throughout Ireland, transcending national divisions.

The special characteristic of the Dominicans was that they were an order of preachers founded specifically for preaching. Originally concentrated in Toulouse, in 1217 St Dominic ordered his brethren to disperse throughout

	DOMINICAN	FRANCISCAN	CARMELITE	AUGUSTINIAN
1220	Dublin: Drogheda 1224 Kilkenny 1225 Waterford 1226 Limerick 1227			
1230	Cork 1229	Youghal: Cork 1229–31		
		Kilkenny 1232–40 Carrickfergus 1232–48 Dublin 1233 Multyfarnham 1236		
	Mullingar 1237–8			
1240	Athenry 1241 Cashel: Tralee 1243 Coleraine: Newtownards 1244	Athlone 1239 Timoleague 1240 Downpatrick 1240–43 Waterford: Drogheda 1240–45 Ennis 1240–47		
		Dundalk 1248 Castledermot 1247		
1250	Sligo: Strade 1252 Roscommon 1253 Athy 1253–7	New Ross: Claregalway: Nenagh 1252 Ardfert 1253 Kildare 1254–60		
		Clane 1258		
1260	Trim 1263 Arklow 1264	Armagh 1263–64		
	Rosbercon 1267 Youghal 1268 Lorrha 1269	Cashel 1265 Limerick 1267 Wexford: Wicklow—1268 Clonmel—1269		
1270	Derry: Rathran 1274	Buttevant 1276–9	Leighlinbridge—1272 Ardee: Drogheda +1272 Dublin 1274	
1280		Trim—1282		Dublin—1282
1290	Kilmallock 1291	Killeigh 1293 Galway 1296	Ballinasmall 1288–9 Kildare 1290	Dungarvan c.1290
1300	Carlingford 1305		Burriscara 1298 Thurles—1300 Loughrea c.1300 Castlelyons 1307–9	Drogheda—1300 Tipperary c.1300 Cork—1306 Fethard 1306
1310			Lady's Abbey +1314? Athboy 1317	Ballinrobe c.1312 Tullow 1314 Adare—1316 Clonmines 1317
1320		Monasteroris 1325 Cavan 1325–30	Caltra: Knockmore c.1320	New Ross—1320
1330		Carrickbeg 1336	Creevaghbaun 1332 Galway c.1332? Kinsale 1334	
1340				

The growth of the Friars, 1220–1340 (+ = after; — = before).

the world, 'preaching the word of God to the nations'. Dominicans reached Oxford in 1221 and had a house in London before 1224. In 1224 they were established in Dublin with the help of Archbishop Henry of London and the Cistercians of St Mary's Abbey. In the same year, aided by the archbishop of Armagh, Luke Netterville, they put down roots in Drogheda. Quickly they spread into the leading towns of the colony: Kilkenny (1225: founder, William Marshal the Younger, earl of Pembroke); Waterford (1226); Limerick (1227: founder, Donough O Brien, king of Thomond. [Map 3] He also founded the Franciscan house at Ennis, c.1240); Cork (1229: founder, Philip de Barry). It will be noticed that an Irish ruler took a hand even in the first Dominican influx. No details are available of the relationship between the citizenry of Limerick (granted a charter by John as lord of Ireland in 1197) and the king of Thomond. But for the establishment of what became one of the most important religious houses in the country, the priory of Athenry, we have valuable information concerning the patrons, English and Irish, who contributed to its foundation in 1241 and the subsequent building programme.

Athenry was the chief town of the de Bermingham family and was destined to grow into an important trading centre. It was Milo, its first lord (d. 1253), who invited the Dominicans there, who bought a site for them at a cost of 160 marks and gave as much again towards the cost of building. In addition, he contributed gifts of English cloth, wine and cart horses. He persuaded his knights and men at arms to help as far as they could. He arranged for regular portions of produce to be paid to the priory from his farms; his son Piers and his grandson Richard emulated him in this regard. Milo died in Cashel but his body was solemnly brought back to Athenry for burial in the Dominican Church: the first of a long line of de Berminghams to find a last resting place there.

Dominican Houses 1224–1305

63

These details come to us from a unique document, generally described as the *Register of the Monastery of the Friars Preachers of Athenry*.[5] It describes itself as a *tabula* or list 'drawn up to record the founders, friends and benefactors of our order and especially of the convent of Athenry'. It is mostly of mid-fifteenth century compilation and much of it is taken up with the largesse of the de Berminghams and of the families who composed the merchant class of the district in the later middle ages: Wallys, Bodkin, Lynch, Godsun, Blake, Butler, Joyce, Simpkin, Walsh and many more. But more important still, the record brings out that the patronage of Athenry priory was not exclusively Anglo-Irish, nor the tombs in its church reserved solely for those of English stock. From the beginning, the Athenry convent was an integral part of Gaelic society as well. The 'Register' records who paid for the various buildings of the first house: Felim O Connor, king of Connacht (and founder of the Dominican house at Roscommon in 1253) is credited with bearing the cost of the refectory; Eugene O Heyne, of the dormitory (he also financed the building of the dormitory of the Clare Franciscan house); Cornelius O Kelly and others, the chapter house: Art McGallogly, the infirmary. Other Irish families financed the erection of the cloister and guest house. Florence Mc Flynn, who was archbishop of Tuam from 1250 to 1253, 'built a house for scholars' and bequeathed to the friars 'optima decreta' (canon law books?). Some Irish bishops chose to be buried there: Maurice O Leayn, bishop of Kilmacduagh (1254–82) and his successor, David O Setachain (1284–90). Given all this Irish interest in a house in an Anglo-Irish town, it is no surprise to learn that the community itself was 'mixed', composed of friars of both nations. We are perhaps entitled to think that the harmonious relationships between the two nations in religious matters exemplified in Athenry was far from unique and that had other such *tabulae* survived there would have been proof that discrimination of nation against nation was rarer, at least among the Friars, than is often suspected.

Within half a century of the arrival of the Dominicans in Ireland, there were twenty-three priories in being. It has already been noticed that at Limerick, Athenry and Roscommon, native Irish leaders were connected with the foundations. Three other priories had Irish founders: Cashel (1243: founder, David O Kelly, O.P., archbishop of Cashel from 1238 to 1253); Coleraine (1244: probable founder, an O Cahan); Derry (1274: founder, Donal O Donnell). The Dominicans also made a significant impact on the Gaelic world in another way. The chapters of Armagh, Cashel, Killala, Raphoe, Cloyne, Ardfert and Lismore all elected or postulated Dominicans for their sees in the course of the thirteenth century. The first friar preacher to be appointed bishop was David O Kelly who ruled Cloyne (1237–9) before being promoted to Cashel where he was archbishop from 1239 to 1253. Another outstanding prelate of this period was Patrick O Scannell Bishop of Raphoe (1253–61) and archbishop of Armagh (1261–70). Throughout his episcopal career he was plagued with conflicts of jurisdiction: with the bishop of Derry, attempting to detach Inishowen from the diocese of Raphoe; with the bishop of Meath, scheming to throw off Armagh's metropolitical authority; with the other three archbishops, rejecting the primacy of Armagh. But he was essentially a reforming bishop. In Raphoe he used his Dominican *confrères*, backed by the secular arm, against enemies of the Faith of whom Pope Alexander IV wrote to the Bishop:

You have come before us in person, and have reported to us that some laymen of your diocese have been instigated by the devil to such a pitch of madness that they not only worship idols, but also marry their own kinsfolk and relations. Moreover, if they are rebuked by you or by others of the faithful for these excesses or if you excommunicate them because of them, these same laymen, like sons of perdition, dare to dispute the catholic faith and that authority which has been divinely granted to the apostolic see and wickedly conspire the death of those who argue against them.[6]

There is no record of his encountering any such 'evident messengers and ministers of Antichrist' (Pope Alexander's words) in his Armagh pontificate. But he was responsible for the founding of the Franciscan house in that city and is credited with a major share in the building of St Patrick's Cathedral there.

Such evidence as comes to us from sources at home concerning the spirituality of these Dominican bishops does not go beyond the rather conventional obituaries characteristic of the Irish Annals. One record, however, of continental Dominican origin, merits mention as a unique if brief glimpse into the spiritual personality of a friar preacher bishop of this period. He is Carbry O Scoba who was bishop of Raphoe from 1266 to 1274:

. . . he was present at the [general] council of Lyons [1274], one of the thirty Dominican bishops who took part in that historic assembly. Humble and devout, yet of cheerful disposition, he had ruled his diocese wisely and well, and had at the same time retained his authority over the neighbouring Dominican convent [Derry?]. As often as a provincial or other official visitor came to the monastery, he took his place in the chapter room with the other friars and as scripture says of the just man [*Prov.* 18.17: 'The just is first accuser of himself.'] he was the first to confess his faults and receive his penance with all reverence. Having come to assist at the council of Lyons and staying with the Dominicans of that city, he repeatedly implored permission from the saintly master-general John of Vercelli, to accuse himself in chapter like the rest of the brethren. This permission was refused as the master-general would not suffer the holy prelate to humble himself in this manner and he was not so open to persuasion as the provincials had been. Shortly after the opening of the council, the bishop was stricken with what appeared to be a slight fever, and sweetly gave up his spirit to God on the eve of the Lord's Ascension in 1274.[7]

Information is scanty about the Irish Dominican connexion with England and the Continent. What is known in some detail however, is the formal legal framework regulating the relationship between the Irish priories, the English province and the central authority of the Order, the General Chapter. Unfortunately, more can be known about the *de iure* constitutional position than about what actually happened *de facto* within and without the constitution.

The Irish houses, together with those in Scotland, formed part of the English province and were therefore subject to the jurisdiction, including visitation, of the English provincial and provincial chapter. The Order as a whole was not very keen on altering its first structure of provincial organisation but in 1275, recognising that some provinces, notably the English ones, were unwieldy, provision was made for subdivisions of provinces to be known as vicariates. It is clear that for long before 1275 Ireland had enjoyed quasi-vicarial status and there is evidence of chapters being held at Athenry in 1243 and Cashel in 1256. The Pope himself in 1256 had referred to the 'vicar provincial of the friars preachers in Ireland' and another source of the same year gives the names of this official and his title of 'vicar of the English provincial'. Ireland like Scotland, formally became a vicariate of the English province in 1275. There were to be ambiguities, however, about all the precise details of the status of vicar-provincial which led finally to the intervention of the master-general himself. When in 1314 Berengar of Landorra was in London for the general chapter of the Order, he took occasion to specify in detail the exact canonical position of Ireland *vis-à-vis* the English province as well as the general chapter and the Order's institutions of higher learning. The result, which may well have been no more than confirmation of the position actually existing, established a reasonable degree of autonomy for Ireland under its vicar-provincial but preserved a real degree of subjection to the provincial and his chapter in England.

The appointment of the vicar-provincial lay in the power of the provincial. But he was required to choose the man from three names put to him from the Irish selectors who were the priors of each house in Ireland reinforced with a representative of each community and the senior theologians of the vicariate known as the preachers-general. The vicar's powers were effectively those of a provincial, subject to the usual safeguards of the Dominican constitutions, except when the provincial was in Ireland on visitation. Authority to appoint visitors remained with the provincial chapter, as had always been the case. The provincial had power to remove the vicar for good cause. Should the chapter in Ireland find it necessary to suspend a vicar, it was for the provincial chapter in England to finalise the sentence. Two representatives from Ireland were required to attend the provincial chapter annually and the vicar-provincial himself was to go every fourth year. Similarly, there should be two Irish representatives at the annual general chapter. Finally, it was ruled that the Irish vicariate might send two students each to Oxford, Cambridge and London to read for degrees, one to Paris and others to other *studia* in the ratio laid down by the constitutions of the Order.

As to the actual working of this skilfully balanced constitution – who became vicar-provincial, what happened at chapter meetings and on visitations and all questions related to the practical administration of the vicariate – we are unfortunately quite in the dark.

The year 1217 was as important for the development of the Franciscan Order as it was for the Dominican. For it was at the General Chapter of that year that the decision was taken to send friars beyond the Alps, and with the creation of eleven provinces under provincial ministers, to take the first steps towards the drawing up of a formal constitution. In 1224 the General Chapter held at the Portiuncula decided to send friars to England. These arrived at Dover in September, the month when St Francis received the Stigmata, a party of four clergy, of whom only one was yet a priest, and five lay brothers. The priest, Richard of Ingworth, was one of three Englishmen in the party, and his is the first name in Irish Franciscan history to be known to us with certainty. Thomas of Eccleston, who spent nearly thirty years collecting contemporary material for his chronicle *On the coming of the Friars Minor to England*,[8] is our source:

[Brother Richard was] a priest and preacher, and first of the brethren to preach to the people north of the Alps. He was later sent by John Parenti [Minister General, 1227–32] of holy memory, to be Minister Provincial of Ireland, for he had shown a wonderful example of exceptional sanctity, and had acted as Brother Agnellus' deputy in England while the latter attended the General Chapter at which the translation of St Francis' body took place [25 May 1230]. He always remained faithful and pleasing to God, and when he had completed his term of office he was released from all responsibilities among the brethren at the General Chapter held under Albert of holy memory [May 1239]. Then, filled with burning zeal for the Faith, he set out for Syria, where he died a joyful death.

Brother Richard, then, was an eminently qualified person to bear primary responsibility for the introduction of *religio seraphica* – that unique blending of humility, simplicity and poverty in the imitation of Christ – into a country which in times distant and recent has been so receptive of the Franciscan spirit. Seven houses were established in the period of his ministership in Ireland.

The passage quoted from Thomas of Eccleston is easily the most solid piece of evidence concerning the notoriously difficult problem of Irish Franciscan origins, the only evidence indeed which rises above the level of pious conjecture. Yet it has not perhaps always received the attention it deserves. It says that Richard of Ingworth came to Ireland after standing in for Agnello of Pisa who had gone to Italy for the General Chapter held in May 1230. This date suggests that Richard came to Ireland in 1231, given that medieval men were reluctant to travel in winter between England and Ireland; but a date in the late summer or autumn of 1230 cannot be ruled out. Tradition, which in fact descends from the fifteenth-century Franciscan Observant congregation which made Youghal its centre, holds that this south-eastern house was the first Minorite foundation in Ireland. There is no contemporary evidence for this. The first certain contemporary dating for a house in Ireland concerns Dublin. In January 1233, King Henry III made a gift of 20 marks to Friars Minor of that city for the *repair* of their church and buildings – evidence which suggests that the convent had been in existence for some time. Taking this evidence into account and accepting that it is not improbable that Richard of Ingworth, like Agnello of Pisa going to England, and indeed like many of the provincial ministers appointed in 1217, was chosen as provincial before there were Franciscan houses in the country of his destination, then it would seem that another hypothesis concerning the coming of the Friars Minor to Ireland is at least as well founded as any so far advanced: that Brother Richard led the first party of Franciscans to be sent into Ireland, that it arrived in 1230 or 1231, and that it first established itself in Dublin. In choosing the capital city as their first base, the Franciscans would be doing what the Dominicans had done before them and the Augustinian friars, and not impossibly, the Carmelites, were to do after them.

The pattern of Franciscan progress was to be very similar to that of the Dominicans. [Map 4] Patronised by baron, knight and burgher alike, receiving regular alms from the kings of England, they established themselves in all the chief towns of the colony and in most of the minor ones as well. They penetrated the Gaelic world too, beginning possibly in Cork, but certainly in Ennis (c.1240) and Armagh (1263–4) and continuing with the foundation of houses at Nenagh (before 1268), Killeigh (1293?) and Timoleague (c.1307–16). Unfortunately there is no Franciscan equivalent of the Athenry list of benefactors extant to throw light on the relationship of a friary with Anglo-Irish and Gaelic patrons. But it is hardly open to doubt that the experience of Athenry was paralleled in Franciscan history.

Some Franciscans were elected bishops in the thirteenth century. Indeed the Irish province very nearly made history in the Order as a whole by being the first to have one of its members elected bishop when in 1244 a part of the Elphin chapter sought the promotion of Thomas O Quin. He did not get the see, however, though later he became bishop of Clonmacnois (1252–79). But the province discouraged its men from becoming bishops. In 1244 they made this known to the king, asking him, that if despite Franciscan reluctance to having friars become prelates, any were so elected, the consent of the minister

Franciscan Houses 1229–1336

provincial should be sought before royal assent was given to the elect. Franciscans are not therefore so prominent among the episcopate of the Irish-speaking areas as are Dominicans – four only were elected in the thirteenth century and of these, three were in the smallest dioceses of all, Clonmacnois and Ross. Only two Franciscans ruled Anglo-Irish sees in this period, both papally provided after disputes. Coincidentally, they were of the same family: Geoffrey Cusack, bishop of Meath, 1253–4 and Nicholas Cusack, bishop of Kildare, 1279–99.

Constitutionally, the Irish Franciscans enjoyed considerably more independence than their Dominican *confrères*. They were not a part of the English province. As has been seen, they were established from the beginning under their own minister provincial, appointed by the minister general. This method of appointment was again preferred when the time came to find a replacement for Richard of Ingworth. Thomas of Eccleston is still our source and once more his narrative gives a thumb nail sketch of a friar of outstanding spirituality.

Brother Henry of Reresby was appointed minister of Scotland, but died before his arrival in the province [*c.*1233], so Brother John of Ketton, guardian at London was appointed in his place. All the houses of friars north of York were included in his jurisdiction, and he later admitted many worthy and valuable men into the Order. Brother John set a high example of devotion and was particularly zealous for the proper recitation of the divine Office. He welcomed our venerable father, Brother Albert [of Pisa, min. gen., 1239–40], with fitting respect in the house at Leicester, and asked him to expound the Rule to the brethren. Having governed the province of Scotland most excellently for many years, that province was reunited to England [May, 1239], and

Brother John was appointed minister of Ireland by our minister general, Brother Albert.

I think it worth mentioning that during the General Chapter at Genoa, Brother John, supported by Brother Gregory of Bosellis, stood firmly in support of Brother William of Nottingham against almost all the other members of the Chapter, and happily obtained that the privilege granted by the lord pope for the Order to receive money through procurators was entirely abolished, and that the interpretation of the Rule approved by Pope Innocent IV [*Ordinem vestrum*, 14 November 1245] should be suspended in any matters where it was more lax than that approved by Pope Gregory. It was Brother John who spoke before the definitors-general of the Chapter, urging that Brother Elias should be reconciled to the Church, and he obtained permission for certain brethren to visit Brother Elias [min.gen. deposed in 1239] and warn him not to delay his return to the obedience of the Church and the Order.

Brother John was also greatly concerned to promote the study of the scriptures, and had a Bible with a full commentary bought in Paris and sent to Ireland. Furthermore, he was so devoted to the welfare of the brethren that many who were unhappy in other provinces came to him, and clearly derived great benefit from his guidance. When he had been minister for twenty years, he was released from office at the Chapter of Metz [1254] . . .

The evidence suggests that choice by the minister general, not election by the provincial chapter, remained the method whereby the Irish provincial minister was appointed. Thus when in 1312, Pope Clement V made a formal statement that the Irish minister provincial, like those of the Holy Land and Greece (Romania), should be appointed by the minister general, under advice, he was apparently declaring what was the established principle, not, as is sometimes said, depriving the Irish province of the right to elect, for some major breach of discipline. Richard of Ingworth and John of Ketton apart, little has survived to tell of thirteenth-century Irish Franciscan personalities and their apostolate. A Thomas of Ireland earned admiration in some Italian Franciscan circles for his humility, because to avoid being forced to become a priest, he cut off his thumb (the physical defect then constituting a canonical disqualification for ordination) and later enjoyed a reputation in Aquila as a miracle worker, both before and after his death. John of Ireland who was minister provincial in 1279 enjoyed considerable standing in the Order. He served on the high powered committee (it included the future Popes Nicholas IV and Boniface VIII and Peter John Olivi) which supplied the matter moulded into Nicholas III's decretal *Exiit qui seminat* (1279), a major commentary on the Rule, especially in respect of the interpretation of the ideal and practice of Franciscan poverty. It is clear that the Irish Franciscans attached considerable importance to preaching because in the second half of the century, a quite extensive literature of the 'helps for preachers' type was produced. Traces survive, but not the books themselves, of *Libri exemplorum*, collections of edifying and cautionary tales for the use of preachers, written by Deodatus who succeeded John of Ketton as minister provincial in 1254, and by a John of Kilkenny, while a 'frater de Wycumbe', of the Irish province, compiled a collection of sermons. Two interesting specimens of preaching literature have survived. The first is a *Liber exemplorum* written in the late 1270's, the author of which remains unidentified, though it is known he was a Warwickshireman, a graduate of Paris and had spent his active life in Ireland, being at one stage *lector* or specialist theologian at Cork. The other enjoyed a wide circulation throughout medieval Europe during the middle ages: the so-called *Venenum Malachie*, a treatise written in 1286 on 'The poisons of the seven mortal sins and their anti-dotes'. Malachy was a native Irishman of the Limerick house, a doctor of theology who was an unsuccessful candidate in a divided election for the archbishopric of Tuam in 1279. He wrote his best-seller, 'for the instruction of simple men whose work it is to teach the people.'

It is from the first of these surviving preachers' manuals that there comes some information concerning the Brother Thomas O Quin who has been mentioned earlier. The English author had a high regard for Brother Thomas, 'a good and faithful man, learned enough, who became bishop of Clonmacnois, after very many years of poverty, humility and correct and uplifting preaching'. The author relates the following *exemplum* (example), which Bishop Thomas himself had given him from his own personal experience, illustrative of the power of faith.[9] It is first-hand evidence which perhaps throws a little light on the man and the times. It has the authentic ring of a medieval preaching friar in action:

When I held the office of preacher in the Order (said Thomas), I came on one occasion to preach in Connacht. And there was at the time an extraordinary but pitiable plague in the diocese of Clonfert. For when men went out to their fields to plough or work or walk in the woods they would see, so I was told, passing armies of evil spirits, which sometimes fought among themselves. Those who saw this vision were at once struck down by illness, becoming powerless and bed-ridden with torpor, and many died miserably thereby. When I heard this, he continued, I gathered the people together in an assembly, a big one, not a small one, and I preached the word of God, saying this to them, among other things: 'Look here', I said, 'you have a great plague among you, brought about by these evil spirits which many of you see frequently in these parts. Do you know why these evil spirits have such power to hurt you? I can certainly tell you: it is because of your lack of faith! You are too afraid of their power, neither believing nor trusting in the thought that God wishes to defend and guard you against any harm they might inflict. If your faith was firm and you believed really firmly that they could do nothing except that which God permitted them to do, and corrected your lives, earnestly imploring the Lord to defend you from their ambushes, then you could be certain they could do you no harm. And you see and know that we [i.e. Friars Minor] are men who in the whole world do most against them and speak the worst things about them. And I am standing here and saying all these things hostile to them and preaching. And I wish and proclaim and pronounce that they come at me and do whatever they can against me. Let these evil spirits come if they dare, I say, and let them all come. Why do they not come? What are they up to? What are they? I hurl abuse at them, as all the people can hear'. And mark you, from that hour the evil spirits disappeared, never thereafter to reappear in that district and immediately there stopped the plague which had for so long so lamentably preyed on the people. You see how little evil spirits can accomplish when they are opposed by firm faith, from this example of how their efforts were brought to nothing by one poor friar whose mocking voice spoke out of a firm faith.

Thomas O Quin, so highly regarded by the English author of the *Liber exemplorum*, was at one stage in his career guardian of the Franciscan house in Drogheda, one of the most English towns in Ireland. That fact suggests that in the Franciscan community in Ireland the two nations had learned to live harmoniously together, the spirit of

St Francis transcending cultural differences. But this situation did not last.

There is clear evidence from 1285 that Irish-speaking Dominicans and Franciscans were held in some suspicion by English officialdom. A committee of enquiry into corruption in high places in the Dublin administration reported *inter alia* that Irish friars 'made much of the Irish language'. The implication seems to be that they discriminated (as the Franciscan bishop of Kildare warned was true of members of many orders at this time), against their Anglo-Irish brethren and fomented civil unrest while, such being the degree of mismanagement in the Dublin exchequer, continuing to receive royal alms, funds administered through that department of government. However this might have been, there can be no doubt that a few years later there was open conflict between Irish and English Franciscans.

Two accounts of the incident have come down to us,[10] both from English sources, neither of them wholly satisfactory, though they are contemporary or near-contemporary. The first is from Bartholomew of Cotton's *History of the English*:

> (1291) At that same time, the minister general of the order of St Francis, making visitation throughout the world, came to Ireland to visit there and in his general chapter, sixteen brothers with their brethren were slain (*in capitulo suo generali XVI fratres cum confratribus suis interfecti sunt*), several were wounded and some were imprisoned by the action of the king of England.

The second is from the *Annals of Worcester Abbey*, recording that on 10 June 1291,

> there was held a general (*sic*) chapter of the friars minor at Cork in Ireland, to which the Irish brothers came armed

with a certain bull. Contention arose over this bull and they fought with the English and many were killed and wounded to the scandal of the order, until finally the English with the help of the town prevailed.

It is not easy to accept that this unfortunate clash took place under the very eye of the minister general himself, though it cannot be entirely ruled out since it is known he was in England in that year. The papal bull which sparked off the dispute has not yet been identified and it is not possible to say more about the nature of the dispute. Nor is it possible to say very much about the consequences of the bloodshed, save that in September of 1291 Edward I ordered the Justiciar and all royal officials in Ireland to put themselves at the disposal of the minister general and his vicars who were seeking the restoration of discipline within the province.

English suspicion of Irish friars, and indeed Irish members of other religious Orders, showed itself again in 1310. A parliament held in Kilkenny instructed all religious living among the English to refuse admission to their monasteries of all who were not of the English nation. Some Irish rulers thought (on the evidence of the O Neill *Remonstrance* of 1317) that this was merely the legalisation of what had long been the practice in the English houses of monks, canons, preaching friars and friars minor. But government policy was still in fact at this stage in favour of mixed communities (*mutua cohabitacio*). The Kilkenny decree was speedily revoked and discrimination against the Irish forbidden just as, in 1297, alleged discrimination against the English in the dioceses of Down and Armagh had been condemned. In the event, however, it first modified the principle of cohabitation by trying to regulate the ratio of Irish to English in certain houses (1324), and then later (1366), abandoned the principle altogether with a reassertion of the Kilkenny decree of 1310.

The real crisis among the friars, particularly among the Franciscans, came with the invasion of Ireland by Edward Bruce in May 1315. His claim to the kingship of Ireland attracted considerable support from Gaelic Ireland and not a little from Anglo-Ireland also. The war which followed, of a uniquely attritional kind, shook the colony to its foundations. Irish friars were in the van of the Bruce faction and were thus inevitably targets of repressive measures by the government.

In September 1315, Edward II warned his Justiciar to be alert to the danger of allowing Irish friars and other clergy of Irish nationality to remain among the English and authorised him to take such action against them as he thought best for the safety of the colony. The king also sought the help of the minister general of the Franciscans, calling on him to discipline friars who were preaching rebellion against the English Crown. A similar request was made of the Pope.

Throughout 1317 the Pope was being told a great deal about the national prejudices and political hatreds of churchmen in Ireland. King Edward II implored him not to elect any 'pure Irishman' to any Irish see, except with his assent previously obtained, because Irish prelates were actively promoting the overthrow of English jurisdiction in Ireland. In particular he asked for the promotion of an English Franciscan to Cashel, whose chapter had divided along national lines to produce two candidates to the vacant see. Edward claimed that the promotion of an Irishman to a diocese situated among the 'brutish and uneducated' Irish (*homines siquidem bestiales et indoctos*) would threaten his loyal people with the gravest dangers.

The Irish, for their part, laid their complaints against the English. The famous O Neill *Remonstrance*, perhaps the first trumpet blast of Irish nationalism, is unquestionably the hardest hitting denunciation of the evils of English rule in medieval history – its Scottish equivalent, the *Declaration of Arbroath* of 1320 is anaemic by comparison. Pope John XXII was presented with a detailed list of English atrocities and oppressions. The one complaint with particular relevance to our present subject matter concerned the attitude of Anglo-Irish monks, canons and friars to the native Irish. They were accused of the 'heresy' of proclaiming that it was no sin to kill an Irishman, no matter what the circumstances. One Simon, a Franciscan, brother of the bishop of Connor, was accused of being one of the most vocal protagonists of this opinion, asserting that should he kill an Irishman, 'he would not for this be one whit less ready to say Mass'. Perhaps, in the absence of supporting evidence, we might be cautious about accepting everything in the highly rhetorical *Remonstrance* as strict truth. But the story about Brother Simon is certainly evidence of the hatred that some Anglo-Irish Franciscans, with other religious, were capable of inspiring at this time. Discord in the Franciscan ranks rumbled on many years after Bruce had lost his life (Oct.1318). In 1325, John Clyn, the Kilkenny Franciscan annalist, recorded that there was trouble throughout almost the whole Franciscan community in Ireland, 'each one taking the side of his own nation and blood while others were ambitious for promotion to prelacies and higher offices.'

Edward II's representations to the Pope and to Michael of Cesena, the Franciscan minister general, had not fallen on deaf ears. The unrest noted by John Clyn was most likely the first reaction to measures initiated by these two authorities. John XXII set up a commission of judges-delegate to investigate the King's charges against friars of the Irish nation. The minister general sent two visitors to work with these judges, who were all English. The result of the investigations was made known in legislation promulgated in a Franciscan provincial chapter held in Dublin in April 1324. The legislator was William of Rudyard, a canonist, later to be a royal judge and deputy treasurer, dean of St Patrick's Cathedral and vicar-general of the Dublin diocese (the archbishop was abroad at this time). As papal judge-delegate in this affair, he was legislating with apostolic authority. The text of his decree tells its own story:[11]

William of Rudyard, dean of the church of St Patrick's Dublin and one of the judges-delegate of the apostolic see, to the reverend religious Brother Henry, minister of the friars minor in Ireland and Brothers Durandus and Romanus, visitors of the Order of friars minor in Ireland, greeting and admonition to firmly obey apostolic commands.

A variety of solemn inquisitions of trustworthy witnesses drawn from your Order and other Orders as well as from the secular clergy and even from lay magnates in different parts of Ireland has shown that the conduct of friars and the presence of Irishmen of your Order in the cities of Cork and Limerick and in the towns of Buttevant, Ardfert, Nenagh, Claregalway, Galway and Athlone is very much to be distrusted and constitutes a danger both to the peace of the lord king and the general welfare of the community unless English and Irish live together. Therefore we strictly command you collectively and individually in virtue of the obedience which binds you to the apostolic see and under pain of major excommunication for contravention or obstruction of this order to remove these same Irish friars from where they are now living and place them in other houses of your Order in Ireland, except for three or four at most drawn from the least suspect whom we permit to remain in each of the houses specified, so that there may be communal living of English and Irish friars judging that in this country they should live together according to circumstances. We will further and command under the same penalties, for the greater peace and security of the country that in none of the eight houses named shall there be guardians of Irish nationality.

To remove all untoward suspicion of your Order in the future we order that theology teachers of Irish nationality at present living in these houses be allocated to houses of Englishmen unless later on another course of action might seem more advisable to us for the achievement of peace; to these and to others so transferred we wish the accustomed consolation of your Order to be shown.

For the greater peace and tranquillity of the country we command that all friars of Irish nationality shall swear a corporal oath to you or one of you that in the future they will neither prompt nor urge rebellion nor hold secret meetings, nor cause them to be made or held, nor do anything by which the peace of the country might in any way be disrupted.

The Dean's instructions, so reminiscent of Stephen of Lexington's of almost a century earlier, carrying the force of papal authority, were stiffened by the co-operation of the Order and also of the secular arm, the Dublin administration. They were repromulgated with clarifications and some modifications in May 1324 on the occasion of a meeting of parliament in Dublin. Dean William thought that his intentions had been deliberately misrepresented and sought, in his second decree, to put his commands beyond question. The new decree made five points. English friars at the discretion of the minister provincial, should be allocated to houses where Irish friars had been in breach of discipline. Having discovered that none of the houses in question had theology teachers except Claregalway and Galway, these two houses were allowed, of special grace, to have theologians of Irish nationality. None of the communities adjudged culpable was to be allowed to have an Irish guardian. But William of Rudyard then went on to except Claregalway and Galway and the other four founded 'within the areas of the Irish'. This must mean that of the original eight mentioned, Cork and Limerick were the only two forbidden to have a superior of Irish nationality. No Irish friar was to exercise general jurisdiction anywhere in Ireland either as *prelatus* or vicar. This veto is a little ambiguous: it probably was meant to exclude Irishmen from holding office as minister provincial or head of a custody or being deputy to such and from being bishops. Finally, 'for the greater peace and tranquillity of this country we will and command that some English friars should be members of communities in all places of pure Irishmen, just as conversely Irish friars should be distributed among the English'.

At this time Philip of Slane O.P., bishop of Cork and member of the King's Council in Ireland, was discussing Irish ecclesiastical affairs with the Pope in Avignon. He complained of discrimination against the English by Irish religious including 'those of the mendicant friars who admit no one into their monasteries unless they are pure Irish'. The English government's suggestion was that 'friars should live together in mixed communities, in all the convents of the Order in the country'. Naturally the Pope favoured this equitable and sensible principle. But by 1366 English policy had apparently abandoned it. The Kilkenny parliament of that year ordained and commanded that:

> No religious house, exempt or not, situated among the English shall for the future receive any Irishmen as professed religious but may receive Englishmen without regard to whether they were born in England or in Ireland . . .

Fortunately for the future history of Catholicism in Ireland, it was not to be clause 14 of the Statute of Kilkenny which determined the relationship of the two nations which made up the Franciscan province in Ireland.

No new Franciscan house was founded for a quarter of a century after 1296, nor, for over half a century after 1305 was there any new Dominican foundation. Nevertheless there was no real slackening of the great tide of monastic advance, since the Carmelites and Augustinians took up where the Franciscans and Dominicans left off.

The transformation of two groups of hermit religious into orders of friars and their subsequent sudden spread, increase in numbers and rise to prominence in public life is one of the most remarkable in the history of medieval monasticism. What was to become the Order of Our Lady of Mount Carmel began in mid-twelfth century as a by-product of the establishment of the Crusader states in the Holy Land, when a group of contemplatives established themselves in small cells on Mount Carmel. As the Latin position in the Near East deteriorated, so these recluses were compelled to seek refuge in Europe. Transmigration brought transmutation. Under the generalship of the Englishman St Simon Stock in the middle years of the century, their way of life was changed to something closely resembling the Dominicans. England became one of the main provinces of the Order. In 1272, taking that as the correct date of the first Carmelite foundation in Ireland, there were approximately thirteen houses in England, founded over a thirty-year period. This rate of growth was almost matched in Ireland. The English houses were generally in the more important towns, but some were in remoter areas, indicating that despite the adoption of the Dominican style, they had not completely shed their eremitical nature. This double settlement pattern is discernible in Ireland too. The Carmelites certainly attracted the support of the burgher class but six of the sixteen houses founded between 1272 and 1334 were in Connacht. All the known names of founders and patrons are Anglo-Irish, but Gaelic co-operation in the establishment of houses such as Caltra (a de Bermingham foundation), on the Athenry model, obviously cannot be ruled out. Constitutionally, the Irish province became autonomous in 1305 on the order of the master general, after an abortive effort in 1294 to establish a Scots-Irish province. The history of the Order in Ireland remains shrouded in obscurity, though it continued to expand in the later fourteenth century.

The Order of Hermits of St Augustine, whose early history is almost as difficult to reconstruct as that of the Carmelites, began as a group of semi-eremitic communities in Italy. A need for organisation in the thirteenth century brought a helping hand from the papacy and the work of uniting various monasteries into a coherent whole was begun by Innocent IV in 1243 and completed by Alexander IV with the 'great union' of 1256. By this decree about seventy houses, some in England, took to themselves the mendicant way of life, Dominican pattern, while retaining contact with their original rule, that of St Augustine. There were about twelve Augustinian houses in England before the first Irish foundation in Dublin. c.1282. The Irish houses, with one exception, were Anglo-Irish foundations, mostly in the bigger towns. Unlike the Carmelites, they did not establish themselves in Connacht to any significant extent. The Irish Augustinians remained an integral part of the English province. Analagously to the Dominicans, they formed a vicariate with the vicar nominated to the English provincial and were expected to send representatives to the provincial chapters in England. Little is known of their history at least in this period of their first expansion in Ireland. But, as with the Carmelites, the absence of documentation should not prevent our appreciation of the significant contribution they made towards maintaining the impetus of the advance of the friars in Ireland.

4 The Changing Episcopate in the Thirteenth Century

The anglicisation of the episcopate

The most solid advance in the reform of the Irish Church in the twelfth century had been in that critical sector of Church life, the episcopate. To compare the state of the episcopate in 1152, at the time of the Council of Kells-Mellifont, with that obtaining a century earlier, is to be made aware that a near-revolution had taken place in its composition and organisation. The coarbial families, monastery-orientated, had given place to a hierarchy ruling within the framework of a defined territorial diocesan system. The hold of ecclasiastical dynasties, of the laity over the monasteries, had been substantially lessened and the quality of episcopal personnel in the new era was made manifest in the life and works of Malachy of Armagh and Laurence of Dublin.

To move on a century from Kells–Mellifont is to become aware that another near-revolution had taken place in the Irish episcopate. But the beneficial effects of this second radical change are by no means so self-evident. In 1254, almost a third of the Irish dioceses was occupied by foreigners: ten by Anglo-Frenchmen and one, the primatial see of Armagh, by an Italian. In Armagh province, the sees of Connor, Down and Meath had Anglo-French incumbents; so had Limerick and Waterford in Cashel province, while all five sees of the Dublin province were likewise filled. This part of the anglicisation process was accomplished in the period 1178 to 1252 but it was not yet

c.1178	—	Connor
1181	—	Dublin
1192	—	Meath
c.1200	—	Waterford
c.1202	—	Down:Ossory:Leighlin
1215	—	Limerick
1223	—	Ferns:Kildare
1253	—	Lismore (previously Anglo-French, 1216–46)
1286	—	Emly (previously, 1212–36)
1306	—	Armagh (previously, 1217–27)
1321	—	Cork (previously, 1267–76?)
1333	—	Cloyne (previously, 1284–1321)

Anglicisation of dioceses, 1178–1333

complete. A chronological chart demonstrates effectively the dates at which the different dioceses began to be held uninterruptedly by Anglo-French prelates (See page 88).

The choice of Anglo-French bishops was the most overt sign of change, but the process went deeper than that. By 1252 when there were still twenty-three Irish bishops, the king of England or his chief representative in Ireland had played some part in the electoral process leading to the appointment of no less than sixteen of these. Records are defective and the figure might have been a little higher. Certainly, in the second half of the century, the number was to increase so that all dioceses, save only four or five were affected in some degree by royal action.

To appreciate the precise degree to which such appointments were influenced by the Crown, it is necessary to understand the electoral procedures in force in Ireland after the Invasion. To say that the king or his justiciar played some part in the electoral process which produced Irish bishops is not to say that he or his representative actually appointed them, any more than the presence of Anglo-French prelates in Irish dioceses means that they were royal nominees. Assessment of the relative degree of freedom of election prevailing in the different Irish dioceses is only possible after examination of the way it was expected episcopal elections should be conducted and the ways in which in practice they were conducted, in so far as this can be known.

By decision of the council of Cashel, the Church in Ireland was to be brought into conformity with the practices of the Church in England. The English way of electing bishops, which had many parallels in feudal Europe, was based on the principle that a bishop was in some sense a double person: he was a member of both the spiritual and temporal aristocracies, being baron as well as bishop. He was a tenant-in-chief of the Crown, holding extensive possessions by knight-service and expected to act towards the king like any other feudal magnate, so far as his order permitted. No king could be indifferent about who became a bishop since, on appointment, such a person became an active member of the ruling class and his obedience and co-operation might be of very considerable political significance. On the other hand, no pope could feel easy about leaving an episcopal appointment in royal hands: there was too much danger of political considerations taking priority over ecclesiastical ones. Churchmen generally, in the second half of the eleventh century, had become increasingly restive about what they considered to be an excessive lay influence in the making of bishops. Different accommodations of the respective viewpoints were reached in the different countries of Christendom. The problem was to distinguish between the baronial and episcopal element in a bishop's status in such a way as to ensure that the king as suzerain had his due, while canonical freedom of election was not impugned. In England, the position obtaining in Henry II's reign had emerged from a vigorous controversy between Henry I and St Anselm and still enjoyed the tacit approval of the English Church and the papacy. The place of the king had been defined in 1164 in clause 12 of the Constitutions of Clarendon:

When an archbishopric or bishopric is vacant, or any abbey or priory of the king's demesne, it must be taken into his own hand, and he shall receive from it all revenues and profits as part of his demesne. And when the time has come to provide for the church, the lord king must summon the more important of the beneficed clergy of the church, and the election should take place in the lord king's chapel with the assent of the lord king and the advice of the clergy of the realm whom he shall summon for this purpose. And the cleric elected shall there do homage and fealty to the lord king as his liege lord for his life and limbs and his earthly honour, saving his order, before he is consecrated.

Clause 11 of the Constitutions had made it clear that bishops as tenants-in-chief held their *temporalia* or diocesan lands and their appurtenances, by ordinary feudal tenure. Hence during an episcopal vacancy, by analogy with royal wardship of *feudalia* during the minority of a baron, these *temporalia* were to be held by the king and granted to the new bishop after he had done homage and fealty to his suzerain. These principles were to be basic in the definitive electoral procedure. That the election should be quite such a royal occasion was not to outlast the pontificate of Innocent III, when the final English adjustment of the two interests was made. But until the early thirteenth century the king's part in the actual selection of a bishop was that envisaged in the Constitutions.

Henry II's two participations in Irish episcopal appointments were in general conformity with what was laid down in 1164. In 1175 at Windsor the King held a council of some importance for Irish affairs, since it was then and there that he received the submission of Rory O Connor, king of Connacht. There came to Windsor Master Augustine O Selbhaigh, the choice of the Waterford electors for their vacant see. Since Waterford was a royal town, it may be presumed that the temporalities of the see had been taken into the king's custody. Laurence O Toole, the archbishop of Dublin, had been engaged in the negotiations between the two kings (the archbishop of Tuam was also present) and it was with him that Augustine was sent to his metropolitan, the archbishop of Cashel, to be canonically examined and consecrated. The English chronicles recorded that Henry 'gave and granted' the vacant bishopric to Augustine. But that phrase would seem to exaggerate Henry's role (unless they mean to refer to the temporalities only) which was rather to give assent and take fealty than actually to nominate the candidate.

Nothing is known of how Reginald became bishop of Connor, about 1178. It seems likely that his appointment owed everything to John de Courcy, the newly victorious earl of Ulster and nothing to Henry II. The appointment of John Cumin to Dublin in 1181, however quite fully documented, reveals a very direct royal intervention. Officials were sent from England after the death of Laurence O Toole in November 1180, to take possession of the substantial temporalities of the Dublin diocese. Roger of Howden described the selection of the new archbishop:

> (The king) granted the archbishopric of Dublin to John Cumin his clerk and intimate friend at the election of the bishops and clergy of England and of certain clerks of the metropolitan church of Dublin who had come to England to the said king in order to have a pastor.

It is clear that in this case, though churchmen participated, there is some justice in the chronicler's claim that Henry 'gave' the see of Dublin to Cumin. But Pope Lucius III himself consecrated him archbishop (21 March 1182) which means that if there had been any canonical irregularity about the appointment, it was validated by papal action.

Between the death of Henry II and the ratification of a new electoral procedure for episcopal elections by Innocent III and King John, Anglo-Frenchmen were appointed to six sees for the first time (Meath, Waterford, Leighlin, Down, Ossory, Limerick) and in two for a second time (Dublin, Waterford). There is very little information available about how these men became bishops. One inference, however, seems permissible: for the most part these were not appointments in which the king had had a hand. Local initiatives were preponderant. The reorganisation of the diocese of Meath, the transfer of

Diocesan structure in the thirteenth century

its seat from Clonard to Trim, the appointment of an Anglo-French bishop were also part and parcel of the consolidation of the de Lacy lordship of Meath. Connor and Down were similarly an important part of the Ulster lordship of John de Courcy. Leighlin and Ossory were in William Marshal's Leinster lordship with its capital and cathedral at Kilkenny. William Marshal was indeed later to claim to the Pope that he held the right of patronage of the diocese of Ossory. Such a claim directly contradicted the principle accepted in England which suffered no rival authority to the king's in a diocese. It is clear that in Ireland the king had not yet secured the full implementation of the English procedure. Whatever the theory, in practice King John did not find it easy to have his way in Irish episcopal elections.

The historian is at some disadvantage when seeking to trace the operation of local forces in the making of bishops in the crucial but confused first two decades of the thirteenth century. There are few or no documents to help him in this respect from sources inside Ireland whether Irish or Anglo-French and he must rely on the records of two governments outside the country: the English monarchy and the papacy. Fortunately for him, the files of these governments sometimes contain reports from men on the spot.

Such a participant in Irish ecclesiastical affairs was John of Salerno, cardinal priest of St Stephen on the Coelian Hill, papal legate in Ireland in 1202. He was caught up in events of great moment. The *Annals of Loch Cé* record baldly that in 1202 Cardinal John held two councils, one in Dublin attended by both Irish and Anglo-French clergy and a second, at Athlone, of the clergy of Connacht. No detail about what was discussed or promulgated has been given by the annalist. It seems likely, however, that the Dublin council considered the highly controversial matter of the succession to Armagh, while it is most probable that the Athlone council considered the almost equally controversial issue of the succession to Tuam.

These were controversies of different types. In Armagh, the issue was a clash between the two nations with King John intervening vigorously if not very successfully. In Tuam, the clash was confined to Irishmen and was between reformers and local interests analogous, perhaps, to that which had brought St Malachy into conflict with Clann Sinaich.

A double election followed the death of Primate Tomaltach O Connor in 1201. The first 'election' was patently uncanonical for it was held in the wrong place, Drogheda not Armagh (at the justiciar's prompting), and the majority of the electors were not present. There were in fact only four electors in attendance: the archdeacon of Armagh, two suffragans of the province and the abbot of Mellifont whose right to be present at all seems highly dubious. This group drew up a short-list of three candidates: Simon Rochfort, bishop of Meath, one of the two suffragans present, Ralph Petit, his archdeacon, and a king's clerk and official, Humphrey of Tickhill. Clearly the Drogheda meeting was very much an English affair.

The archdeacon of Armagh then summoned the electors, who were the suffragan bishops of the province (all but two of them were Irish), to assemble at Armagh. The bishop of Meath and the abbot of Mellifont (who was Irish) declined to go there 'on account of the Irish'. There was now elected the prior of the Augustinian house at Bangor, Eugenius. The legate told Innocent III that this election brought very great strife between English and Irish, for the English firmly declared that they were utterly unwilling to accept any Irishman as their archbishop and argued along with some Irishmen, it was said, that the appointment of an Englishman would be conducive to the good of Armagh and the peace of the whole realm. King John complained to the Legate that the (Irish) bishops of

Clogher, Clonmacnois, Kells and Ardagh were hostile; he also tried to bribe Eugenius into renouncing his candidature. The Legate put his problems to the Pope who responded with a masterly analysis of the legal technicalities of the case which passed into the *Decretales* to become part of the common law of the Church. His conclusion was to advise the choice of a candidate of neither nation. There may be a longterm consequence of this recommendation in the appointments of the German, Albrecht Suerbeer (1239–46) and the Italian, Reginald (1247–56). But it was Eugenius who was to carry the day. The circumstances of his victory are obscure. It seems he appealed to Rome but no record of Innocent's formal approval has survived. However, despite John's peremptory command to all in Armagh that Eugenius was not to be accepted as their archbishop but that Ralph Petit should be, by 1205 he had been accepted as primate by both Irish and English clergy. For in that year he took part in a clerical assembly, possibly presiding over a council, at Mullingar, in the heart of Petit territory and attended by clergy of both nations, including two of his former rivals, Ralph Petit and Simon Rochfort. John made his peace with Eugenius in 1206 though it cost the Archbishop money. But it seems to have been a genuine peace for in 1207, the see of Exeter being vacant, John informed its keepers that he was sending the archbishop of Armagh to act as bishop during the vacancy. Eugenius seems to have successfully overcome the English animosities so violently expressed earlier.

The Armagh vacancy would give the Legate insight into the problems that the growth of the Anglo-French clergy had brought to the Irish Church. The Tuam vacancy gave him, and the Pope, experience of another Irish problem: hereditary tenure of bishoprics and lesser ecclesiastical offices. The ecclesiastical dynasties yielded ground more slowly in the Connacht province than elsewhere. But the reform was still going on even after the Invasion. Thus the *Annals of Clonmacnois* record that in 1172(?) a council at Clonfert legislated against lay control of churches and ecclesiastical business, against the ordination of the sons of bishops and priests; seven laymen were dispossessed of episcopal lands they were holding. Cadhla (Catholicus) O Duffy, a member of the family already noticed in connexion with the Cross of Cong, died in 1201. The vacancy had already been filled, after a fashion, before the Legate arrived in Ireland. The see had been held by Cadhla's father and grandfather before him, so the Cardinal told Innocent III, and in order to continue the succession he had uncanonically consecrated his nephew in his own lifetime and he had taken up the family inheritance. It was only with difficulty that the Legate got rid of the usurper. The suffragans of the province, who were the electors, were summoned, and by his advice and command elected the Augustinian prior of Saul, Felix O Ruadhain. Archbishop Felix, an outsider, was not welcomed by the king of Connacht. The *Annals of Loch Cé* record that in 1216 the Archbishop was 'cruelly and violently taken prisoner by the Connachtmen and Maelisa O Connor and put in chains; a thing that we have never heard of before, namely, an archbishop being manacled.' The entry recalls St Malachy's fears of martyrdom if he challenged the Ui Sinaich in Armagh. There is some evidence that Archbishop Felix made peace with the O Connors at least for a time. Ultimately, however, his tenure proved impossible. He found refuge in Dublin, resigning his see in 1233, becoming a Cistercian and dying in St Mary's Dublin in 1238.

The Armagh and Tuam elections were the outstanding events of the Legate's mission in Ireland but he was concerned with two, and possibly three, diocesan issues of some importance. It was possibly at his Athlone council that he negotiated the union of Mayo (held by an O Duffy) with Tuam. There were to be strong attempts to reverse this decision but it was upheld by Honorius III in 1217 and, definitively, by Gregory IX in 1240. His action in another diocesan union was indecisive. In 1202 Felix, bishop of Lismore, resigned his see to the Legate. This was the beginning of a squalid attempt by successive bishops of Waterford to assimilate Lismore. The Legate apparently allowed the bishop of Waterford to hold Lismore in 1202 but both Innocent III and Honorius III were to condemn the Waterford attacks in no uncertain terms. When the dispute began, it was between an Anglo-French prelate and an Irish one and should be considered along with the Armagh election dispute as evidence of the ill-feeling between the nations in the early thirteenth century. But even when Lismore was held by a foreigner the ambitions of the Waterford bishops were in no way diminished nor did the morality and legality of their tactics tend to improve. The Legate's final concern with the affairs of the episcopate was, it seems, with the diocese of Meath. It is very likely that it was he who gave the necessary permission in 1202 to Simon Rochfort to transfer his see from Clonard which had been burned by a local Irish prince 'to injure the foreigners that were in it' to the protection of the de Lacy garrison town of Trim.

The Armagh election had exposed the limitations of King John's power to overrule local interests. This was far from being the only time he was to meet a rebuff. In fact, of the five other episcopal elections in which he decided to take a hand, one only was to see his candidate successful.

For Cashel in 1206, he was a warm supporter of Ailbe O Maelmuidhe, bishop of Ferns from c.1186. But the Cashel electors did not pick him. For Limerick in 1207 the King instructed his justiciar:

This is to inform you that we have granted the vacant bishopric of Limerick to Master Geoffrey, parson of the church of Dungarvan and we wish for and assent to his promotion to the episcopal see of Limerick. We therefore command you that you cause him to have that bishopric and that you warn and induce the clergy of that diocese to elect him and receive him as bishop.[1]

But Geoffrey did not get the see. The King was also unsuccessful when supporting Geoffrey White for Cork in 1214, despite his efforts to enlist the help of the archbishops of Cashel and Dublin. The effect of his intervention in these two sees seems to have led to protracted vacancies. John indicated his support of Robert for Waterford in 1210 and he was elected. But then the candidate was a kinsman of the justiciar and for that reason, likely to get the see in any case. Mention must be made of the appointment of Henry of London to Dublin in 1213. This was by capitular election and nothing is known of any part John may have played in influencing the electors. One of the King's last governmental acts was to put the temporalities of the diocese of Killaloe into the hands of Bishop Ailbe of Ferns, until he should be appointed to that see. But this was not to be. This vacancy at Killaloe was to become, like the Armagh dispute of 1201–07, something of a *cause célèbre* as a clash between Irish and Anglo-French interests. Indeed it was even more celebrated since it was linked to a new and radical government policy: a plan to prevent the election of Irishmen to any bishopric or chapter.

Neither Henry II nor King John had shown any special anti-Irish prejudice in ecclesiastical matters. No doubt they preferred men of their own nation in key sees like Dublin and Armagh. But they did not insist on the absolute exclusion of Irishmen from the episcopate. Henry had accepted Augustine for Waterford without demur. John, after failing to place his candidate in Cashel, accepted the new archbishop as his clerk and *familiaris* (member of his household). The classic instance of co-operation between the monarchy and the Irish Church – which after all was the declared policy of the whole hierarchy after Cashel II – was the former abbot of Baltinglass, Ailbe, who ruled Ferns from *c*.1186 to 1223. He had an especially strong bond with John, formed even before he became king; he ministered occasionally in England; he was John's candidate for Cashel. Ironically, it seems to have been this bishop who caused in part at least, the change in English governmental thinking. For Ailbe was no lick-spittle. Sometime before May 1216, he had excommunicated one of the leading figures in England and Ireland, William Marshal, alleging that he had as lord of Leinster, mis-appropriated lands belonging to the see of Ferns. The Earl, who was to die in 1219 still under excommunication and whose sons also were to incur the Bishop's wrath for the same offence, was primarily responsible for the policy of exclusion. The veto against the promotion of Irishmen was promulgated under his name only, not in the name of the regency council then ruling England for the nine year old Henry III. The instruction was also connected with the Killaloe vacancy in which Marshal had an interest. There was also a vacancy in the primatial see of Armagh which, as has been seen, had already been the scene of one attempt at anglicisation. The relevant mandates, all issued in January 1217, some three months after John's death, were terse but clear:[2]

> The King to his justiciar of Ireland, greeting. We order you in virtue of the faith by which you are held to us that you shall not allow any Irishman to be elected or promoted in any cathedral church in our land of Ireland since by this our land (God forbid!) is disturbed . . . Witness, count [Marshal], Oxford, 13 January.

> The King to his justiciar of Ireland, greeting. This is to inform you that we have given our assent to the canon-ical election of Robert Travers to the bishopric of

Killaloe. We therefore order you to arrange that the same Robert shall have full seisin of the said see with all its appurtenances . . . Witness count Marshal, Oxford, 15 January.

The King to the archbishop of Cashel, greeting. This is to inform you that we have given our assent and favour to the election made of Robert Travers to the see of Killaloe and we send him to you, asking you to confer on the same Robert the favour of confirmation and consecration . . . Witness as above.

The King to his justiciar of Ireland, greeting. Since the peace of our land of Ireland has been disturbed more frequently through elections there of Irishmen, we command you, in virtue of the faith which holds you to us, that you should not for the future allow any Irishman in our land of Ireland to be elected or promoted in any cathedral. With the advice of our venerable father, Henry lord archbishop of Dublin and your own, you will by every means obtain that our clerks and other honourable Englishmen necessary to us and our kingdom be elected and promoted to bishoprics and dignities as they become vacant. Witness, 17 January, as above.

The King to his justiciar in Ireland, greeting. This is to inform you we have committed to our beloved and faithful Richard Marsh, our chancellor, the custody of archdiocese of Armagh with all its appurtenances. And therefore we command you to cause the same chancellor or his deputy, nominated as such in his letters patent to you, to have the said archdiocese. Witness the same, Gloucester, 22 January.

The King to the dean, archdeacon, chapter of Armagh, greeting. We order you that as you love the good and honour of your church you shall not presume to elect anyone as your archbishop without our assent . . . Witness the same, Gloucester, 23 January.

Similar letter to the suffragans of Armagh province, same witness, same date.

William Marshal, as lord of Leinster, was the obvious man in the regency council to take the lead in Irish affairs. Smarting under sentence of excommunication by an Irish prelate, he had taken advantage of his new position of authority in England. But there was more in it than just pique. That there should be a vacancy at this time in Killaloe was a tempting opportunity to establish Anglo-French power in an area where Marshal had important interests and had some years earlier met rebuff. There were ears in Ireland ready enough to hear the new message, not least those of the justiciar to whom these mandates were addressed. For Geoffrey Marsh, with the Marshals, Butlers and others, had been in the van of the settlers' penetration into Ormond. It had been in 1207 that William Marshal and Geoffrey Marsh had together tried to construct a castle in the episcopal town of Killaloe and had failed. Further, Robert Travers, the chosen Anglo-French candidate for Killaloe was of a family settled in the area (their name survives in the place-name, Traverstown). They were tenants of the Butlers. Geoffrey Marsh was currently administering the Butler lands during the minority of Theobald Walter II; Robert Travers was his nephew. One of his sons had married a niece of the Archbishop Henry of London mentioned in the last mandate cited above. Thus behind the new anti-Irish policy lay a mesh of personal, family and territorial interests, whilst the three principals held supreme governmental positions: William Marshal exercising virtually the royal power in the context, seconded by Geoffrey Marsh his representative in Ireland and advised by the archbishop of Dublin who, from April 1217, was papal legate in Ireland with a broad commission to uphold the king's interest there.

The archbishop of Cashel, Donal O Longargain mentioned in these letters, was not a party to the anti-Irish policy. He was in fact in France in self-imposed exile from his see because of infringements of the liberty of his church of Cashel. His deputy, whose rank, name and nationality remain unknown, was however, prepared to help. He exercised metropolitan powers to confirm the election of Travers who was then consecrated by three of his fellow countrymen, the bishops of Waterford, Limerick and Emly. Before that consecration had taken place, the Killaloe chapter elected their archdeacon who went to Rome to lay his case before Honorius III. The pope made a meticulously fair examination of the whole affair which lasted for several years. He finally concluded, however, that Travers was a manifest intruder, made bishop by the force of lay power and must be ejected and those who consecrated him disciplined. But as late as 1226, such was the tenacity of Travers, the strength of the new settlers in at least parts of the Killaloe diocese and their convenient ability to ignore unwelcome papal mandates, that Travers was still in possession. It is likely he held on until death. A contemporaneous case of intrusion into Ardfert, also through the agency of Geoffrey Marsh, ended more successfully for the papacy when, by 1224, the intruder had been persuaded to remove himself permanently to the monastery of St Alban's in England. Honorius III was in no doubt as to what was the real issue in Killaloe. The Irish had complained bitterly to him, probably through Archbishop Donal of Cashel, that the English were grievously and iniquitously oppressing them. Henry of London was forbidden to show favour to Robert Travers or to any others of his nation who were guilty of acts of aggression against the Irish. The pope warned the archbishop that to discriminate in favour of one's own nation as against another was against the divine law: 'non enim est acceptio personarum apud Deum' (*Rom.* 2.11): 'For there is no respect of persons with God' or (in a more modern translation), 'God has no favourites'. *Acceptio personarum* in episcopal elections must stop.

It is possible, though the evidence is not conclusive, that the termination of Henry of London's legateship, somewhat tersely announced by the pope on 6 July 1220, was the pope's censure of his equivocal attitude in the Killaloe dispute. James, canon of St Victor's in Paris, his new legate, bore this commission into Ireland:[3]

> Honorius bishop etc. To his beloved son Master James his chaplain and penitentiary, apostolic legate, health etc. It has come to our ears that certain Englishmen, with unheard-of temerity, have ordered that no cleric from Ireland no matter how educated or good-living, shall be promoted to any ecclesiastical office. Not wishing to turn deaf ears to an abuse of such audacity and evil, we order you by authority of this letter to make public denunciation of this order as void and to prohibit these English from maintaining it or attempting anything similar in future. Irish clergy should be freely admitted to ecclesiastical offices if their learning and conduct are fitting and their election canonical. (6 August 1220)

James' mission was not very obviously successful. Honorius III's condemnation of discrimination did not prevent two recurrences of it in 1225 (Waterford) and in 1226 (Cloyne) even after the pope had again condemned it in 1224. It is not possible to follow the detail of these two elections. In the first, the instruction to appoint an Englishman would seem to have been unnecessary; in the second, it was unsuccessful. After the regency period, the Crown seems to have been content to let the matter rest with the local chapter providing it conformed to the established procedures agreed for England between King John and Innocent III and extended to Ireland by virtue of the Cashel II decision that the practices of the Church in Ireland should conform to those in use in England.

The new arrangement, superseding *c*. 12 of the Constitutions of Clarendon read, in King John's charter:[4]

> Hence it is that, whatever custom has been so far observed in the English church during our own and our predecessors' reigns and whatever jurisdiction we have so far claimed in the election of whatever grade of prelate, this we have now conceded at their petition, for the salvation of our soul and the souls of our predecessors and of our successors as kings of England, voluntarily and entirely of our own free will, and with the general consent of our barons; and we have decreed and hereby by our charter confirmed that for the future in all and each of the churches and monasteries, cathedral or conventual, through our whole realm of England there should be for ever free elections of whatever grade of prelate, great or small, – saving only the securing to us and our heirs of the custody of vacant churches and monasteries that belong to us. We also promise that we will not hinder, nor permit or instigate our agents to hinder, the electors in all and each of the said churches and monasteries from freely appointing a pastor over them whenever they so wish after the prelacy has become vacant, provided that permission to elect be first sought of us and our heirs, a permission we will not refuse or postpone. And if (which God forbid) we should refuse or postpone, the electors will nevertheless proceed to make a canonical election. Similarly after an election let our assent be sought, which similarly we will not refuse unless we have offered, and lawfully proved, some reasonable cause to justify our refusal.

It is in the light of this agreement that we must consider

the significance of the Armagh vacancy in which William Marshal and Geoffrey Marsh, as documented above, also began to take part in January 1217. The new procedure envisaged capitular election, preceded by request of the chapter (or the canonical electors if they were other than a chapter) for licence to elect, custody of temporalities during vacancy and for the bishop-elect to present himself to the king for his assent before consecration. An important consequence of the new position was the enhanced importance and freedom of the chapter or electing body. It had become very important from the Crown's point of view that chapters should not be allowed to evade the obligation to seek royal licence and royal assent, for if they did so, royal participation in episcopal elections would be further diminished and possibly be removed altogether. Hence the government was particularly insistent on adherence to the new procedure. Accordingly, in 1217, governmental policy towards episcopal elections in Ireland was two-fold: to secure the appointment of Englishmen and also to ensure that chapters sought royal licence and assent. If the Killaloe vacancy is an excellent example of the implementation of the first part of this policy, the Armagh election is an equally revealing illustration of the second.

The Armagh electors chose an English archbishop, Luke Netterville, who was already archdeacon of Armagh. If the argument be accepted that the absence of any recorded objection to his selection, particularly the absence of any appeal against it to the papal curia, means the election was canonical, this was a canonical election. But it was not legal as far as the English Government was concerned because licence to elect had not been sought. Luke was sent back for the proper procedure to be implemented and he did not get assent, and therefore custody of temporalities, until royal licence had been properly requested. That the government was able to take custody of temporalities and withhold them until the proper forms had been observed was doubtless a powerful inducement to chapters to toe the line.

Nevertheless, in England as well as Ireland, chapters remained reluctant to seek royal licence. The reason for their distaste for this procedural form was doubtless their desire to retain the temporalities until they presented a bishop-elect for royal assent. Early in 1219, however, the regency council appealed to the pope for action against chapters which evaded their electoral obligations towards the Crown. Honorius III instructed the prelates and chapters of England and Wales, as well as Ireland, to seek royal licence to elect under pain of ecclesiastical censure. But in Ireland, where sees were so poor, custody of temporalities was particularly resented and evasion continued. Opposition to the taking of temporalities into the king's hand in vacancy came to a head in 1231 when Hubert de Burgh of Limerick, ordinarily a very 'safe' bishop politically, was deputed to appeal to the pope against the practice. Henry III made a counter-attack so successfully that the view of the bishops of Ireland was not apparently put to the pope. The papacy continued to uphold the king's right to temporalities during vacancy. Neither *de facto* nor *de iure* did the bishops and chapters gain their point and throw off the escheator's control during vacancy. As colonial settlement spread, so the effectiveness of governmental control of temporalities increased. By 1237 some twenty dioceses were within the English sphere of influence. That temporalities were with the escheator during vacancies was a most potent factor in this development.

Though the Crown's role was important and the papacy had its part, it is clear that the most important voice in the making of a bishop was that of the chapter or its equivalent. In colonial areas, chapters became anglicised and elected their fellow-countrymen. Areas unaffected by settlement continued to appoint Irishmen. In a number of dioceses the balance of power between the nations was more precarious. Cashel and Killaloe were important examples of sees which managed to retain a succession of Irishmen who, nevertheless, found it expedient to reach a *modus vivendi* with the Crown. The Crown, for its part, was satisfied with the elect of the chapter, no matter what his nationality, providing licence and assent had been sought and it was satisfied that the elect was not a political risk. The papacy held itself available for the resolution of conflicts, decision of doubtful points of law, ratification of institutional changes. It was also responsible for the canonical confirmations of archbishops-elect.

This remained the general position as anglicisation proceeded apace throughout the thirteenth and early fourteenth centuries. The Crown, as the colony grew, came to make its influence felt in virtually every diocese in Ireland. It is instructive to review the position at the time when Edward I, in whose reign (1272–1307) the colony reached its apogee, came to the throne. In 1272 there were twenty Irish bishops, thirteen Anglo-Irish or English (Dublin was vacant; it was invariably held by an Englishman) and one Italian (in Clonfert, 1266–95). No native Irishman was bishop in any of the five dioceses which formed the Dublin province. This had been the position for about half a century and was to remain so throughout the rest of the medieval period. In Tuam province, on the other hand, no Englishman had as yet held a see. The archbishopric itself was to be held by Englishmen from 1286 to 1313, otherwise without significant exception, the province remained under the control of Irish prelates throughout the medieval period. The situation in the other two provinces was not so clear-cut. In Armagh, there were seven Irish-held sees: Armagh itself, Clogher, Clonmacnois, Derry, Dromore, Kilmore and Raphoe (though its bishop is found acting as a suffragan of Canterbury in 1273) as against the English-held dioceses: Ardagh (though it was very exceptional for this diocese not to be ruled by an Irishman), Connor, Down and Meath. The Irish dioceses of Armagh province were to remain relatively free from Crown intervention. Edward I made a determined effort to force Derry, Raphoe, Dromore and Kilmore to conform to English-style electoral procedures but his success was limited and only temporary.

In Cashel, however, the situation was very different. Many parts of Munster which contained some of the most fertile land in Ireland were among the most densely colonised by the invaders. But they had not succeeded in making themselves indisputable masters throughout the province. The respective strengths of the two nations was overall very even, and this position was reflected in the composition of the episcopate. Six sees were generally ruled by Irish bishops in this period: Cashel, Ardfert, Emly, Kilfenora, Killaloe and Ross, and five by English bishops: Limerick, Lismore, Waterford, Cloyne and Cork. But the situation was fluid and there were changes at various times in the century and even in the fourteenth century the position had not everywhere finally stabilised itself.

Space does not allow a detailed examination of the degree to which all the dioceses of the province were affected by the anglicisation process. But the archdiocese itself represents the balance of the nations at its nicest and its history, therefore, allows a glimpse at the problems which the new order posed for Irish bishops. It too succeeded in keeping intact the succession of Irish prelates throughout the century, despite the town itself being predominantly English (though the archbishop was its lord) and the see, small in extent, lay mostly within *terre Engleis*. The respective experiences of anglicisation of Cashel and Dublin (and of Archbishop Nicholas Mac Maol Iosa of Armagh discussed in the next chapter) form an instructive contrast.

The archbishops of Cashel, 1186–1316
Matthew O Heney, O.Cist. 1186–1206
Donal O Longargain, O.Cist. (from 1220) *c.*1208–1223
Marianus O Brien, O.Cist. (from 1231) 1224–37
David O Kelly, O.P. 1238–53
David Mac Carwill, O.Cist. (from 1269) 1254–89
Stephen O Brogan, 1290–1302
Maurice Mac Carwill, 1303–16

In common with the other major Irish sees at this time, Cashel built a new cathedral, developed a chapter organisation to go with it and consolidated the organisation of the temporalities of the diocese. Donal Mor O Brien had in 1169 built a cathedral dedicated to St Patrick which lay between Cormac's Chapel and the Round Tower. This was rebuilt in the period 1224–89, not without some financial stress, in a style which reflects the influence of the new Anglo-French churches in the area. The chapter with major dignitaries, was in existence in the first decade of the thirteenth century. The first intimation that it was of mixed national composition comes *c.*1230 when an Anglo-Irishman is found to be chancellor. It is in the 1230s also that the Crown, for the first known time, collated to a benefice when the see was vacant. This power to collate during vacancy was an extension to Ireland of a power exercised by the king in England (it was also exercised in vacant French sees by the kings of France) and it was repeatedly exercised in Cashel throughout the century. Generally these collations were of Englishmen but not invariably, for on at least one occasion Edward I presented an Irishman. Use of this power was an obvious method wherewith to try to pack a chapter. It is known that the Dublin administration was collating to benefices during episcopal vacancies without the king's knowledge or approval in the 1220s. This probably explains the Cashel chapter's petition to Pope Honorius III that the number of canons should be restricted to twelve and any increase without its consent forbidden, a request which the Pope granted in 1224. For clearly if the chapter were to be increased in size by the government during a vacancy in the see (Cashel was vacant in 1223), there would be an opportunity of changing the balance between the nations within the chapter. The final vindication of the chapter's independence, this time from a threat of a different sort, came with Innocent IV's ruling in 1254 that it was the Cashel chapter, and not the suffragan bishops of the province, which was the proper electoral body for the archbishopric.

The political geography of thirteenth-century Ireland made it impossible for the archbishops of Cashel to avoid some degree of co-operation with the Crown. In the course of the century it became clear that in most circumstances where an archbishop found himself at odds with the English government, the government would have the better of it. It thus became established Cashel policy to maintain a *modus vivendi* with the Crown, even if, from time to time, it is apparent that the different archbishops pursued it with different degrees of willingness. Few of the archbishops in this period failed to incur the suspicions of English officialdom in one way or another. But, equally, few of them were able to stand outside the ambit of Crown influence and power.

Archbishop O Heney belonged to that generation of Irish churchmen who thought, in the spirit of Pope Alexander III, that co-operation with the invader was in the best interests of the Irish Church. Not that he was an uncritical admirer of the foreigners, as his famous remark about their propensity for making martyrs of bishops suggests (the allusion was of course to the Becket murder). But he was papal legate for Ireland (1192–98) and as such held a position of authority in respect of each of the two nations. There can be little doubt that he impressed the foreign clergy. The Annals of the Cistercian abbey of St Mary's, Dublin, recorded his death in 1206 with this panegyric: 'Matthew, archbishop of Cashel, legate of all Ireland, the wisest and most religious of all Irishmen, after founding many churches, having triumphed over man's ancient enemy in working many miracles and after voluntarily abandoning all worldly pomp, went happily to his rest at Holy Cross abbey'. Unfortunately we have no means of knowing more intimately of his spirituality or pastoral activities. Dublin had special cause to remember him because when, in the early years of the century, Archbishop Cumin was in exile after a dispute with King John, Matthew administered the see in his absence. The Legate was involved in disputes in the diocese of Ross, Leighlin and Ardfert. The precise manner and degree of his involvement remains unknown but it may well have overfavoured the English interest for Innocent III relieved him of his legateship.

After Archbishop Matthew's death, King John hoped to continue the harmonious relationship of Cashel and the Crown by pushing the promotion of Ailbe, Cistercian bishop of Ferns, whose attitude to the newcomers was very much that of the late archbishop. In this aim, John was unsuccessful though he accepted Donal without protest, confirming the properties of the see, including lands granted to it by the Lord of Thomond. However, this initial accord over the archiepiscopal lands was not to last.

Disputes about ecclesiastical properties were commonplace in this period in both English and Irish controlled dioceses, due partly to the impact of the invader, partly to inevitable adjustments in the diocesan system so recently set up at Kells in 1152. In Cashel the starting point of the dispute concerned the justiciar's alleged arbitrary seizure of episcopal property in the town of Cashel in order to build a castle. Complaints to both King and Pope having failed to achieve any satisfaction for the Archbishop, he withdrew to France, putting Cashel under interdict (1216–17). But the dispute grew to more serious proportions. The Archbishop protested that in the giving and receiving of evidence in the case, English legal practice countenanced discrimination against Irish witnesses and, further, that there was discrimination against Irishmen being promoted to sees in Ireland. This latter charge clearly had reference to the policies of William Marshal in the province of Cashel, described earlier. Archbishop Donal's complaint was apparently sufficient to bring about the removal of Henry of London from the papal legateship and the despatch of the legate James to rectify the abuses complained of (July–August 1220). However, later evidence suggests that the Crown eventually was able to mount a stronger lobby at the curia and was winning the Pope round to its point of view. The archbishop was ordered by the Pope to lift the interdict (May 1222). He resigned his see at some date before August 1223 and retired to a monastery.

When national animosities threatened the successful filling of a vacant archbishopric, inevitably the papacy gave thought to whether provision of a complete outsider might afford a satisfactory compromise solution. Innocent III had suggested this in connexion with Armagh in 1202 and Innocent IV was to act on it when providing the German Albert Suerbeer to Armagh in 1239 and the Italian Dominican Reginald in 1247. But this course of action was not a success. Suerbeer resigned in 1246 and Reginald was an almost permanent absentee. Honorius III had recourse to this solution on the resignation of Archbishop Donal. But his nominee, Michael Scot, refused on the grounds that he did not know the language. The Pope then translated Marianus from Cork, conscious when he did so that he was selecting a native Irishman who had been 'clerk and intimate' of King John, as he reminded Henry III. What little is known of the new archbishop's work suggests that he was in favour with the Crown. But having become a Cistercian in 1231, Stephen of Lexington found him excessively partial towards his own fellow country-men in the great Cistercian upset of these years.

Little is known either, of David O Kelly translated from the see of Cloyne to Cashel in 1238. He was sufficiently integrated in the Anglo-Irish ecclesiastical world to make common cause with Archbishop Luke of Dublin to resist the primatial claims of Armagh, and successfully vin-dicated the autonomy of the province from visitation. On the other hand, he attempted to assert his independence as metropolitan in respect of one of the powers of the Crown by proclaiming in 1251 that he would confirm the bishop-elect of Limerick (an Anglo-Irishman) whether or not royal assent was forthcoming. He was forced to back down. So too, in a similar context, was his successor, David Mac Carwill. The archbishops of Cashel were unable to disregard the common law procedures in the confirmation of their suffragans, irksome though they undoubtedly found them.

David Mac Carwill was caught up in a series of dis-putes, some concerned with points of principle connected with the welfare of his see, some concerned with personal antagonisms. It is not easy, given the state of the evidence, to know exactly where the rights and wrongs of these various quarrels lay. But certain features of his pontificate stand out as unusually revelatory of the position of Irish bishops at this period when the tide of anglicisation was at its flood.

Henry III opposed Mac Carwill's election on the grounds that he was associated with, and even related to, known enemies of the Crown. Innocent IV, however, prevailed on the King to accept him but he was never to be wholly trusted by the Dublin administration. A bitter feud with some of the English in the town of Cashel and aspirations to independent action in confirming bishops-elect in his province no doubt did little to allay suspicion. It became overt after 1274, and the context was changes in Cistercian organisation.

There was a noteworthy connexion between the see of Cashel and the Cistercians which Archbishop David continued when, in 1269, he himself joined the Order. The evidence of the General Chapter Statutes shows that he was actively promoting Irish Cistercian interests in the early 1270s; he founded a Cistercian house in 1272 at the foot of the Rock of Cashel, having first unceremoniously expelled the Benedictines; in 1274 he persuaded the General Chapter to reverse the filiation arrangements completed by Stephen of Lexington and to restore Mellifont to its former pre-eminence. This last was looked on with a jaundiced eye from Dublin where it was thought that the Archbishop was deliberately promoting the specifically Irish section of the province at the expense of the English. In other contexts, too, he was accused of favouring his own nation and with seeking to humiliate the English. But if David Mac Carwill was in fact actively anti-English, he manifested his nationalistic tendencies in a strange way in the late 1270s when, with three of his compatriots, the bishops of Emly and Killaloe and the abbot of Holy Cross, he led a movement to obtain the admission of native Irish (at least in Munster) to full English citizenship. These prelates, claiming to speak in the name of the 'community of the Irish tongue' sought 'an end to evil law' with the granting of English law to the Irish. They offered the huge sum of 10,000 marks for this grant and were ready to pressurise with the whole force of ecclesiastical coercion any Irish who would not co-operate in this integration scheme. The plan foundered apparently on crude Anglo-Irish self-interest. Perhaps it never had a chance of acceptance on either side. But that such an offer should be made demonstrates the strength of anglicisation pressures in Munster in this period. Perhaps, too, it reveals Archbishop

David Mac Carwill as a 'last representative of those native churchmen who retained something of the hopes with which the twelfth-century reformers greeted the Normans'[5].

However this might be, archbishops of Cashel continued to work closely with English officials. Stephen O Brogan, for services rendered, could count on the considerable support of the archbishop of Dublin, John of Sandford, who was also a leading figure in the Dublin administration. Maurice Mac Carwill was present at the Kilkenny parliament of 1310 which forbade the reception of Irish religious into monasteries among the English. Another of the same family, Thomas, likewise gave his support, and threatened his censures of those who disregarded it, to the similarly discriminatory legislation of the Statute of Kilkenny in 1366. How far the adoption of such positions was the price these archbishops deliberately chose to pay for the maintenance of peace essential for the care of souls and in order to safeguard the welfare of their Irish subjects, we have no real means of knowing.

The archbishops of Dublin 1181–1306
John Cumin, 1181–1212
Henry of London, 1213–28
Luke, 1228–55
Fulk of Sandford, 1256–71
John of Darlington, O.P., 1279–84
John of Sandford, 1284–94
William of Hotham, O.P., 1296–98
Richard of Ferings, 1299–1306

Anglicisation of the Irish Church came earliest to Dublin and took root there much more thoroughly than elsewhere. In personnel, institutions, liturgical practices, architectural styles, wealth and government connexions the Church of

Dublin developed into something very akin to that of an English secular cathedral, and for many purposes was treated as such by Crown and papacy.

In the period with which we are here concerned, all the archbishops were English born. The ordinary reason for their promotion was service at a high level to the kings of England, frequently in colonial administration based on Dublin but often also in England and on the Continent. John Cumin had some twenty years of faithful service as bureaucrat, judge and diplomat before Henry II arranged his promotion to Dublin. Henry of London was to be justiciar from 1213 to 1215 and again from 1221 to 1224. Luke, dean of the chapter of St Martin's-le-Grand in London, that pool of royal clerks, was an official of the King's Wardrobe in England and became a member of the justiciar's council in Ireland. His successor, treasurer of the other London chapter which supported so many royal officials, St Paul's, became justiciar in 1265.

There were of course hazards in this close connexion between high ecclesiastical office and political service, common enough though it was in feudal Europe. One such was perhaps typified by Henry of London. This archbishop had been appointed papal legate in 1217. In 1220, however, he was relieved of this post by Pope Honorius III in a letter that reads very like a curt dismissal. It is not improbable that the Pope's displeasure with Henry of London was because of the archbishop's support of that policy of discriminating against the appointment of Irishmen to bishoprics, initiated, as was seen earlier, by William Marshal and put into practice by Geoffrey Marsh. No doubt there were other instances where political interests were allowed to take precedence over ecclesiastical ones.

A second hazard was absenteeism. This evil became frequent with the archbishops of the second half of this period. The first absentee archbishop was John of Darlington. Trained in the Dominican *studium* at Paris, John had gained a reputation as a scriptural scholar. By 1256, however, he had left the academic life for court circles and had become both the confessor of Henry III and a member of his council. His loyalty to that king and his son in the Baronial Wars ensured his continuing favour with Edward I. He was employed by the king in 1278 on an embassy to the papal curia to discuss certain taxation matters between the papacy and England. Due to a divided election and a succession of vacancies in the papacy, the vacancy of the Dublin see had lasted seven years. Nicholas III took advantage of John of Darlington's presence in Rome to promote him to Dublin. However, the new archbishop proved indispensable to Edward's plans to collect taxes from the English clergy. He died without ever having set foot in Ireland. Dublin had been, in effect, without an archbishop from 1271 to 1284.

No doubt an able vicar-general might do much to mitigate the administrative inconvenience of archiepiscopal absence. Such a one was John of Sandford, dean of St Patrick's who held the position in this period and it was fitting, therefore, that he should eventually succeed to the see. Archbishop John was also a royal official, holding posts in the judiciary, treasury and chancery and finally becoming *custos* (keeper), 1288–90.

From 1296 to 1306 Dublin was again held by absentee prelates who owed their positions to the inability of the Dublin electors to agree on a candidate. This gave popes the chance to nominate English prelates who were either royal protégés or happened to be on royal embassies to the curia. William of Hotham and Richard of Ferings were able men but the only significance for Dublin in their busy careers was their absence from their see. The appointment by Clement V of Richard of Havering illustrates yet a third hazard to which the intimate connexion of Dublin with the Crown exposed the see. After another divided election, the

Pope appointed a royal favourite whose flagrant unsuitability for ecclesiastical office was shown when he did not bother to be consecrated archbishop, contenting himself with enjoying the considerable revenues of the see.

Dublin churchmen were to come to speak with pride of 'our metropolis, handmaid of the English church'. For almost a century after the appointment of John Cumin, the organisation of Dublin according to the norms of ecclesiastical practice of the Church in England went ahead very vigorously. Thereafter, because of the long vacancies and periods of absenteeism by several archbishops, the reforming impetus slowed down considerably, to pick up again, fitfully, in the fourteenth century. The historian is considerably hampered in his attempt to portray the archbishops at work in their diocese and province because of the total absence of episcopal registers, an absence the more surprising in anglicised Dublin because of their considerable abundance in England at this time. However, there is more source material existing for Dublin affairs in the thirteenth century than for any other Irish see, though for the most part, it is concerned with the rights and properties of the institutions of the diocese and the disputes at law which these often occasioned. Information on the more spiritual side of a bishop's jurisdiction such as would be provided by, for example, visitation records or ordination lists, does not exist. Further, no evidence exists which enables us to fathom the spirituality of individual prelates; no personal insights are possible. Hence, if only from the nature of the surviving evidence, the archbishops and diocesan officials have come to appear to us as men of affairs preoccupied, perhaps too much so, with defending the alleged legal rights of their see. Thus the history of the diocese seems often little more than a chronicle of property deals and of conflicts between rival jurisdictions. Nevertheless, though the evidence has its limitations (and indeed in this respect Dublin is no different from many a score of dioceses in thirteenth-century Christendom), it is adequate to reveal developments of consequence.

An important piece of diocesan reconstruction was begun shortly after the Invasion. The amalgamation of Glendaloch with Dublin was accomplished in stages between 1185 and 1216. Though not all Irish historians have been satisfied that the union was accomplished without political chicanery on the English side, it was approved by the pope on evidence drawn at least as much from Irish sources as from English. At the Fourth Lateran Council of 1215, Innocent III received the following testimony of Archbishop Felix O Ruadhain of Tuam and his suffragans:[6]

Lord John Papiron, legate of the Roman Church, when he came to Ireland, found Dublin with a bishop who then exercised the episcopal office within the walls. In the same diocese he found another church, in the mountains, which likewise was called a city and had a certain *coepiscopus*. Delivering the *pallium* to the bishop then ruling the church of Dublin, the legate constituted the excellent city of Dublin to be metropolis of that province and directed that the diocese containing both cities should be divided so that part should be granted to the metropolis and part should remain to the church in the mountains, intending, as we firmly believe, that on the death of him who then ruled that church, this part should revert to the metropolis, and he would have brought this about at the time had not the arrogance of the Irish who then had power in the area deferred it. Henry, king of England, heard of this intention from several persons, conforming to the action and will of the legate he granted the other part to the metropolis. Similarly, after John now king of England had listened to important and experienced men in that land, he granted it to John, predecessor of the present archbishop.

Furthermore, although that holy church in the mountains was from early times held in great reverence on
account of St Kevin who lived there as a hermit, it is now
so deserted and desolate and has been so for forty years,
that from being a church it has become a den of thieves
and pit of robbers, and because of the deserted and
desolate wilderness there are more murders committed
in that valley than in any other part of Ireland.

Innocent III accepted this account and the union was
promulgated. Honorius III confirmed it, 6 October 1216.
Save for a brief reappearance of titular bishops of Glendaloch in the late fifteenth century, this ancient monastic
centre, was an archdeaconry of the Dublin diocese *inter
Hibernicos* (among the Irish). On at least one occasion the
archdeacon of Glendaloch was a native Irishman. When in
1290 he was promoted to the see of Cashel, Stephen
O Brogan asked that his replacement should also be of his
nationality. Clearly this made sense and might well have
helped to a better understanding between the two nations
in the diocese. But no tradition of appointing an Irish
archdeacon of Glendaloch was established.

Another important change made in the early period of
anglicisation concerned the chapter of the diocese. It is
clear that by the early thirteenth century, the cathedral
Chapter had become a very important institution in
Ireland since, for the most part, it had the decisive voice in
the making of the episcopate. We are, however, signally
ill-informed about the origins and development of this
new institution. Clearly its rise to importance began before
the Invasion. The development of a territorial diocesan
system and the building of new cathedrals which went
with it, created the need to make regular provision for the
services of the cathedral church and the upkeep of its
fabric and properties. The general trend of the twelfth-
century reform movement made recourse to outside

models inevitable. There is some evidence emanating from Arrouaise, of somewhat dubious quality, that the reformers thought priories of Augustinian canons of the Arroasian rule would afford a satisfactory pattern for Irish cathedral chapters. But it was only in Holy Trinity, Dublin, that such a congregation was established by St Laurence O Toole in 1163.

Within a century of the council of Kells-Mellifont, the only dioceses in Ireland which did not have a chapter of secular canons were Meath and Down. In neither case was this the result of any pre-Invasion arrangement. That the electors in Meath were the senior clergy of the diocese was a result of Simon Rochfort's transference of the see to Trim, where the church of the Augustinian priory was to serve throughout the middle ages as the bishop's seat. It was John de Courcy who was responsible for the establishment of the Benedictine community which elected to Down. For the vast majority of dioceses, the dates when chapters came into being is quite unknown. There is, however, firm evidence that the Irish dioceses of Cork, Ross, Ardfert and Tuam had secular chapters in the 1190s. It may well be that there was widespread imitation of English capitular organisation by Irish prelates. This would have been in conformity with the decision of Cashel II to accept the usages of the Church in England. Certainly when Donnchadh O Brien established a secular chapter in the cathedral of St Mary's, Limerick, he deliberately followed English custom.

That the anglicised dioceses adopted English patterns will not of course occasion surprise. But in Dublin anglicisation led to an unprecedented development: the existence of two cathedrals a few hundred yards from each other, one with a chapter of Augustinian canons (Holy Trinity), the other with a chapter of secular canons (St Patrick's). The rivalry between these bodies, especially in archiepiscopal elections, was to be a great source of weakness to the see in the thirteenth century. As has been seen, it caused long vacancies which were frequently ended only with the appointment of an unsuitable, absentee archbishop.

This remarkable institutional development began in 1191 when Archbishop John Cumin 'determined to make the church of St Patrick, Dublin, a prebendal church, and to place within it a college of clerks of approved life and learning, who may supply an example of life to others and minister instruction to the simple'.[7] The new establishment was consecrated on St Patrick's day 1192, with the presence of the archbishops of Armagh and Cashel to testify to a degree of friendship between metropolitans of the different nationalities. Thirteen prebendal churches and a common fund for the canons were set up but no officials or dignitaries were appointed. This gap was filled by Henry of London in 1220–21 with the creation of the offices of chancellor, precentor, treasurer and dean, the constitution of Salisbury cathedral supplying the model. The reason why archbishops should prefer a secular to a regular chapter seem clear enough: it was easier to control and the prebends were at the disposal of the archbishop, not the community. But why Cumin and Henry of London chose to allow the anomalous situation of two cathedrals and two chapters to develop instead of demoting Holy Trinity from cathedral status is not at all clear. The constitution of St Patrick's received papal confirmation at each stage. Whether or not the papacy fully appreciated what it was helping to bring about is also something of a mystery.

Most prominent English ecclesiastics who settled or held an appointment in Ireland seem to have accommodated a flock of relatives and clients with positions in the country. It was perhaps inevitable that relatives of the archbishops should be awarded canonries in St Patrick's chapter. Its first dean was a nephew of Archbishop Henry of London and another nephew was the chapter's chancellor, *c*.1229–31. John of Sandford, first member of the chapter to become archbishop, owed his first ecclesiastical advancement to his archbishop-relative. In the early fourteenth century, there were two Hothams in the chapter after Archbishop William of Hotham, and John of Havering is found as archdeacon of Dublin in the wake of the occupation of the see by the archbishop-elect, Richard of Havering. No doubt the bulk of this archiepiscopal patronage escapes the historian's search. The chapter too was something of a reservoir for supplying the suffragan sees of the Dublin province. This is particularly noticeable for the dioceses of Kildare and Ossory, in the period before their chapters became the closed local oligarchies, that they became in the second half of the thirteenth century, electing almost exclusively from among their own number.

More importantly, St Patrick's came to form a prominent element in the civil administration of the colony. In Henry III's reign, eight members of this chapter are to be discovered as ministers or judges whilst in the reign of Edward I it was openly stated in parliament that it was composed for the greater part of king's clerks and servants. The statement can be put to the test and found accurate. There exists from 1306 a document issued in the name of the dean and chapter who pledge themselves to work for the restoration of the former state of their church, allegedly lost 'through neglect in recent times'.[8] There were twelve signatories. Of three of these no trace can be found in the lists of office-holders in the civil administration. But the others either had long careers behind them, like Thomas of Chedworth, who had first come to Ireland as early as 1265, or were just embarking on one, like William of Rudyard, still active in government in the early 1340s. No less than seven of the nine canons who held posts in the civil administration were officials in that key department of state, the Exchequer. The reason for this close tie between the chapter and the colonial government is not hard to find.

The prebends, the richest in Ireland, formed so to say the basic salary of these civil servants.

Development of the chapter of St Patrick's ran *pari passu* with the building of St Patrick's cathedral. The marshes of the river Poddle were not the best of foundations for what was to become the biggest cathedral in medieval Ireland and throughout its history moist-clay foundations and flooding have been a problem to this necessarily crypt-less church. The explanation of John Cumin's choice of this unsuitable site lies in his wish to build on a place of special veneration traditionally associated (erroneously, it would seem) with the mission of the national Apostle. The small existing St Patrick's church was built beside St Patrick's Well. Foreign ecclesiastics generally showed themselves eager to associate themselves with the saints of Ireland, and Cumin was no exception. Indeed he was active in promoting the cause for canonisation of his predecessor, Laurence O Toole.

Just before the Reformation, Archbishop John Alen noted in his *Liber Niger* that 'our church of St Patrick is as it were the noted follower (*insignis pedisequa*) of the church of Sarum.' Salisbury was the model adopted by the earliest English archbishop of Dublin. The cathedral of St Patrick's, built between 1220 and 1254, with its beautiful Lady Chapel of *c.*1270, clearly owed more than a little to Salisbury which was consecrated in 1225. (Henry of London was present at the ceremony). Capitular organisation, architectural style and also liturgical usages came to Dublin from Salisbury. The Sarum rite was adopted for the services in St Patrick's. It was to be to Salisbury that recourse was had in 1284–85 when the chapter needed advice on certain problems of interpretation of its statutes.

The first English archbishop initiated other building projects and jurisdictional arrangements. The palace of St Sepulchre, home of archbishops of Dublin for six hundred years, was begun by John Cumin, with the establishment of its adjacent area as a liberty, subject to the archbishops' jurisdiction. The lands held by the archbishops, apparently some 50,000 acres in pre-Invasion days, and added to thereafter, were organised in a group of archiepiscopal manors north and south of the City, from Swords to Dalkey. Planning of new buildings and the regulation of manorial courts in those estates were among the earliest works of John Cumin and Henry of London. Royal officials though they were, the establishment of this archiepiscopal secular jurisdiction brought them into conflict with the Crown and in Henry of London's case, with the City authorities. John Cumin's conflict was severe enough to drive him out of Dublin and for Pope Innocent III to espouse his cause against King John.

Though overshadowed in many ways by the new foundation of St Patrick's, the senior Dublin chapter, Holy Trinity, was not thereby reduced to insignificance. It remained a house of Augustinian canons down to the suppression of the monasteries and with its acres of land in co. Dublin, was the wealthiest monastery in Ireland. St Laurence O Toole, together with Strongbow, the first conqueror of Leinster, had undertaken the building of a new cathedral. This prospered under Archbishop Cumin, Henry of London and Luke to produce an impressive building in west-of-England stone and idiom. Jealousy of St Patrick's provided most incident in the history of the Holy Trinity canons for much of this period. The story of the relationship is long and involved. Its key is the attempt of Holy Trinity to exclude the rival chapter from archiepiscopal elections, or at any rate for it to 'compete' on equal numerical terms with the bigger body. The position agreed in Archbishop Luke's time and confirmed by Pope Nicholas III in 1279 was that the chapters should come together for elections which were to be held at Holy Trinity. But conflict was renewed regularly at successive vacancies with disastrous consequences, as has been seen.

A settlement was negotiated between the chapters in 1300 and was confirmed by Pope Boniface VIII. After some early hesitation the 'composition of peace' proved workable. The status of Holy Trinity as 'mother church' and her superiority of honour was recognised. Archbishops were to be consecrated in Holy Trinity, the holy oils blessed and a dead archbishop's insignia retained there. Archbishops were to be buried alternately in the two cathedrals. When an archbishop went to Rome, he was required to take with him an equal number of canons from each chapter. Diocesan synods were to be held in the cathedrals alternately, but Holy Trinity was to be the scene of the opening and closing of provincial councils should they be held in Dublin. Perhaps what contributed most to the settling of these tedious but damaging quarrels was that in the fourteenth century archbishops came to be appointed by papal provision not by capitular election and thus the major occasion for conflict was removed. Neither by provision nor election did the Holy Trinity canons succeed in having one of their number appointed archbishop.

The two chapters were associated with one of the more promising developments in Anglo-Irish intellectual life, the attempt to set up a university of Dublin. When Richard of Havering resigned his claim to the Dublin see in 1310, the two chapters for once readily agreed on a candidate. But Edward II persuaded Pope Clement V to appoint one of his clerks, John Lech, whom he had recently failed to have put in possession of the Scottish see of Dunkeld. It was this archbishop who petitioned the Pope for authorisation to establish a university in Dublin. He pointed out to Clement V that no *scolarium universitas vel generale studium* (medieval language for a university) existed in Ireland, that study abroad involved great difficulties and that as a result there were few in Ireland trained in higher education. On 13 July 1312 papal permission was granted, subject to the consent of the suffragan bishops. The University was still only a 'paper' one when Lech died prematurely and further developments were delayed when the Dublin chapters reverted to their customary habit and produced two candidates for the see. Some four years elapsed before an appointment was made: that of Alexander Bicknor, Oxford graduate, canon of St Patrick's, royal judge and Exchequer official. He was to be Justiciar in 1318–19. Bicknor's career as archbishop exemplifies most of the dangers intrinsic in a situation where episcopal office was unusually closely bound up with royal favour and government service. In the first place, his personal character must be accounted gravely suspect in that there is little doubt he was guilty of serious peculation when in office as Treasurer of Ireland (1308–14). Then he was frequently absent from his diocese on protracted embassies on the Continent. Finally, he was caught up in political intrigue in high places – accused by Edward II of plotting the downfall of his ministers, the Despensers, he threw in his lot with that monarch's infamous queen, Isabella, and was thereby associated with the party which deposed Edward II. Loss of Edward II's favour brought about the seizure of the Dublin temporalities in 1326 and loss of Edward III's, a similar penalty until he had paid back what he owed to the Exchequer. It was not until 1344 that he received the king's pardon for falsifying treasury accounts.

Despite his chequered career, however, Bicknor made some impression on the Dublin scene: in forwarding the university project, in promulgating an important series of constitutions for his province and in vigorously upholding Dublin's alleged right to the primacy of Ireland. The latter two issues will be examined in due course. At this point it is necessary to register that despite his support (or because of it?), the university of Dublin did not prosper. In February of 1320, Bicknor, 'with consent and assent of our chapters of Holy Trinity and St Patrick' issued detailed regulations for the masters and scholars of 'our university of Dublin'.

The ordinances were based on the practice of Oxford, Bicknor's own university. Three masters of theology were appointed and a master of canon law, the dean of St Patrick's, William of Rudyard, was appointed chancellor. But the embryo was still-born. Money, leadership and scholarship all seemed to be lacking. Further attempts, in 1358 and 1363, to put life into this important scheme also failed. There is no suggestion in the evidence that native Irishmen would have been excluded. But all that is known of Dublin in this period suggests that it would have been primarily an Anglo-Irish institution and this very likely was another factor in its failure to take root.

5   The Rule of Law

Ireland and the Papacy

IN common with the other countries of Christendom,
Ireland became increasingly subject in the thirteenth and
fourteenth centuries to the universal jurisdiction of the
omnium ecclesiarum mater et magistra (mother and mistress of
all Churches), the Roman Church. The papacy embodied
the principle of the unity of the Church, a unity expressed
essentially in the Church's common faith, of whose purity
and integrity the Roman Church was the especial guardian. It was expressed too in that universal system of
jurisprudence of which the pope was the unquestioned
master and whose creation was so much the particular
hall-mark of this period of papal history. This system of
law, common to the whole Church, fashioned in response
to its expressed needs and wishes, stood as surety against the
ever-insistent disintegratory pull of local particularisms.
The unity of faith was buttressed by a uniformity of cult,
discipline and institutions. The pope was legislator for the
universal Church, the supreme judge in all cases pertaining
to ecclesiastical jurisdiction, the ultimate authority for the
solution of doubts or difficulties concerning the faith or the
law or administrative procedures. The ever-increasing
number of matters reserved exclusively to his jurisdiction
(*iura reservata*) was a sure sign of the growing extent and
effectiveness of papal government in this period. The
papacy supplied that measure of rational, authoritative
central government for which the Churches of the West

had come increasingly to feel the need and canon law was the chief instrument of that government.

The classical law of the Church (*Corpus iuris canonici*), systematised, standardised and expanded in this period, consisted of three main components. The first was compiled about 1140 in Bologna by Gratian. His collection of nearly four thousand texts – *Concordia discordantium canonum* (Harmony of dissonant canons) or *Decretum* – enshrined a thousand years of the Church's experience in the governmental and administrative spheres. The second, composed for the most part of conciliar and papal legislation issued since 1140 was promulgated by Pope Gregory IX in 1234 – five books of Decretals. Sixth and seventh books came to be added to form the third part of the *Corpus iuris canonici*: *Liber Sextus*, promulgated by Boniface VIII in 1298; the *Clementinae*, constitutions mostly of Pope Clement V, promulgated by John XXII in 1317. Around this body of law there grew up a very considerable technical literature, often the product of university teaching, especially in Bologna and Paris. It was this jurisprudence, one of the most impressive intellectual achievements of medieval civilisation, which welded the Latin Church into a coherent juridical society.

Ireland's stock of medieval canonist manuscripts, which constitute the most obvious relics of the Church's medieval legal system in most European countries, has disappeared virtually without trace. Moreover, the abortive university of Dublin apart, for which a canon law faculty had been planned, nothing is heard of canon law schools until the later middle ages. We are therefore restricted in our ways of charting the reception of canon law in Ireland. Nevertheless, it is not open to doubt that Ireland came under the powerful sway of this highly articulated legal system. Here, as elsewhere, local customs yielded to Roman standards or were harmonised with them. That the ecclesiastical leaders of Ireland were eager so to yield was a main theme of the reformers of the pre-Invasion period, as has been seen in Chapter I. Nor was the impetus lost after the Invasion, for the principle adopted at Cashel II of establishing in Ireland the liturgical and legal advances and practices of the Church in England, was a push in the same direction. So too was the attendance of Irish prelates at two of the most important of all medieval papal legislative occasions – to Lateran III (1179) went Archbishops St Laurence O Toole (Dublin) and Cadhla O Duffy (Tuam) as well as Bishops Constantin O Brien (Killaloe), Brictius (Limerick) and Felix (Lismore). Four archbishops, fourteen bishops and two bishops-elect (of whom fourteen were native Irish) attended Lateran IV in 1215. The work in Ireland of legates sent from Rome was a further impetus no doubt. They were: Cardinal Papiron (1152), Cardinal Vivianus (1177–78), Cardinal John of Salerno (1202–3), James, papal penitentiary (1221). Personal visits to the papal curia by individual bishops and correspondence with the popes were also important channels of legal communication between Ireland and the Holy See.

Correspondence in the form of applications to the curia for definitive rulings in legal matters about which the enquirer was in doubt allowed Ireland to make a modest contribution to the Gregorian Decretals. For some of these queries raised issues of more than local significance and were found important enough for incorporation into the general law of the Church. In reply to a question of Archbishop Matthew O Heney, Clement III ruled in 1190 that the son of a bishop, born before his father's ordination, could become a priest and hold a benefice in his father's church (Greg. Decr. 1.17.12). Answering Archbishop Tomaltach O Connor, Innocent III put on record that Mosaic custom notwithstanding, under the law of Christ, there was no restriction on a woman's entering a church after childbirth (Greg. Decr. 3.47.1). The king of Connacht, Cathal O Connor sought advice about the sanctuary of criminals in churches. Innocent III, in reply, made a distinction between the legal standing in respect of sanctuary of freemen and those who were unfree which was deemed significant enough to become Gregorian Decretals 3.49.6. A series of questions arising from the disputed election at Armagh put to Innocent III by his legate Cardinal John of Salerno produced a decretal (1.6.20) destined to become famous among canonists for its clarification of some important points of principle in a period when the law of capitular election was still in its formative stage.

The legation of John of Salerno, a member of the Sacred College from 1193 to 1208, left its mark in other ways. He was appointed legate to Scotland as well as to Ireland in 1201, his terms of reference including the whole of this country, not just the parts subject to the king of England and his decisions concerned matters of weight in all four provinces. It is known from the *Annals of Loch Cé* that in 1202 he held two synods: one was in Dublin and brought both native and foreign prelates together and the other, of clergy and laity of the western province, at Athlone. Both his brief and the circumstances attending his stay in Ireland (1202–3) made diocesan arrangements and episcopal appointments his predominant concern. He was anxious to stop hereditary tenure of prelacies in Connacht and his bringing to Tuam as archbishop, Felix O Ruadhain prior of Saul in co. Down, which proved so unpopular with the king of Connacht, is to be seen in that context. So too, most probably, has his suppression of the diocese of Mayo and its incorporation in Tuam. Another of his rulings made Ardagh diocese a suffragan see of Tuam but later in the century it was subjected to Armagh. In Armagh province, he was at the centre of the bitter dispute over the succession to the archbishopric after the death of Tomaltach O Connor in 1201. This quarrel he was not able to compose before leaving Ireland. His promotion of the abbot of the

Scottish Cistercian house of Melrose to the see of Down in 1202 was, however, successful and so too was his authorisation of the transfer of the see of Meath from Clonard to Newtown, Trim. In Cashel province, he supported Lismore in its fight against the unscrupulous and violent attempt of the Anglo-French bishop of Waterford to annex it to his own jurisdiction. That his mission involved the settlement of numerous cases of lesser moment we may well believe but other than that of the property dispute between the Augustinian canons of St Mary's, Louth, and a local knight, which went to Rome because he failed to achieve a settlement, no record of such cases survives.

John of Salerno's work showed how important a role a legate might play in the reorganisation of the Irish Church. The problems remained formidable and Innocent III expressed his impatience with the lack of legal *savoir-faire* shown by prelates in Ireland. Yet relatively little use was made of legates after Cardinal John. His only successor was James the Penitentiary whose mission in 1221 was an undistinguished one. The *Annals of Loch Cé* record his stay with the one comment that 'he collected horse-loads of gold and silver from the clerics of Ireland through simony'. This particular complaint of papal financial extortion was to receive many a sympathetic echo among English chronicles in the thirteenth century. Nor was it the last time that Irish opinion showed its hostility to the agents of the papal fiscal machinery.

After 1221 the representatives of the pope who came to Ireland were appointed specifically for financial purposes, most commonly for the collection of the crusading taxes which were levied at fairly frequent intervals throughout Christendom in the thirteenth century. The precise process whereby these levies were collected in Ireland has perhaps still to be worked out, but its general pattern seems clear enough. At the centre was a papal *nuntius* (envoy), generally an Italian, who directed a team of collectors and preachers, working in all parts of Ireland. It included friars, Italian bankers and representatives of the king of England (whose coffers were not infrequently, with papal assent, the ultimate destination of these crusading monies or at least of a part of them).

One such *nuntius* was John of Frosinone, sent to Ireland by Pope Innocent IV to organise the collection of the tax on clerical incomes ordered for the relief of the Holy Land by the General Council of Lyons in 1245. He had the co-operation of King Henry III and obtained a canonry in St Patrick's, Dublin. John of Frosinone was to spend most of the rest of his life in this country, dying here in 1274. For some part of his career as resident papal tax collector he had the support of another Italian, John of Alatre, strategically placed in the western diocese of Clonfert, which see he ruled from 1266 until 1295 when Boniface VIII translated him to the archbishopric of Benevento. These tax-collectors had no easy assignment. John of Frosinone was excommunicated in 1249 by the bishops of Achonry and Killala – uncanonically since a papal *nuntius* could not be excommunicated without the pope's express permission. But the Italians apparently had more resolution than English collectors. In 1254, Laurence Somercote (known otherwise as a canonist of some standing) was acting in Ireland as collector of the crusading tenth. Writing to some correspondent in England he protested that he would never again set foot in Ireland on such a mission, even if his commission were to be doubled, and declared himself ready to go to prison rather than 'to go to Ireland again to be crucified for the sake of the crusade tax'.

However, in the thirteenth century finance was some way from being the biggest single item in Hiberno-papal relations. Much the most important individual issue was the episcopate. High on the list of papal *iura reservata* stood all matters connected with dioceses and their incumbents. Reserved to the pope's jurisdiction were: translations of

bishops from one see to another, depositions and resigna-
tions, alterations in diocesan boundaries and changes in the
locations of episcopal seats, solutions of election disputes
and canonical confirmations of bishops-elect where there
was no other superior to act. Such matters were referred to
the papal curia as a matter of course in this period and the
papal registers contain numerous examples of each of these
issues coming up for settlement at Rome. They do not
need detailed recapitulation here; some of the more important of them have been mentioned in other parts of this
book. It should always be borne in mind, however, that
because a papal judgement was sought and obtained it does
not necessarily follow that it was immediately obeyed.
Ireland was a very long way from Rome, lying on the
'very edge of the world' as Roman scribes liked to say,
and bad communications often made the information
available to the curia out of date or one-sided and facilit-
ated the task of anyone seeking to exploit the law's delays
to his own advantage. Nevertheless, this qualification
made, papal government, so far as it went, was effective
government.

The papacy's part in the making of bishops is a good
example of this effectiveness. The papacy had a part to
play in this fundamental matter in a number of different
ways. In the first place, it was the papacy which laid down
the basic rules by which elections of bishops were to be
conducted. The bishop-elect was to be canonically examined by superiors to check his suitability for high office.
Also laid down was the manner in which episcopal consecrations were to be performed. By the end of the pontificate
of Innocent III the law of episcopal elections for general
application throughout the whole Church had been completed: all canonical procedures were clear and uniform;
failure to observe them invalidated the election and
brought the election to the pope for decision. Secondly, in
addition to these general rules, the papacy had agreements,

explicit and tacit, with the different countries of Christendom, aimed at preserving ecclesiastical independence in episcopal elections from excessive or arbitrary intervention by the lay power but giving the latter a recognised legal position in the bishop-selecting process. As has been seen earlier, this was done for Ireland by the agreement between Innocent III and King John. There is evidence of Innocent III allowing the kings of Connacht, though technically vassals of the English Crown, to play a role in the episcopal elections of the Tuam province similar to that allowed to John in the areas subject directly to his jurisdiction.

The papacy, then made the legal framework within which chapters exercised the substance of the power of appointing their own bishops. By far the greatest number of episcopal appointments in thirteenth-century Ireland were by capitular election with the elect canonically checked by his metropolitan, the archbishop of his province. The papacy did not intervene unless the canon law of election had been broken. When it had, the pope took to himself the right to have the last word in the appointment, though the precise way in which he arrived at a settlement in any disputed election might vary with circumstances. Such occasional interventions, and they were never very numerous, constituted the third way in which the papacy had a hand in the composition of the episcopate. The fourth concerned appointments of archbishops. These too were normally elected by chapters but, as they did not have canonical superiors in Ireland, confirmation of the validity of their elections and of their own personal suitability for their posts was the responsibility of the pope.

The over-all picture may be summarised in this way: the popes had an important influence in the establishment of the electoral procedures whereby bishops were appointed in thirteenth-century Ireland, the papal role in the actual making of the episcopate was marginal. Capitular election was the rule in practice as well as in theory. The popes administered the law primarily as a court of appeal, acting when things had gone wrong, at the request of others, rather than on their own initiative. In this appellate capacity, popes acted very much according to established law – not for nothing was the thirteenth century the age of the lawyer popes – in the first place according to canon law, but also in accordance with the established compromise of canon and English law relating to the secular aspects of the episcopal office. To this extent, therefore, the popes upheld the *dominus Hiberniae* and the principle that the Irish Church should follow the practices of the English Church. But the king of England was not allowed to push the compromise to extremes. He might not legally follow a policy of racial discrimination in ecclesiastical appointments. His rejection of candidates on political grounds (though this was not common) might be overruled if independent ecclesiastical examination established the canonical regularity of the election proceedings and the canonical suitability of the elect. There was a noteworthy regard for the rights of the electors and no suggestion of any arbitrary overruling of them by exercise of the *plenitudo potestatis* (fulness of power). Of the cases of disputed election investigated at the curia, many were solved simply by establishing who was the chapter's real nominee. In at least one case – that of Florence Mac Flynn (Tuam, 1250) – an uncanonical election was voided but the chapter's candidate provided. In cases where it was decided that provision was the only solution to the deadlock, wherever possible, the popes associated the electors, or their proctors, with the provision. Hence provisions tended to be successful appointments, at any rate as far as avoiding the complications that could ensue through disregard of the racial situation.

In the period of the 'Avignon papacy', which began in 1305 with the election of Clement V and continued until the return to Rome by Gregory XI in January 1377, the

Roman Church moved appreciably nearer to Ireland. Almost at once, there was a significant increase in the amount of Irish business in which the curia had a hand. Thus in the pontificate of John XXII (1316–34), of some forty episcopal appointments made, twenty seven were by papal provision. Papal tax-gatherers had never been more active. Judicial business grew apace.

But perhaps the most striking call on papal services in this pontificate was in the political field. In the disturbed decade of the Bruce Invasion and its bitter aftermath, both the king of England and his officials, as well as Irish princes, sought to enlist the political co-operation of the pope.

The princes under the leadership of Donal O Neill petitioned John XXII for recognition of Edward Bruce as their lawful king. The *Remonstrance* in which they set out their case, is by any standards a remarkable document. On the negative side, it was a sweeping indictment of the injustice of English rule and, on the positive side, a vivid assertion of the historical and cultural uniqueness of the Irish nation. That it should be addressed to the pope will cause no surprise. The papacy had for long professed its championship of all those, great or small, individuals or groups, clerical or lay, who felt themselves deprived of justice. But further, it had been the papacy which had legalised the English lordship of Ireland and it was especially with this bond between England, Ireland and the papacy that the princes were concerned. They sent a copy of Adrian IV's *Laudabiliter* to John XXII and, in the *Remonstrance* itself, condemned Adrian for favouring the ruler of his native country, for placing the Irish in a miserable predicament. They argued that Henry II and his successors had violated the terms on which the grant of the lordship of Ireland had been made to them in *Laudabiliter*:

For Henry promised, as is specified in the said bull, that he would extend the boundaries of the Irish Church and preserve her rights inviolable and secure; that he would bring the people into a state of obedience to the laws, improve them by the introduction of good morality implanting new virtues in the land and eradicating the weeds of vice and pay to blessed Peter the Apostle, a pension of one penny annually for every house. This promise concerning Ireland, however, as well he himself as his successors and their wicked and deceitful English officials have in every instance violated, entirely departing from the terms of the grant made to them and studiously and intentionally exhibiting in their actions a line of conduct directly contrary to all those conditions which they had promised to fulfil.

The document went on to demonstrate in detail how the terms of the grant had been violated. It argued that the kings of England, their officials and the English colonists in Ireland,

who, after having bound themselves, according to the ordinance of the court of Rome, to govern our people in a just and moderate way, have made it the object of their unprincipled study to exterminate them from the country.

They compelled the Irish people,

to shake off the cruel and insupportable yoke of their bondage and to recover our natural liberty[1]

by renouncing English jurisdiction and accepting that of Edward Bruce.

John XXII was not prepared to ratify such a translation of lordship. He contented himself with an earnest appeal to the conscience, sense of duty and kingly honour of Edward II that he should 'Proceed to command and enforce a just and speedy correction and reform of the grievances' of the Irish. However in one studiedly ambiguous passage of his letter to Edward he seemed to suggest that he did not consider a request for a transference of jurisdiction because of misuse of power an unreasonable or irrelevant one:

> Duty requires that you should give your earnest attention and apply yourself with readiness and zeal, to the introduction of such measures as may be acceptable in the sight of your creator, and that you should scrupulously refrain from all such courses as may justly provoke against you the wrath of God, the Lord to whom vengeance belongs, who never disregards the groaning of those who are unjustly afflicted [cf. *Judges* 2.18], and who is described as having rejected his own particular people, and made a transfer of their kingdom to others, on account of the unrighteous acts of which they had been guilty [cf. *Eccles*. 10.8].[2]

Edward II got somewhat more from John XXII than did the Irish princes. Two senior members of the Dublin administration were promoted by the Pope to important sees: Alexander Bicknor, who was Treasurer of Ireland was made archbishop of Dublin and William Fitz John, Chancellor of Ireland, became archbishop of Cashel. He obtained also stern papal condemnation, under sanctions of apostolic excommunication, of all supporters of Edward Bruce especially those friars, 'agents of the devil', who were promoting rebellion. He was permitted to retain for himself the crusading tax ordered in 1312 by the General Council of Vienne. He also secured papal approval, at least in principle, of an ambitious and radical scheme to restructure the diocesan system in the provinces of Armagh, Tuam and Cashel. The proposal was to reduce the number of dioceses in these areas to ten, with the Dublin province remaining as it was. This would have cut the number of dioceses by more than half. Edward pleaded that such was the poverty of most of the sees that they were not administratively viable. However, his leaving Dublin unscathed and his proposal that wherever possible the episcopal seats should be located in royal cities, make the political nature of his scheme abundantly clear. It was intended as a measure to facilitate the subordination of the Irish dioceses to the English sector of the Church and to the colonial government. In the event, however, nothing came of this scheme. John XXII's first tentative steps towards implementing it were failures. It is not without interest however, that two of the unions of dioceses he proposed in 1327 in the wake of this general reconstruction plan, came to fruition later: the union of Lismore and Waterford in 1363 and of Cork and Cloyne in 1411.

The English Crown received a fairly substantial measure of co-operation from John XXII. Despite the sympathy he expressed for the Irish labouring under injustice, the Pope was not a whit less committed to supporting the English lordship of Ireland than had been his predecessors. However, he was not prepared to allow himself to be persuaded into adopting any extremist positions. When, about 1331, the Justiciar and the King's Council in Ireland presented the Pope with what can perhaps be best described as a Counter-Remonstrance, charging the Irish with numerous excesses of both faith and morals and asking the pope to preach a crusade against the guilty, he turned a deaf ear.

The considerable increase in the volume of judicial, financial and administrative business transacted at Avignon led to the development of more sophisticated organs of papal jurisdiction. Correspondingly, it led to the development of more specialised ways in which the governments of Christendom and other parties concerned had their interests represented at the curia. It remained standard practice for the kings of England to despatch special embassies for special purposes. But increasingly more use was made of resident agents (*procuratores*) whose function was to act for royal, baronial and ecclesiastical clients in the routine business of papal government. The more complex the machinery of papal government, the more the need for men who were expert in threading a way for their clients through its processes.

The Crown made use of numerous agents of this type in the period of Clement V and John XXII but it favoured especially the firm of Sapiti, a family business of which the head was Andrew Sapiti a Florentine lawyer.[3] For over thirty years he acted as 'King's clerk in the Roman court' or 'King's agent (*procurator*) in the Roman Court', as the sources described him. His career affords an unusual insider's view of papal government in general and in particular, of aspects of Hiberno-papal relations. For the firm he built up handled much Irish business both for Edward II and Edward III as well as for Irish and Anglo-Irish bishops.

At first glance it is perhaps surprising to find the kings of England and prelates from Ireland employing Italians in this way. The explanation lies in the pre-eminent position of Italians, especially Florentines, as the bankers of Europe, not least of the papacy itself and of the English government. The Sapitis owed their rise to their connexions with different firms of Florentine merchant bankers, especially with the Frescobaldi and the Circuli Nigri, both of which firms were extremely active in England and Ireland in the early fourteenth century. The Frescobaldis were expelled in 1311 but the business activities in Ireland of the Sapitis continued for some decades longer.

The name of Andrew Sapiti first occurs at the papal court in 1304 when he became a public notary by papal authority. He moved to Avignon and in 1309 is found employed by Henry VII, aspirant to the Holy Roman Emperorship, and Edward II of England. He was already a clerk of Edward II as also of Walter Reynolds, bishop of Worcester and Treasurer of England, who was paying him an annual fee. Sapiti was to continue to represent the interests of the English Crown and of members of the English hierarchy and baronage down to his death in 1338. We should not think of him as an ambassador or consul in our modern understanding of diplomatic representation. Sapiti was essentially a lawyer, running a legal practice at the papal court. He took clients as they came, drawing up their petitions to the pope, supervising their progress through the formal stages of process in the papal chancery, watching over his clients' financial interests in the papal *camera*, representing them in the papal courts of justice. He was not the only 'solicitor' used by the kings of England but he was the most used. He acted for a substantial number of continental bishops and abbots, but he acted for more bishops from England and Ireland than from anywhere else.

The Sapiti family business was a highly successful one. Andrew Sapiti had the assistance of two brothers, six sons and numerous kinsmen. They were all extensively bene-ficed on the Continent and in England. Two examples will suffice to testify to the extent to which popes, cardinals and kings patronised the members of the firm. Andrew himself was canon of Florence and papal chaplain (1331) and a member of the household of Cardinal Peter of Spain. His brother Simon, who died *c*.1340, held benefices at various periods of his busy career in the dioceses of Laon, Durham, Florence, Coventry and Lichfield, Chichester, Volterna and Lyons.

Businessmen in Ireland, lawyers of the English Crown in Avignon at a time when Irish affairs were of some significance in Anglo-papal relations, the Sapitis inevitably attracted business from bishops of Irish sees. The survival of two registers – one which contains copies of the petitions Andrew forwarded to the pope on behalf of his numerous clients in the period 1332–37 and another concerned with a miscellany of other business which he was handling in the years between 1316 and 1337 – allows a glimpse of Sapiti at work on Irish affairs. The full investigation and editing of these important documents has still to be completed. But preliminary examination in conjunction with the cameral records finds the Sapiti firm acting for twelve bishops from seven sees in Ireland: Armagh, Cashel, Tuam, Meath, Cork, Cloyne, Kildare. Half of these bishops were native Irishmen. The archbishops of Dublin conspicuously preferred to use other firms. Sapiti acted for the English Crown in 1324 when the proposal to reorganise the diocesan system in Ireland was put to the pope. It was he too who was engaged by the Justiciar and King's Council in Ireland to present the Counter-Remonstrance to John XXII in 1331.

Much of the business which the bishops employed Sapiti to transact was routine, with payment of dues into the papal treasury a prominent item. We may note a few examples illustrative of the sort of service he was expected to provide.

One of Sapiti's earliest native Irish clients was John Mac Carwill, bishop of Meath from 1321 to 1327 (he was incidentally the only one of his nation to rule this see in the middle ages). The Mac Carwill family, it will be recalled, had already supplied two archbishops to Cashel and in 1327, John was himself provided to that see. Since translation from one diocese to another necessarily involved direct papal action, the new archbishop was liable for payment to the pope of the fee known as common service (*servitium debitum*) which was ordinarily assessed at one third of the annual revenue of the see. However, it had somehow come about that the assessment of 3,640 florins, placed on Cashel for the purpose of this *servitium* was enormously disproportionate to its real income; where Armagh's assessment, for example, was less than a third of that sum, and Tuam's 200 florins. Sapiti set about securing a reassessment and succeeded in obtaining an enquiry by the chief papal tax-collector in England into the financial state of Cashel diocese. Unfortunately, before he had made his report, John Mac Carwill died and his successor Walter le Rede, translated from Cork, was liable not merely for his own *servitium* but also for the outstanding arrears (some 2,750 florins) of his predecessor. In his turn, however, Walter died prematurely, in 1331, with the reassessment still not concluded.

At this stage, Edward III lent a hand in the case. He told the pope that the see of Cashel was a great worry to him: it was situated among unconquered Irish who were responsible for considerably wasting that Church's material resources. His ministers in Ireland had recommended a prelate as suitable for this diocese. If the pope saw fit to lower the fee the new prelate would be required to pay, he might the better be able to defend Cashel against the incursions of these very violent enemies. The recommended candidate proved to be a native Irishman, John O Grady and he was duly papally provided to Cashel. When he came to pay what he owed, he found that his obligation had been cut to 400 florins. He was required to pay also 400 florins for each of his four predecessors.

Another Mac Carwill to make use of Sapiti's good offices was Thomas, whom the Cloyne chapter chose to be its bishop in 1333. When he presented himself at Avignon, however, he found that the pope had promoted someone else. Sapiti was asked to petition the pope that a suitable benefice in Ireland be found for the disappointed Thomas. It is not clear how immediately successful he was but he was to go on to be archbishop of Tuam (1348–65) and archbishop of Cashel (1365–72).

Malachy Mac Aodha, archbishop of Tuam from 1312 to 1348, was a frequent client of Sapiti. The most significant business negotiated for him concerned the union to Tuam of the dioceses of Annaghdown, Kilmacduagh and Achonry. Such a union of course needed papal approval and this the archbishop, through Sapiti's efforts, secured in a bull of 31 July 1327. The unions were scheduled to take place on the deaths of the then incumbents. When in due course, however, these occurred in Achonry (1344) and Kilmacduagh (1357), the papacy quashed the projected unions. In relation to Annaghdown, however, the archbishop had more success. Annexation of this diocese had long been a cherished aim of the archbishops of Tuam and it had always been resisted. It was again resisted after 1327. One Thomas O Mellaig was elected by the chapter and with the support of Edward III, went to fight the case at Avignon. He was still active there at the time of his death in 1330. It looks very much as if in this instance, Sapiti, acting for Archbishop Malachy against the bishop-elect of Annaghdown was opposing the wishes of Edward III in this question. Annaghdown elected a successor to O Mellaig, a Franciscan of the Claregalway house, Walter Okeloyn. Sapiti arranged for him to be bought off. The archbishop was to pay him annually either one quarter of the fruits of the church of Claregalway, in the archbishop's gift, or five marks sterling.

The detailed history of Hiberno-papal relations after the pontificate of John XXII has yet to be written. There were apparently no further requests for any dramatic political initiative from the papacy from either Irish princes or English officialdom. It seems clear that the story of the papal-Irish connexion in the later fourteenth century revolves round two main themes: Ireland's place in the papal fiscal system and the increase in the number of papal provisions to bishoprics. As to the former, one important hypothesis has already been formulated. The effect of the increased papal eagerness to raise money made the curia more willing to grant dispensations for clerical bastards to become priests, thereby opening the way for Irish clerical families, against which the reformers, with papal help, had struggled for two centuries, both to disregard the obligation to celibacy and to facilitate hereditary succession to bishoprics, abbacies, rectories and other benefices. Undoubtedly papal financial policies fostered this trend in the fifteenth century, as will be shown in a later chapter. K. W. Nicholls has argued that the process began with John XXII. The matter needs further research.

As to papal intervention in the making of bishops, a comparison of the position generally obtaining in the reign of Edward II with that a century later, in the reign of Richard II, reveals a very pronounced change. In the thirty five years of Edward's reign, there were only thirteen papal provisions to Irish sees and four of these were to Dublin, the consequence of the inability of the two chapters there to agree at election time. By 1399, virtually the whole episcopate held office in right of papal provision. But this was not the only change. Whereas in the time of Edward I the English Crown played a part in the appointments made by the majority of Irish chapters, by 1399, such had been the recession of English power, common law procedures had almost disappeared outside the Dublin province and adjacent dioceses. The increase in provisions does not necessarily mean the local clergy were deprived of a voice in the appointment of their bishop. While the position in the later fourteenth century stands in need of detailed examination, it would seem that generally the chapter selected a candidate who repaired to Avignon for the pope to provide him to the see. There was a fee to be paid for this provision. In the case of the number of dioceses still amenable to English influence, the pope would normally expect a supporting recommendation from the king (which he would have got from the royal administration in Ireland) to accompany the candidate's request for provision.

The Crown never quite gave up hope of persuading the papacy to influence the composition of the episcopate in a pro-English way. In 1381, for example, English ambassadors are to be found telling Pope Urban VI that experience in Ireland showed that language differences brought wars and other tribulations. It was urged, therefore, though in somewhat contradictory fashion, that since 'the better and greater part of that land' spoke English (referring only to the *terre Engleis* presumably), all prelates should be ordered to command their subjects to learn English. Nor should anyone be appointed to ecclesiastical office unless he could speak English.[4] The petition, unrealistic though it was, was in the spirit of clause 3 of the Statute of Kilkenny, frequently reiterated, which commanded 'that beneficed persons of holy Church, living amongst the English, shall use the English language; and if they do not, that their ordinaries shall have the issues of their benefices until they use the English language . . .'

It is no surprise to find Ireland figuring in Anglo-papal discussions in 1381. For in these years to the already existing divisions in Ireland, there had been added another. The Great Schism divided the whole Latin Church and threatened, in the Irish Church, to make wider and deeper the gulf between the two nations.

In April 1378 the College of Cardinals having apparently elected a new pope, Urban VI, rejected him in July on the grounds that the election had been invalidated by their having had to conduct the election in fear of violence by the Roman mob. A new pope was selected, the French Cardinal Robert of Geneva, who took the name Clement VII. The powers of Europe, however, took sides and lined up with one or other of these popes, thereby dividing the Church between the Urbanist or Roman obedience and the Clementine or Avignon obedience. This was the period of the Hundred Years War and England therefore inevitably took the anti-French line and supported Urban VI, whose uncanonical election, in any case, had not been convincingly demonstrated. Scotland, however, taking an anti-English line, supported Clement VII. It was to be expected that English Ireland would be Urbanist. What, however, of Gaelic Ireland? Was Ireland to be split ecclesiastically according to the country's cultural dualism?

There is evidence from Armagh provincial legislation that there was some support for the Avignon pope in the province. It is known too, that Clement VII attempted to appoint an Irish Franciscan to Armagh in 1381. There is evidence that Franciscans in Cashel and Galway were actively pro-Clement and in 1382 Clement provided the Franciscan minister provincial to Cashel, though he did not get possession. In Tuam Archbishop Gregory O Mochair (d.1383) was openly for Clement VII and so too were some at least of his suffragans. However, there is no very substantial evidence to warrant the conclusion that Gaelic Ireland was solidly anti-Urbanist and there seems no evidence of pro-Avignon activity in Ireland later than the dates given in this paragraph. It is more than likely that there was no significant division in Ireland between the obediences after the 1380s.

Provincial legislation
Ars artium est regimen animarum : the government of souls is the art of arts. The classical dictum (it comes from St Gregory the Great's *Pastoral Rule*) was frequently invoked in the canon law of the thirteenth century. One of the pastoral techniques most favoured by the popes of this period was the council, both the provincial council where the metropolitan presided over an assembly of the bishops of his province or the diocesan, where the bishop assembled his diocesan clergy, or the senior of them. At the Fourth Lateran Council in 1215, Innocent III ruled that every metropolitan should hold a provincial council once a year, the decrees of which should be reiterated in diocesan councils also to be held annually by each bishop. These councils were essentially pastoral occasions. They were at once an opportunity for an archbishop or bishop to exhort his clergy to more strenuous pastoral activity, to instruct them with precise directives on how this should be done –

with particular reference to clerical conduct and example – and to restrain them from practices incompatible with the 'art of arts' or at variance with the common law of the universal Church. The decrees of these councils were sometimes the fruit of the bishop's first hand experience in visitations of his diocese, sometimes, perhaps usually, adaptations of papal decretals, sometimes plain borrowings from other diocesan codes. They came to form, so to say, the standing orders of a province or diocese, added to, modified and clarified by successive prelates. From the council, they would be passed on in other groupings of clergy (deaneries, for example) and where appropriate, read in church to the faithful laity.

No province or diocese in Christendom seems to have obeyed to the letter the Lateran Council's decree about annual councils. But provincial and diocesan councils did become a regular feature of thirteenth-century church life. Henry of London has often been credited with being the first or among the very first, to implement the Lateran Council ruling when he summoned a Dublin provincial council in 1217. The statutes of this council have unfortunately not survived and no doubt many councils were held in both Irish and colonial Ireland of which we have no record at all.

Five sets of conciliar statutes of Dublin provenance have survived from the twelfth, thirteenth and fourteenth centuries. It is in itself a miserably small dossier of local canon law as compared with many other areas where very much of this material has not been lost. But it is easily the largest from an Irish source and it commands attention as affording some insight into at least one aspect of diocesan administration.

Generally speaking, the only record of these councils which has survived is merely the text of the decrees themselves. Other records, of liturgical occasions such as sermons, informal discussions outside the council meeting place (usually the cathedral), speech-making in the formal sessions, have vanished.

There is one exception to this wholesale loss of documentation of councils. We are unusually well-informed about the provincial council which John Cumin opened in Holy Trinity Cathedral on Laetare Sunday, 1186. The reason for the existence of this fuller report is because Giraldus Cambrensis was an active participant in the proceedings and never a man to minimise his own contribution, wrote it up twice, once in his Autobiography (*De rebus a se gestis*) and again in his *Topographia Hiberniae*. When Archbishop Cumin held his council, Irish clergy were still very numerous in his diocese and province. We may take it that the suffragan bishops, heads of religious houses and other clergy who attended were predominantly of the native race. This most interesting feature of Giraldus Cambrensis' vivid account of the council concerns the clash of opinions between the personalities of both nations. His narrative, along with the decrees of the council which have survived in Pope Urban III's letter confirming them, for once in the history of medieval Irish church councils, allow a fairly detailed reconstruction of what happened.

As was customary, the archbishop opened his council with a sermon. Giraldus has not recorded its text but he does tell us that its subject-matter concerned the sacraments. It will be recalled that the first English-controlled ecclesiastical council in Ireland, Cashel II, had paid especial attention to the administration of the sacraments as being a matter on which contemporary Irish practice was thought to be less than adequate. It is perhaps reasonable to see the decrees of this Dublin council as in this respect continuing reform undertaken earlier. The bulk of the legislation was designed to correct certain malpractices in the administration of Holy Eucharist, Baptism and Holy Orders and to promote due observance of marriage law.

It was apparently the Irish custom to use as an altar just a wooden table. The council enacted that for the future a stone altar or table with an altar stone should be used, as was universal practice. Detailed instructions were issued concerning hosts, altar cloths, chalice, wine, *piscina*, vestments, baptismal font and baptismal vessels. Other decrees concerned ordination. No bishop was to ordain a cleric from another diocese without commendatory letters from the candidate's bishop or archdeacon. No candidate was to be ordained without a clear title to a benefice for his support, 'for it is dishonourable and shameful for ministers of the Lord's table to have to beg in public'. Those of illegitimate birth should not be promoted to holy orders (papal dispensation from this prohibition was very common). The prevalent custom whereby two orders were received in one day was forbidden as being contrary to the general law of the Church. Considering how much the reformers of the earlier twelfth century had to say about the sexual laxities of the Irish laity, it is perhaps surprising that the council did not have more to say on the subject of marriage than its decree enjoining marriage on fornicators and excommunication of those who persisted in their sin.

It is not known at what precise point in the council the decrees were promulgated. As the information comes to us from Giraldus,[5] the next important event after the archbishop's sermon was an intervention, on the second day, by the Cistercian abbot of Baltinglass, Ailbe O Maelmuidhe who, with English assent, was to be appointed bishop of Ferns shortly after the council.

Giraldus described the abbot's intervention as a sermon. In fact it was much more. A vigorous discourse on clerical chastity was but the prelude to a denunciation of priests who had come over from England and Wales who were living in concubinage, some of whom had even gone through a public form of marriage. The abbot deplored this departure from celibacy the more because of the high standards of clerical continence characteristic of Ireland. Ailbe actually produced some of the guilty priests and had them make public confession of their crimes. The indignant archbishop ('on my advice' claimed the self-important Giraldus) took immediate action and those whose confessions were confirmed on reliable evidence were promptly suspended from benefice and office. The Irish among the assembled clergy jeered and derided the offenders.

These judicial proceedings left their mark on the archbishop's legislation:

> Since the clergy of Ireland among other virtues have always been remarkably eminent for their chastity, it would be wrong and disgraceful if, in our time, through the negligence of us, who though unworthy has been called under a most holy pope and a most Christian king to the government of souls, lilies of outstanding chastity should be corrupted by the foul contagion of strangers and the example of a few incontinent men: wherefore we forbid under penalty of loss of office and benefice any priest, deacon or subdeacon to keep any woman in their houses either under pretext of essential service or any other excuse whatsoever, unless it be a mother, sister or such persons of an age which removes suspicion of unlawful relationship.[6]

It can be imagined that the English and Welsh clergy present were no little taken aback by the trial of their delinquent brethren. There is evidence from this very time that they considered themselves very much the leaders of reform and thereby superior to the Irish clergy. It was at this time that the Cistercian Jocelin who had come from Furness abbey in Lancashire to help to establish John de Courcy's new monastery at Inch, completed his *Life of St Patrick*.[7] Jocelin wrote under the patronage of the earl of

Ulster but also under that of two Irish prelates, the archbishop of Armagh and the bishop of Down, both sees with recent and important connexions with St Malachy. In the course of his book, Jocelin came to make some observations on the post-Patrician history of Patrick's see. He spoke of 'the time of darkness' when the attacks of Scandinavian pagans wrought havoc with the Irish Church and led to the adoption of practices, by untrained clergy, which were contrary to the law of the Church. There were two views, reported Jocelin, about whom should have the credit for reform of these abuses. The Irish claimed that it was St Malachy who had led the Irish Church back to Christian law. But the English, for their part, claimed that it was entirely due to their efforts. Jocelin prudently declined to take sides in the argument.

Giraldus Cambrensis, we may take it, did not share this inclination towards neutrality. When the Archbishop instructed him to preach, on the third day of the Council, on the subject of pastoral care, his sermon became a counter-attack. With the humiliating sound of Irish jeers at Welsh and English priests still ringing in his ears, he spoke with no little enthusiasm of Irish clerical excesses, and of the negligences and vices of the Irish laity.

Giraldus praised the Irish clergy for their chastity, their devotion to prayer and observance of the canonical hours, their perseverance in fasting and abstinence. But they were given to drunkenness, he declared. Their days were spent in strict religious exercises, their nights in convivial drinking. He admitted that this did not lead to sexual misconduct, as the moralists generally insisted was the consequence of excessive drinking; for once, *ubi vina dominantur, Venus non regnat* (where drink is in charge, the goddess of love does not hold sway). Further, Irish clergy were negligent about pastoral care. Irish bishops were usually monks and though often good ones, monks tend to make bad pastors. Irish saints had been confessors rather than martyrs – no pastor had been found prepared to shed his blood for denouncing the failings of his flock. The result of this shirking of pastoral responsibility can be seen in the quality of the Irish laity: *gens spurcissima, gens vitiis involutissima, gens omnium gentium in fidei rudimentis incultissima* (an impure people, a people most enveloped in vices, the people among all peoples most uninstructed in the elementary principles of the faith). He spoke of their deficient matrimonial law. His other charges – of non-payment of tithe, failure to catechise before baptism, disrespect for churches, laxness in burial rites – hardly seem to match the extreme violence of his language. But then Giraldus was anxious to blacken the laity in order the better to upbraid the clergy for neglect of their duties.

Giraldus stepped down from the pulpit well satisfied with his work, 'to a murmur of approval' from his fellow-countrymen, he claimed. He had the good grace, however, to record one telling Irish rejoinder to his sermon, that of Archbishop Matthew O Heney O.Cist. of Cashel: '(Irishmen) were ever wont to show great honour and reverence to churchmen and never to show force to God's saints. But now a people has come to our country who know how to make martyrs and make a practice of doing so. Ireland soon enough will have her martyrs just like other countries.'

The remainder of the decrees show affinity with points made by Giraldus in his sermon. It was ordered under canonical penalty that tithe be paid, 'from provisions, hay, the young animals, flax, wool, gardens, orchards and from all things which grow and renew themselves yearly.' It was decreed that no one should be buried in any churchyard which had not been consecrated by a bishop as a burial ground and that no burials should take place without the presence of a priest. Laity who violated ecclesiastical liberty, especially by intruding priests into benefices, were put under sentence of excommunication, as also were those priests who accepted benefices or ecclesiastical possessions uncanonically.

Giraldus has presented a picture of the rivalries between the native clergy and the invader. But it is clear that though the exchanges were sharp, it was not an antagonism that made co-operation impossible. There is other evidence from this period that prelates of each nation found it possible to work together. In 1192, when the new St Patrick's was consecrated, the occasion was graced by Tomaltach O Connor, archbishop of Armagh and Archbishop O Heney of Cashel. The latter, in his capacity as papal legate, then presided over another reforming council. Unfortunately, its decrees have not survived, nor have we any account of its proceedings.

These councils permit a first glimpse of relations between the higher clergy of both nations in Dublin. But it is also the last. The progress of anglicisation meant the disappearance of Irish bishops and abbots from the Dublin province. It seems likely that Archbishop Henry of London presided as papal legate over a council of the whole Irish Church in 1217. But no information about this council has survived. Thereafter no council under the presidency of a papal legate, Irish or English, and composed of bishops of both nations ever again met in Dublin, or indeed anywhere else in Ireland.

By the second half of the thirteenth century, a code of diocesan standing orders was in being. In the form it has come to us, it was probably the work of Archbishop Fulk of Sandford (1256–71) who was one of the most energetic of Dublin administrators in the thirteenth century. He did not draft the individual decrees himself however. Rather he collected them ready-made from a variety of sources outside Dublin. The way in which he built up his compilation of diocesan law is an interesting specific illustration of how the influence of papal law spread into local areas and of how the norms of ecclesiastical discipline as understood in England were adopted in colonial Ireland. The law promulgated by Archbishop Fulk derived ultimately from the law of the universal Church as laid down by the papacy but more immediately from law enacted already in both the York and Canterbury provinces.[8]

Archbishop Fulk's code numbered forty-eight laws. The first thirty-one of them came from York where they had been drawn up, under some Durham influence, in the years between 1241 and 1255. A second group, of six canons, are a somewhat abridged version of legislation promulgated in a Canterbury provincial council held at Lambeth in 1261. These decrees are mostly about wills, administration of which, in the English legal system, pertained to the ecclesiastical and not the civil courts. It is possible that the remaining eight canons were of Dublin provenance, but their style and content is of a type commonplace in thirteenth-century English dioceses.

The decrees were not systematically classified and they dealt with a wide variety of administrative and disciplinary topics. The biggest single subject concerned the selection, ministrations, behaviour and income of priests. A very prominent place was occupied by what the canonists called the *honestas externa* or public respectability of the clergy. They were wont to discuss this matter of correct clerical conduct under four headings: diligence in performance of the priestly office; moral rectitude; dress and deportment; abstention from unsuitable activities. All these occur in the Dublin decrees in one form or another. Priests must be punctilious about performing the services of the Church, about sick-visiting, proper maintenance of the fabric and furnishings of churches and the custody of the Blessed Sacrament and holy oils. Just as their lives must be separate from the life of the people, so their dress and deportment should demonstrate that separation. Considerable attention was given to the preservation of chastity; the prevention, detection and punishment of breaches of it figure prominently in these decrees. Priests' concubines were to be compelled under pain of excommunication to do penance; if they defied this censure, they would be coerced by the civil power. Priests were required to observe the precept of St Paul: 'In the army, no soldier gets himself mixed up in civilian life, because he must be at the disposal of the man who enlisted him' (2 *Tim.* 2.4).

They were not therefore to engage in professional or commercial activities nor act as agents for laymen nor undertake any venture which would distract from their spiritual functions. Nor were they to frequent taverns or worldly entertainments, gamble or bear arms. They were to shun avarice, and to be particularly on their guard when administering the sacraments of Penance and Holy Communion so that they should not appear more grasping of temporal advantage than zealous for the spiritual good of the penitent or communicant: the Body of Christ should not be distributed in such a way that, 'in holding out the Eucharist in one hand, and receiving money in the other, the ministry of our redemption is made venal'. Tithe and related matters touching priests' income were carefully regulated in this code.

The laity figured as 'subjects' (*subditi*) whose vices were to be tracked down and denounced. The clergy were to hold regular meetings to prepare and issue such denunciations. Excommunication *ipso facto* was the punishment for a wide variety of offences against ecclesiastical liberty (i.e. the freedom of churchmen in their own concerns) and public order. The common use of excommunication perhaps in part explains the provision that no parish priest should hear the confession of, or give Holy Communion to, anyone from another parish, without licence of the parish priest. The absence of such a check would enable an excommunicate to frequent the sacraments of which his sentence had deprived him. Another characteristic feature of these decrees as they affected the laity concerned marriage.

Clandestine marriages (i.e. those contracted without the presence of a priest) were strictly forbidden; even betrothals should be contracted in the presence of a priest.

In the fourteenth century, this code was refurbished in provincial councils: Alexander Bicknor's, c.1320; John of St Pol's, 1352; Thomas Minot's, 1366. The matter of this legislation is very comparable to that of the thirteenth-century compilation and is too, for the most part, borrowed directly from English legatine and provincial decrees. Significantly, those are often of thirteenth-century origin. The norms governing clerical discipline, ecclesiastical organisation and legal procedures had become standardised and the reissue of existing legislation was thought adequate to meet current needs.

In all this Dublin legislative and conciliar activity, we look almost in vain for evidence of the situation of native Irish clergy and laity within the province. There is one exception. Archbishop Minot's provincial council held at Kilkenny in 1366, at a time near to that of the parliament which promulgated the notorious Statute of Kilkenny, included some decrees of great interest in this respect. It may well be that Minot was merely putting into formal legislation for use throughout the province what had been common practice in different parts of it for some long time.

It was alleged that priests and other clergy ministering among the Irish had contributed greatly to lawlessness either by giving evil advice or by tacitly approving of wrong-doing. For the future, Irish clergy were ordered to restrain Irish rulers from violating the oaths they had taken to keep the peace. Should priestly admonitions go unheeded, the clergy must denounce the malefactors to their bishop who would excommunicate them. The clergy would then be ordered to refrain from saying Mass and administering the sacraments (except penance and baptism). If those priests who lived among the Irish did not obey this instruction, they would be suspended. Further, for the future, all ordinands of Irish nationality, were to take an oath not to go to war 'against the peace of the Irish Church, the king and his faithful people nor give advice or help or encouragement to those who did go to war'. Major excommunication was to be the *ipso facto* punishment for violation of this oath.

The provincial council considered that the native Irish were particularly liable to be preyed upon by bogus questors for alms. Charlatans, men of dissolute life, selling false indulgences, by lying preaching, forged documents and false relics, exploited the pious credulity of the faithful. In addition, they were found to be a serious menace to public order in that they persuaded both Irish and English people to swear oaths of peace on their false relics and then, at a price, granted pardons for breach of them. Thereby the sacrament of penance, proper use of indulgences and the canonical censures of the Church were brought into disrepute and all manner of serious crimes committed. Immediate steps were to be taken to abolish such abuses.

One further decree throws some light on the position of Irish clergy in this anglicised area of Ireland. The council promulgated a law forbidding anyone to harbour apostate religious. It mentioned *inter alia* a class of religious who did not follow any established rule such as that of St Benedict or St Augustine but followed a customary rule (*consuetudinalis observancia*). Because this customary observance had been in vogue for a long time and officially tolerated by successive bishops, apostates from it were to be subject to the same penalties as other religious. The reference to this observance must mean that pockets of Celtic monasticism had survived in the Dublin province (perhaps at Glendaloch) into the fourteenth century. It is a remarkable testimony to the endurance of early Irish institutions and the conservatism of medieval Irish society.

The archbishops of Armagh were equally active as legislators in the fourteenth century, though their legislation has not survived in any comparable quantity. The principal extant collection of provincial constitutions though found in the register of Archbishop John Swayne (1418–39), was promulgated at a council held in Drogheda in October 1411 by Archbishop Nicholas Fleming (1404–16). About thirty canons have survived, some are Fleming's own but most are reissues of the decrees of several of his predecessors, David Mageraghty (1334–46), Richard Fitz Ralph (1346–60), Milo Sweetman (1361–80) and John Colton (1382–1404). Their range is not as comprehensive as the Dublin constitutions, but for the most part they are pronouncedly local in character. It should be noted that though Armagh province was part *inter Hibernicos* and part *inter Anglicos*, its provincial councils were regularly attended by suffragans from both parts.

These Armagh 'standing orders' contain much that is familiar, at least in their general import. They are in part a penal code, laying sanctions of excommunication and, where appropriate, loss of benefice or suspension, on those who live in concubinage, impede the testamentary jurisdiction of the ecclesiastical courts or the appellate jurisdiction of the archbishop's metropolitan court, seize or alienate ecclesiastical property or oppress tenants on ecclesiastical estates. Property and income matters are the subject of other constitutions, aimed at safeguarding parochial contributions to bishops and to ensure due payment of tithe. A local adaptation of a well-known canon law ruling insisted that there should be no lay taxation or levy of any kind on ecclesiastics or their properties or their tenants without licence of the local ordinary. The evidence of the fifteenth-century Armagh registers makes it clear that the rules laid down for the protection of the sources of episcopal incomes were among the most invoked and the most ignored of all.

A second batch of constitutions concerned administration of the sacraments. Bishops were instructed to hold ordinations three times each year if candidates were forthcoming, to administer the sacrament of confirmation to children in each deanery at least once a year (if they can get access to them added the decree, thus briefly drawing the historian's attention to another of the hazards of episcopal life in war-torn Armagh) and to consecrate the holy oils on Maundy Thursday. There was an instruction permitting the solemnisation of marriage throughout the year (providing banns had been published, and except in the period between Palm Sunday and Low Sunday) in order to cut down the incidence of clandestine marriages. *Omnis utriusque sexus*, the famous canon of the Fourth Lateran Council commanding the faithful to go to Confession and to receive Holy Communion in their own parishes at least once a year, was reiterated.

Another group of canons concerned devotional practices, particularly of the laity. Particular stress was laid on the proper observance of Holy Week, so that the faithful might receive Holy Communion on Easter day as 'most purified vessels'. On the negative side, some undesirable Eastertide practices were forbidden: the practice of hunting hares on the Monday of Holy Week because it was thought that the blood of the animal killed on that day was of special medicinal value was condemned as superstitious and unlawful; the game of galbardy (as yet unidentified) traditionally played on Easter Monday and at other times in the Easter season was condemned as a dangerous occasion of sin. Finally, full observance of the feasts of SS Patrick, Brigid and Columcille was enjoined throughout the province, and of SS Fechin and Ronan in the diocese.

One constitution helps to throw some light on an important subject in Irish medieval history on which for the most part we are conspicuously uninformed: the extent to which the episcopate set itself to preach peace between the nations:

Also, following [the constitutions of] Milo [Sweetman] by the authority of this present council we command and ordain under penalty of excommunication for disobedience, that all our suffragan bishops shall labour to the utmost they can to bring about and preserve peace between the English and Irish of our province of Armagh, preaching peace between them and compelling by all possible ecclesiastical censures each and everyone of their subjects to keep the peace. If any bishop, however, should become a sower of discord between English and Irish, which God forbid, he shall not only be suspended from his office, but shall be *ipso facto* excommunicate.

There is some evidence from Sweetman's register that his pacificatory endeavours were not confined exclusively to legislation. In 1373, for example, he brought about peace between Niallan Mac Guinness, king of Iveagh, Mac Donald, captain of the Scots in Ulster and the justiciar, sheriff of Louth and other prominent English officials and magnates. Other recorded instances make it very likely that he was an active mediator and preacher of peace between Irish and English.

Sweetman is not the only archbishop of Armagh of whose concern to ameliorate the strife between the nations we have evidence. Archbishop Richard Fitz Ralph's register has not survived but the survival of his Sermon Diary is some compensation for the loss. This document gives some insight into his pastoral life particularly into that part of it which he accounted his special vocation, preaching. The record of his vigorous preaching activity both at the papal curia and in the English parts of his province (preaching in English) affords some indication of his hopes and fears for peace in Ulster.

Preaching before Pope Clement VI in Avignon in 1349, Fitz Ralph depicted a scene of savagery in his province:

'the two nations are always opposed to one another from a traditional hatred, the Irish and Scots being always at variance with the English: so much so that every day they rob and slay and kill one another: nor can any man make any truce or peace among them, for in spite of such a truce they rob and slay one another at the first opportunity'.[9] Fitz Ralph was to have first-hand experience as a thwarted peace-maker.

The Archbishop spent substantially less than half of his thirteen and a half year pontificate in Ireland and perhaps his contribution would have been the greater if he had concentrated more on assuaging bitterness in Ireland than on stirring-up controversy about mendicant privileges in England and Avignon. Nevertheless he was an unremitting upholder of the laws of justice and charity against those English guilty of discriminatory practices, legislating against those who refused to recognise the legality of wills made by Irishmen, condemning the guilds of Drogheda for their practice of excluding the Irish from membership. But it was his own involvement in mediation between Irish rulers and Dublin administration which led to his most violent condemnation of the conduct of Englishmen towards the Irish. After negotiating a peace between the English and Hugh O Neill in 1355, he found it ignored by many individual Englishmen who, in pursuit of their own private ends, continued hostilities in blatant disregard of what lawful authorities had constituted for the public good. Morally and legally the acts of such peace-breakers amounted to murder and robbery, but they sought to justify themselves by recourse to the law of the march (*lex marchie*) and the custom of their forebears. Archbishop Fitz Ralph denounced such alleged law and custom as contrary to God's law of charity. But he found that even upright and experienced priests would tell them in confession that what they had done was not sinful. It would seem, then, that the accusations made in the O Neill

Remonstrance addressed to John XXII in 1317 of Anglo-Irish religious claiming it was no sin to kill an Irishman were less exaggerated than they seem. For the *lex marchie* and ancestral custom condemned by Fitz Ralph must have been in existence for some long period and would apparently correspond substantially to the Irish complaint.

The constitutions of 1411 touch the career of Fitz Ralph at another point, and that an important one. Archbishop Fleming had reissued *Omnis utriusque sexus*, as had become customary in Ireland and elsewhere, with particular emphasis on the authority of the parochial clergy: if a parishioner claimed he had been to confession to some other priest, he might be required to show proof of this before being admitted to Holy Communion. The regulation was intended to be a safeguard against confessions being heard by the unauthorised. Fleming's decree went on to say that it was not the intention of the council to detract in any way from the power of those religious who had apostolic authority to hear confessions from so doing. This qualificatory clause obviously refers, in general, to religious exempt from episcopal jurisdiction but more specifically, to the friars and to that rivalry over the hearing of confessions between them and the diocesan clergy which, in different parts of the Church, had a history going back to the early days of mendicant expansion. If there had been similar clashes in Ireland in the thirteenth century they do not appear to have reached any significant proportions. But from 1350 the position became different. The full significance of the obviously pacificatory attitude of Fleming's council towards the friars appears only after an appraisal of the period of tension between mendicants and diocesan clergy which preceded it.

The traditional mistrust of mendicant privilege in the diocesan sphere was reawakened in 1349 when Pope Clement VI was approached by representatives of the friars with a request to reexamine an earlier papal ruling,

Boniface VIII's *Super cathedram* of 1300, regarded by the diocesan clergy as a definitive statement of the legal standing of the friars in respect of preaching, hearing confessions and rights of burial. A number of prelates at the papal curia were alarmed by this new initiative aimed at changing the status quo and persuaded Fitz Ralph who was in Avignon on some other business, to act as their spokesman. It is natural to ask if in his acceptance of this role, personal experience in Armagh played any part. There is no evidence before 1354, however, of any tension between the archbishop and the friars of his diocese. This was not the only theological debate at the curia in which Fitz Ralph took part; it is clear he had an aptitude and taste for controversy. But as he became more involved in the mendicant controversy, so much the more critical of the friars of his own diocese did he become until eventually he ascribed to them the primary responsibility for that abuse of the confessional which, as has been seen, he considered lay at the heart of the failure of the clergy to preserve peace between the two nations.

Fitz Ralph began his attack on 4 July 1350 with a sermon, *Unusquisque*, demanding the withdrawal of all privileges granted by the papacy to the friars which touched pastoral care because, he claimed, they disrupted diocesan and parochial life and thus spread confusion among the laity. He was to go on to argue that the very exercise of the pastoral ministry was in contradiction to the purpose for which the mendicant orders were founded. As the friars counterattacked, so Fitz Ralph reacted in turn. He wrote a voluminous hardhitting treatise *De pauperie Salvatoris* (Concerning the poverty of the Saviour) which examined in minute detail the theological and canonical status of the mendicant vocation. In December 1356 he commenced a trenchant frontal attack on the friars and their alleged neglect of their true calling in a course of sermons preached in London and concluded the following March. In

November he produced a final climacteric denunciation of them before Pope Innocent VI and his consistory (*Defensorium curatorum contra eos qui privilegiatos se dicunt*. A defence of parish priests against those who call themselves privileged).

Fitz Ralph was back in Armagh in 1351 where he remained until he went to London late in 1356. It was a period of vigorous provincial and diocesan government, punctuated with strong action such as putting Drogheda under interdict in 1352 for failure to clear arrears of tithe. His first recorded complaint against the friars dates from February 1354 when the archbishop suggested rather forcefully that friars were failing to insist on restitution and satisfaction being made whenever sins of theft and fraud were confessed to them – the implication is that they were letting off penitents lightly in order to curry favour. A year later, in a sermon preached at a provincial council, Fitz Ralph made a much more blunt assertion in denouncing certain 'exempt mendicants' as thieves and plunderers of the ecclesiastical revenues of others. But it was at Avignon in the *Defensorium curatorum* that he produced his most damning indictment:

I have in my diocese of Armagh, so far as I can reckon, two thousand subjects who every year are involved in sentences of excommunication by reason of the sentences I have decreed against deliberate murderers, public robbers, incendiaries and suchlike; and of all these, scarce forty a year come to me or my penitentiaries; and yet all these receive the sacraments as other men, and are absolved or are said to be absolved; and they are believed to have been absolved by the friars beyond doubt, for there are no others to absolve them.[10]

However accurate Fitz Ralph's diagnosis of the contribution of the friars to pastoral confusion in Armagh and elsewhere, Innocent VI tried to steer a middle course between the warring parties. On the one hand, he instructed the subjects of the king of England to maintain the privileges of the friars and to continue benefactions to them. In 1359, as a further gesture of support to the friars, he confirmed *Vas electionis*, the decretal issued by Pope John XXII in 1321 which had condemned the opinions of the French theologian John of Pouilly. John had declared that the canon *Omnis utriusque sexus*, which stated that the obligatory annual confession should be to a person's 'own priest', disqualified the friars from hearing confessions and not even the pope could dispense from this obligation. Hugh Bernard, Franciscan minister provincial of Ireland, was prominent among those who had secured these measures of papal support. On the other hand, however, the pope did not amend *Super cathedram* nor did he silence Fitz Ralph. The archbishop died in 1360 – to the friars' chant of *Gaudeamus* rather than that of *Requiescat*, recorded one chronicler. But all their efforts had not been able to secure papal condemnation of his views.

The hornets that Fitz Ralph had helped to stir up did not readily return peaceably to their nests. In Ireland the continuation of the conflict between diocesan clergy and friars was an unwelcome addition to the tensions which beset the Church in the later middle ages. Trouble flared on a number of occasions about two of which in particular documentation remains.

In 1375 the Franciscans at Limerick claimed that the bishop of Limerick, Peter Creagh was oppressing them grievously. They had at hand an appropriate champion in the archbishop of the province. Philip Torrington was himself a Franciscan and a doctor of theology, who had been a prominent member of the English province. He went in person from Cashel to Limerick claiming that as archbishop he was by long-established right, conservator of the privileges of the Minorites in Ireland. There is no record of the archbishops of Cashel holding such a position but it is not unlikely. Such conservators had been appointed in different countries in the early part of the century and the archbishops of Armagh, Dublin and Cashel had been appointed conservators of Dominican privileges in 1317. But Bishop Creagh resisted him by force, 'abusing him like a madman', reported the Archbishop to the Pope, and turned the more furiously on the Franciscans, oppressing them as much as he could, excommunicating all who attended the Franciscan church or arranged burials there. The bishop kept up his campaign of hostility against his metropolitan and the friars. The case was referred to Pope Gregory XI who entrusted the archbishop of Canterbury with the task of putting an end to the strife. As to what Archbishop Simon Sudbury managed to accomplish, we can only echo James Ware's words: 'I am at loss how this tempest came at last to be appeased.' But whatever did come, the appeasement was not general throughout Ireland. For in the early years of the fifteenth century, the controversy between the friars and the diocesan clergy was renewed.

Quite where in Ireland it was renewed is not known but the conflict was clearly of a wide and serious nature, at least in English Ireland. The apparent leader of the attack on the friars was one John Whitehead who took up the cudgels as a self-professed disciple of Richard Fitz Ralph. His precise position, however, was much more that of John of Pouilly than of Fitz Ralph – if the views attributed to him by his friar enemies are to be accepted as at least a broadly accurate statement of what he and his supporters were teaching. They were accused *inter alia* of maintaining that John of Pouilly's views were true, even though Pope John XXII had condemned them and that *Vas electionis* was void; that *Omnis utriusque sexus* laid down an inviolable principle of divine law when it commanded that confession should be to a person's own priest and neither God nor the Pope could dispense from that obligation; that friars seeking privileges to hear confessions or conduct burials were in mortal sin and popes who granted them or confirmed them were themselves in mortal sin and excommunicate; that friars were not pastors but robbers, thieves and wolves. Pope Alexander V duly condemned these views in his decretal *Regnans in excelsis* (October 1409) and in effect re-asserted the right of friars to minister to the faithful and to receive oblations from them. The decretal provoked some noises of dissent in the university of Paris, whereupon all the orders of friars in Ireland banded themselves into a league of self-protection (1410) and urged other provinces to close the ranks similarly. That their movement of self-defence was not unsuccessful in Ireland is demonstrated by the implicit acknowledgement of the principle reasserted in *Regnans in excelsis* by Archbishop Fleming's provincial council in 1411.

Alexander V's condemnation was not quite an end to the controversy in Ireland, however. Eugenius IV found it necessary to reaffirm it in 1440 when Philip Norris, formerly vicar of Dundalk (where Fitz Ralph was now looked on as a saint), doctor of theology of the university of Oxford, canon of St Patrick's Dublin, had been cited to Rome for propounding views substantially the same as John of Pouilly's. Philip was imprisoned by King Henry VI from 1441 to 1443 and finally excommunicated in 1452. But Pope Calixtus III came to his rescue in 1456, reinstating him and ordering the friars not to molest him. He was dean of St Patrick's Dublin from 1457 down to his death in 1465. It is probable that his views attracted more attention in the university of Oxford and the papal curia than in Ireland. For there is nothing to suggest he ignited any fires in Armagh or Dublin where he ministered.

Courts ecclesiastical and civil
Medieval men, clergy and laity alike, lived under the

jurisdiction of two powers, spiritual and temporal, and therefore of two legal systems, the law of the Church, canon law, and the law of the civil power. In most general terms, 'temporal' matters were the concern of the civil courts and 'spiritual' matters belonged to the jurisdiction of the ecclesiastical courts. In practice, of course, such a distinction was far too simple to be meaningful. Cases meriting the attention of the courts invariably had both spiritual and temporal implications. All were in one way or another 'mixed': there were very many temporal matters over which churchmen were concerned to have cognisance and the converse was equally true. In most European countries, however, there was substantial agreement on the extents of the respective jurisdiction and co-operation between them, though their precise practical workings varied from country to country. But as well as agreement and co-operation, there was a continuous dialogue, in differing tones of acrimony, which sometimes exploded into serious conflict, about the niceties of exactly where the dividing line between the jurisdictions should be drawn.

The kings of England sought to introduce into Ireland the common law interpretation of the relationship of the two legal systems. This was a logical consequence of the Cashel II principle that the Church in Ireland should adopt the practices of the Church in England. The whole process of this aspect of the anglicisation of the Irish Church in the thirteenth century has been much studied in recent years. It has been established beyond doubt that the jurisdiction allowed to the courts Christian in colonial Ireland was exactly that in operation in England. The introduction was successful in Anglo-Ireland, even though it was often disputed by the Anglo-Irish clergy, just as the clergy in England often protested, almost invariably in vain, against the alleged encroachments of the Crown on ecclesiastical liberty. The Anglo-Irish bishops, often joined by Irish bishops whose dioceses came also under the influence of the common law, from time to time drew up lists of grievances (*gravamina*) against the operation of the common law in what were considered to be ecclesiastical preserves. These were presented for redress to the Justiciar and King. Sometimes this would take place in association with a meeting of parliament and then the bishops would counter a request for royal taxation of their property with a demand for redress. But they did not make very much headway. The Crown was quite prepared to promise correction of abuses of the system and to clarify doubtful points of procedure. It was not prepared to make any concession of principle. In disputed matters it was the Crown which decided where the dividing line between the civil and ecclesiastical jurisdictions should be drawn. When in the later middle ages, the power of the Crown in Ireland had declined, the story is somewhat different, just as it had always been in the purely Irish areas which were not within the Crown's reach. Unfortunately, however, the sources have little to tell about the working of ecclesiastical courts in these areas.

Not that they have much to tell us at first hand about their operation in the *terre Engleis*. It can be deduced from the submissions of the clergy and the replies they elicited from either the Dublin administration or the Crown, just what cases were handled in the ecclesiastical courts. It is not until the later middle ages that there are records from the courts themselves.

The full ecclesiastical claim was a very comprehensive one. The Church claimed jurisdiction over a case either *ratione materiae* i.e. if the *matter* in dispute was spiritual or ecclesiastical, or *ratione personae* i.e. if the *person* or persons involved were by reason of their status especially the subjects of ecclesiastical authority. English law, however, admitted relatively little of the claim, though what it did admit was not negligible. It would not concede that litigation about church lands was a matter for the ecclesiastical court. On the other hand, testamentary jurisdiction was such a matter and with it some jurisdiction over personal property. The very important matter of matrimonial jurisdiction, which also had significant property implications, was also the preserve of the ecclesiastical judge. English law guarded its monopoly of criminal jurisdiction as jealously as that of real property cases. But a number of offences which the Church knew to be sins were not regarded as crimes by the Crown and they came to the ecclesiastical judge for 'correction of souls'. This was a fairly numerous category including, most importantly, the whole province of sexual morality.

Canon law saw the clergy as a privileged class, 'immune' from secular jurisdiction and therefore claimed for the ecclesiastical courts competence over all cases, whether criminal or civil, in which a clerk (he might be only in minor orders) was involved either as plaintiff or defendant. But English law severely circumscribed 'benefit of clergy' and for all intents and purposes the position of the clergy was just the same as a layman's. There was one major exception to this principle. A clerk accused of felony was entitled to trial in the ecclesiastical court. The lay court, before handing him over, would make enquiry by jury about his guilt – not technically to try him but to establish whether he should be sent to his bishop or not. The real trial took place in the ecclesiastical court. Since canon law did not impose the death penalty, many clerical criminals got off more lightly than their lay counter-parts.

It may be readily imagined that two sets of professional lawyers, canon and common, wrangling over the finer points of what was, and what was not, spiritual and temporal produced a much more complex and technical debate than the above simplified account suggests. Some examples will perhaps convey something of the realities of the practical operation of the two jurisdictions.

Three very different case histories may be selected. The

first demonstrates the sort of jurisdiction exercised in the courts Christian in Ireland and how that jurisdiction was exercised under the surveillance of the Crown. The king's itinerant justices sitting at Limerick in 1290 heard charges against the bishops of Limerick and Emly and the exercise of ecclesiastical justice by their principal legal officials. The charges were of two sorts. One consisted of accusations of abuse of the jurisdiction that was properly theirs: they were accused of charging excessive fees for proving wills and over-sentencing in cases of usury and sacrilege. The other charged them with exceeding the bounds of ecclesiastical jurisdiction. Thus the courts Christian were permitted to try cases of breach of faith since the violation of an oath, the breaking of a promise made to God, was a spiritual matter. But the Crown did not allow that it followed that jurisdiction over the promise gave jurisdiction over the matter about which the promise had been made. Thus the ecclesiastical judge could punish the sin of breaking faith but he had no jurisdiction, for example, over debts. Similarly, he was allowed to punish the sin of assaulting a priest by the infliction of a penance but not to punish the crime of breach of the king's peace by fining the assailant. The royal judges also found fault with the levying of fines on weavers who had worked on holy days. Presumably their objection was to the levying of pecuniary punishments rather than the imposition of penances, for the issue itself was clearly ecclesiastical.

The second illustration shows the two powers in contention over jurisdiction in the experience of a distinguished Irish prelate Nicholas Mac Maol Iosa, archbishop of Armagh from 1272 to 1303. In thirty years of a very active episcopal career, Archbishop Nicholas came to know at first hand every shift and twist of this particular politico-legal game. His career is the classic thirteenth-century example of the Irish prelate forced to come to terms with the common law system. But he fought for his concept of ecclesiastical liberty on two fronts, for he saw his jurisdiction threatened too by Irish princes.

Nicholas was very concerned about the financial state of his diocese. In 1279 he told Edward I that that part which lay in the 'land of peace' (the somewhat euphemistic term applied to the English area) was worth but 100 pounds annually to him. He was therefore anxious to resuscitate the dwindling income of his see – a necessary work which indeed had already begun under his predecessor Patrick O Scannell, O.P. (1261–70). Nicholas sought respite of Edward I from certain royal pressures on Armagh resources. One type of pressure was being exerted on the archbishop in his capacity as metropolitan of the province, the other in his capacity as tenant of the Crown in respect of the episcopal manors of Termonfeckin and Dromiskin.

On the first head, the archbishop complained about the English insistence that during vacancy in the episcopal sees of the province, the temporalities of the diocese were claimed by the Crown. Nicholas maintained, with good reason, that by long-established custom, custody of temporalities as well as spiritualities in vacancies of the suffragan dioceses belonged to the archbishop. After investigation into this claim, which if conceded would have put Armagh in a different position from the rest of the Irish dioceses, it was rejected by Edward I. On the second head, the archbishop petitioned for relief from certain financial obligations and this was granted. When, however, he claimed that he held the lucrative right to 'wreck of the sea' (in English law a royal monopoly) at Termonfeckin, this too was rejected after investigation. In 1289, Nicholas again pressed his claim for custody of temporalities during Armagh vacancies and was refused again. In this period he was litigating in the Justiciar's court over various properties in co. Louth to which he felt he had a claim.

Nicholas perforce pursued his objectives by legal process.

But he did not neglect the possibility that good relations with English officialdom might serve his cause. Before 1285, the Dublin administration was dominated by the Fulbourn family: Stephen, bishop of Waterford, was both Justiciar and Treasurer, his uncle was Chancellor and he was to be succeeded by Stephen's brother, Walter. When there was a vacancy in the diocese of Meath, Nicholas lent a hand in the promotion of Walter Fulbourn. The archbishop refused to confirm Thomas St Leger the candidate selected by the Meath clergy and then, claiming that their right of election had lapsed to him, the metropolitan, through their neglect, provided Walter Fulbourn to the Meath see. The manoeuvre did not work because the Meath electors appealed to the papacy and eventually were to win. Nicholas' incursion into Dublin politics did little to serve his ends. One John of Kells, archdeacon of Meath and supporter of Thomas St Leger was also an official of the Dublin exchequer, with a strong sense of grievance against the rule of the Fulbourns. He denounced Archbishop Nicholas to the Chancellor in England for chicanery in the Meath election and the Fulbourns for their exploitation of government for their own private gain. His denunciation of Nicholas shows how easy it was to express ecclesiastical and political disputes in simple terms of national antagonisms. He told the Chancellor: 'You know the Irish are hostile to the English and never cease from disturbing their peace whenever possible. Their leaders know nothing of self-control. They seek to crush their subjects under foot in tyrannous domination'. The complaint against the Fulbourns led to a full-scale investigation by commissioners sent from Westminster. Nicholas found himself charged with arrogating to himself custody of temporalities during vacancies; consecrating a bishop of Meath without licence to elect having been asked for, nor fealty to the king taken from the elect; usurping pleas of the crown in his courts; harbouring felons; coining money without licence. Like the Fulbourns (Stephen became arch-bishop of Tuam and Walter bishop of Waterford), Archbishop Nicholas in the end escaped serious harm, but he suffered a series of fines for various offences of usurping royal rights. He seems to have managed to evade paying them, however.

The Fulbourn set-back did not put an end to Nicholas' inventiveness. In 1291, Edward I made a determined attempt to levy a tax on the Irish Church and elaborate arrangements for its assessment and collection were drawn up. Few ecclesiastics in Ireland, Irish or Anglo-Irish, had the slightest intention of paying anything and there were hostile reactions of different kinds from different parts of the country. When parliament met in Dublin to consider the royal demand (there was to be a tax on lay property too), the king's representative was presented with a for-midable list of *gravamina*, amounting to a severe criticism of the lack of respect of the Dublin administration for ecclesiastical immunities and jurisdictions. Archbishop Nicholas had his own individual reaction to this. He summoned an Armagh provincial council to meet at the Dominican house in Trim and with his suffragans, attempted to form a confederation of all the bishops and chapters of Ireland for mutual support against lay violation of their 'privileges, jurisdictions, liberties and customs'. All were to unite to resist 'undue impediment, annoyance, encroachment, oppression or grievance from person or persons invested with any lay jurisdiction or power what-soever'. There would be a common policy of resistance, a pooling of legal expenses, upholding of each other's sentences of excommunication and interdict, all binding under pain of fine for non-observance, part of which was payable to the pope and part to those who were observing the terms of the confederation. This singular scheme did not, however, get beyond the paper planning stage.

The archbishops of Armagh did not have to contend

only with the initiatives of the kings of England. They needed to be alert also to the protection of ecclesiastical rights against inroads made on them by the numerous clan rulers of Ulster. In 1296, Pope Boniface VIII reiterated a principle long cherished by the papacy: no secular ruler might tax churchmen without papal permission. The context of this declaration, made in the decretal *Clericis laicos*, was Anglo-French preparations for war and both Edward I and Philip IV reacted sharply to this attempt to shackle their freedom in their own countries. Archbishop Nicholas, however, with his customary ingenuity, turned the papal action to his own profit. He used *Clericis laicos* as an opportunity for drawing up formal agreements concerning ecclesiastical liberty between himself and the Irish rulers of his province.

He summoned Donal O Neill and the leading lords of Tír Eoghan to his presence, expounded *Clericis laicos* to them, along with certain other constitutions relating to the 'liberty of the Church and the salvation of souls' and persuaded them to attach their seals to these documents as indicating their acceptance of the principles they contained. Then, accompanied by the bishop of Clogher, a great company of clergy and relics of the saints (some years earlier Nicholas had claimed the discovery of the relics of Patrick, Colmcille and Brigid in Saulpatrick), he betook himself to Brian Mac Mahon, king of Oriel. Brian, with his leading men, went through a similar ceremony. In addition, they gave their consent to a long list of specific undertakings, breach of which was punishable according to a carefully assessed scale of fines payable in cows. Lay rulers were obliged to refrain from oppressing the ecclesiastical power, especially by not making exactions of any kind whatsoever on the clergy and their tenants and to permit a much broader principle of benefit of clergy than English law allowed. They were too to co-operate with the clergy in protecting ecclesiastics and their property and in helping in the arrest of excommunicates. The whole is a view of ecclesiastical liberty fashioned according to an amalgam of Irish, common and canon law principles. It is clear that Nicholas considered O Neill and the other Irish rulers as little regardful of clerical rights as the Dublin administration. Agreements to refrain from molesting ecclesiastical tenants, occupying ecclesiastical lands, usurping ecclesiastical jurisdiction, with promises to lend the aid of the secular arm, often made and often broken, became a regular feature of the Ulster scene in the later middle ages.

The third illustration, drawn from the actual records of an ecclesiastical court in action, will be considered in the next chapter (see pp. 206–8).

6 The Century before the Reformation

The Church in Decline

Relatively little has been written about the Church in the later years of medieval Ireland, a period when all over Europe there were ominous signs of decay in the traditional institutions of medieval Christendom. It seems true to say that in so far as there is an established interpretation of this unhappy period of Irish Church history, it is based on a series of reports of early sixteenth-century origin which purport to describe the state of Ireland in general and after that of the Church in particular.[1] Perhaps the best-known of these, standing at the very beginning of the published *State Papers (Ireland) Henry VIII,* set out to describe the general condition of the country before going on to sketch a 'plan of its reformation'. The preparation of such plans and their presentation to Henry VIII was a feature of this period of Irish history. The anonymous author painted a very black picture of the decay of English sovereignty in the Irish lordship, to which historians frequently have had recourse to describe the condition to which Ireland had been reduced by three and a half centuries or so of English rule. It had trenchant things to say about the state of the Church.

The author recalled the report of one of his contemporaries of a conversation alleged to have taken place between St Brigid and her guardian angel about the state of religion in Ireland. The angel 'did show to her the lapse of the souls of Christian folk of that land, how they fell down into hell as thick as any hail shower'. This is a variation on a theme well known in medieval Ireland. Archbishop Fitz Ralph, for example, told Pope Clement VI in 1349 of the Toledan necromancer who asked the devil which country supplied him with most subjects. The answer was Ireland, because everyone there robs everyone else, never making restitution and therefore dying impenitent. Further the nations always oppose each other in hate and so, living without charity, die without grace. The sixteenth-century moralist, however, has another explanation for the 'lapse of souls':

> Some sayeth that the prelates of the church and clergy is much cause of all the misorder of the land; for there is no archbishop, ne bishop, ne prior, parson, ne vicar, ne any other person of the Church, high or low, great or small, English or Irish, that useth to preach the word of God, saving the poor friars beggars; and where the word of God do cease, there can be no grace, and without the special grace of God the land may never be reformed; and by teaching and preaching of prelates of the Church and by prayer or orison of the devout persons in the same, God useth alway to grant his abundant grace; ergo the Church not using the premises is much cause of all the said misorder of this land.

Numerous other reports of the same period, the more convincing for being less comprehensive in scope and more specific in local detail, have served to confirm this bleak picture. There are accounts, for example, of the decay of cathedrals (and therefore of parishes) in some of the smaller dioceses of Armagh and Tuam; accounts from the Anglo-Irish areas such, for example, as that of Hugh Inge, bishop of Meath (1523–28), writing to Cardinal Wolsey lamenting 'the sorrowful decay in good Christiantie' in his diocese or that of the earl of Kildare giving his view that 'If the king do not provide a remedy there will be no more

Christentie [in Tipperary and Kilkenny] than in the middle of Turkey'. Examples could be multiplied. In their relative bulk they have been seen by historians as indicating an over-all degree of disorder in the late medieval Irish Church not far short of total breakdown of organised religion in that war-torn country.

It is no doubt prudent to treat these early sixteenth-century assessments of the state of the Church with caution because of the subjective nature of their origins. Nevertheless, no one who has examined the Irish ecclesiastical scene in the fifteenth century will minimise the seriousness of certain defects in the administrative structures of the Church, nor the short-comings of ecclesiastical leadership in this period. The fifteenth century, in Christendom generally, is seen conventionally as the age of the decadence of the medieval Church. Ireland knew its share of the common experience of religious decline.

It is not difficult to isolate the chief features of the Irish Church in its period of decline. They were four in number.

The first was the continued insistence by the English authorities on a policy of maintaining the Englishness of the Church in the areas subject to English law. The policy had received its most formal enactment in 1366 in clauses 13 and 14 of the Statute of Kilkenny wherein the admission of native Irishmen to bishoprics, canonries of cathedrals, care of souls in parishes and all the different types of religious community among the English was strictly forbidden. It is true that in practice these decrees were operated, in so far as they were operated, far from strictly. They were used as a controlling mechanism, regulating the admission of Irishmen to the English ranks by establishing a licensing system whereby Irish priests and religious were required to obtain a grant of English denization if they wished to live and work in the English areas. But the existence of such legislation, and it was frequently reiterated, and the system of dispensations from it, is in itself indicative of a political, legal, cultural and psychological barrier between the two nations which was essentially divisive and therefore detrimental to the full living of the Christian life. As Fitz Ralph had seen so clearly, it perpetuated the negation of charity.

By the end of the middle ages, the natural process of intermarriage between the two peoples had, despite all legislation to the contrary, brought about a considerable degree of assimilation of the two cultures on all social levels. Nevertheless, in that period, as in all periods since the Invasion, bitterness between native and colonist was always a poison to envenom the sores of the medieval ecclesiastical body politic. A typical case comes from 1431 when John Gese, bishop of Waterford and Lismore attempted to impeach his metropolitan, Richard O Hedian, archbishop of Cashel, in a parliament at Dublin. Among the charges were that of 'making much of the Irish, loving none of the English,' of refusing benefices to Englishmen and urging other bishops to do the same, of 'seeking to make himself king of Munster'. O Hedian survived to rule his see down to his death in 1440.

Tensions between clergy of the respective nations still continued to influence decisions made in high places about matters of grave import. For example, in 1445, after more than two centuries of Franciscan activities in Ireland, the Irish province had for the first time a native Irishman, William O Reilly, as minister-provincial. He was formally recognised as such by King Henry VI. However, a group of Anglo-Irish friars opposed him, on the spurious grounds that he had secured his appointment by deceit and that he was a rebel against English authority. Henry VI was persuaded to withdraw his earlier recognition of Brother William, who was incidentally a doctor of theology of the university of Oxford, and to command the reissue of legislation forbidding anyone of 'Irish blood, name and nation' to be minister or vicar of the Order in Ireland. This legislation had a history going back at least to the 1320s, as has been seen earlier. However, appeal to Pope Eugenius IV brought William's reinstatement, fortunately for the Irish Franciscans, for he proved to be an earnest reformer of the Order in times when such were in conspicuously short supply. The incident typifies how easy it was for the disgruntled to exploit the discriminatory legislation for purely self-interested ends, impeding the promotion of leaders of quality.

This first cause of regression in the Irish Church of the later middle ages was the responsibility of colonial Ireland. The second was the distinctive contribution of Gaelic Ireland. The dynastic nature of episcopal and abbatial succession had always been a feature of the Church *inter Hibernicos*. The efforts of reformers from the twelfth century onwards had done much to replace the principle of succession from within particular families by the principle of free canonical election. But familial control of individual dioceses, parishes and religious houses had never ceased completely. By the fifteenth century, it had again become widespread, being endemic in the provinces of Tuam and Armagh.

The total extent of hereditary succession of ecclesiastical office is hidden from us by the sparsity of source material. But the Annals, genealogical tracts and papal letters leave no room for doubt that it was very widespread throughout Gaelic Ireland in the fifteenth century. Its inevitable consequence was the large-scale abandonment of clerical celibacy.

A typical example of such an ecclesiastical dynasty may be selected from the Fermanagh diocese of Clogher where the Maguires were the ruling family and the Mac Cawells a leading ecclesiastical family. The union of the two families constituted in a very real sense the essence of the relationship of Church and State in that area of Ulster and has its parallels throughout Gaelic Ireland.

The two families between them controlled the see

virtually throughout the whole century.[2] Art Mac Cawell, bishop of Clogher 1390–1432, Pierce Maguire, 1433–47, Ross Maguire, 1447–83. There was also a Bishop Eugene Mac Cawell, 1505–15. The ecclesiastical implications of the intermarriage of these two families left their first mark on the records, to all seeming, with the marriage of Joan, daughter of Bishop Brian Mac Cawell (1356–58) to the archdeacon of Clogher, Maurice Maguire, known in the Annals as the 'Great Archdeacon'. Their eldest son, after graduating in canon law at the university of Oxford, succeeded his father as archdeacon before becoming bishop of Clogher by papal provision in 1433, in succession to his uncle (?), Art Mac Cawell. A second son became abbot of the Augustinian house of Lisgoole and a third, also an Oxford man, prior of the Augustinian house of Devenish. All three married. The Ross Maguire who became bishop in 1447 may have been the son of Bishop Pierce but this is not certain. Pierce Maguire's sons did obtain important positions in the diocese: Edmund became archdeacon and then dean of Clogher, William was a canon of Clogher and abbot of Lisgoole, Turloch, prior of the Augustinian house of Loch Derg. The first two of these at least had sons who apparently had to be content with merely parochial benefices. It is not clear exactly where Bishop Ross Maguire fits into the family tree though it is certain that he contributed much to its ramification, for he had ten sons. One of them, Cathal Óg Maguire, canon of Clogher and of Armagh, rural dean of Loch Erne, achieved fame as the chief compiler of the *Annals of Ulster*. He had at least twelve children, -- one of them married a daughter of Thomas Mac Brady, bishop of Kilmore (1480–1511). The *Annals* recording Cathal Óg's death in 1498 noted in the panegyric that he was 'a gem of purity and a turtle-dove of chastity'. We may share Fr Canice Mooney's feeling: 'here a certain puzzlement possesses us'. It is possible that Cathal Óg was a layman even if he did enjoy ecclesiastical benefices. But more likely, the entry in the *Annals* is an exact demonstration of Fr Mooney's point that little or no social stigma attached to concubinage (i.e. clerical marriage) or illegitimate status (which priests' children had in canon law).

The third major area of deterioration in the fifteenth-century church lay in the religious orders, canons, friars and monks alike. The history of the Mac Cawell and Maguire families and their connexion with Lisgoole, Devenish and Loch Derg is one example among many of the decline of the Augustinian canons in Gaelic Ireland. The English houses of Augustinians were often little better, with canons few in number, lax in discipline. Sometimes the monastery itself was no more than a frontier block-house in the wars against the Irish.

But the Order which had most comprehensively fallen on evil days was the Cistercian, once the glory of monastic Ireland, vanguard of the reform movement. *Corruptio optimi pessima*. Cistercian discipline derived its strength from its uniformity and that submission to the central authority of the General Chapter which guaranteed it. But by this period the General Chapter had virtually lost its power to enforce its will in Ireland. Efforts to fill the void by establishing a strong national congregation (1496) foundered on the inability of the two nations to pull together for the good of the Order. With the failure of authority came a total breakdown of the visitation system. The General Chapter appointed special *reformatores* to try to reform the Cistercians in Ireland but their efforts came to nothing. One of these reformers, John Troy, abbot of Mellifont, in a report to the General Chapter in the closing years of the fifteenth century, has left a detailed assessment of the generally depressed state of Irish Cistercianism at the end of the middle ages.

Troy confessed his despair of finding any remedy for the ruin and desolation of the Order in Ireland where, he stated, the monks of only two communities, Dublin and

Mellifont, kept the Rule or even wore the habit. His analysis of the root causes of the disaster singled out particularly the ceaseless wars and hatred between the two nations, which left the Order especially vulnerable to oppression; the lack of adequate leadership, a lack compounded by the action of the papacy which appointed abbots who sometimes were not Cistercians and occasionally not even ordained; the control of so many monasteries by the great families who treated the monastery simply as part of their property complex, placing their own relatives in command. Small wonder that the numbers of Cistercians shrank away. At the time of the suppression of the monasteries, the total number of monks in St Mary's Dublin was fifteen; in Mellifont, fourteen. These, as we have seen, were reputedly the two houses of best observance in Ireland. At Granard the number was six; Jerpoint and Inislounaght, five; Kilcooly and Hore, two. The only redeeming feature of the Cistercian scene was the continued effort, though it was on too small a scale and remained ineffectual, to accomplish some improvement.

The fourth characteristic feature of the Irish Church in decline was not one for which Irish churchmen were responsible. It is well known how, in the later middle ages, the papacy made of its right to provide to benefices a major industry. This centralisation of the control over the whole complex system of ecclesiastical office was exploited often as a purely fiscal operation of which the aim, at least in practice, was more financially than religiously motivated. In England the traffic in benefices was controlled by legislation denying the papacy powers to override the ordinary collators. This legislation applied, too, in colonial Ireland. But most of Ireland by now lay outside the scope of the English kings' veto. As far as Gaelic Ireland was concerned, this papal centralisation led to a considerable increase in 'Rome-running'.

In principle, this was no bad thing. In earlier periods, the universalism of Rome had counterbalanced the insularity of Ireland. But in the fifteenth century, papal action, far from eradicating abuses prevalent in Ireland, served only to encourage them. The evidence comes from the nine published volumes of the *Calendars of entries in the papal registers relating to Great Britain and Ireland* which cover the period up to 1492. The bulk of the entries in these calendars concern provisions to benefices and the majority of them are benefices in Gaelic Ireland.

Two typical examples may be selected for reproduction *in extenso*. They illustrate the provisory system in action. They demonstrate how that system was an abuse in itself and how it contributed to the continuance of other abuses.

The first case comes from 1484 the first year of the pontificate of Innocent VIII (1484–1492). That his immediate successor was Pope Alexander VI will warn us that this was not the most edifying period in papal history.

It has been seen earlier that hereditary succession to all manner of ecclesiastical offices had become extremely common in Gaelic Ireland. Here is an example of how that system was encouraged by papal co-operation in its continuation. The deanship of Clonfert was the particular preserve of the Mac Egans and the case cited here shows the papacy itself devising a legal means of getting round the stipulation of canon law that a son might not succeed immediately to his father's benefice: an intermediary was substituted by legal process.

To Carbry Mac Egan, dean of Clonfert. Collation etc., as below. His recent petition contained that his father, Carbry the elder, then dean of Clonfert, being old and desiring to resign the deanery in order that with the consent of the apostolic see his son should obtain it, sent him to the Roman court to get the matter expedited; that, learning when he got there, that on account of his illegitimacy, as the son of Carbry the elder, a priest, and an unmarried woman, related in the fourth degrees of kindred and affinity, he could not obtain the deanery without an intermediate person after his father, he, at the advice of the lawyers, got the deanery to be freely resigned by Carbry the elder, to a certain judge or commissary appointed by Sixtus IV; that the said judge admitted the resignation by papal authority, and by the said authority made collation and provision of the deanery, thus void, to John Ochonoyul, priest, of the diocese of Clonfert; that after John had obtained possession of the deanery, and had held it for some time, he freely resigned it, also to a certain judge or commissary appointed by the pope; and that the judge or commissary admitted the resignation by the said authority and by the same authority made collation and provision of the deanery, thus void, to Carbry the younger, who had been made a clerk, and had been sufficiently dispensed by the pope, on account of the said defect, to hold the deanery, in virtue of which collation and provision he obtained and still holds possession. His petition added that he feared that on account of the foregoing, and for other reasons, the said collation and provision did not hold good. The pope, having learned that the deanery is still void, hereby makes him collation and provision of it, a major dignity with cure, yearly value not exceeding 30 marks sterling, howsoever void, etc., and orders the bishop of Clonfert, the prior of the monastery of Clontuskert, in the diocese of Clonfert, and John Odo[n?]ay, a canon of Annaghdown to induct him into possession.[3]

The second text, one of a very large number of similar cases to be found in the papal registers, illustrates an established process of obtaining a benefice. The petitioner would go to Rome and denounce the existing holder of the benefice he sought as guilty of crimes for which the appropriate canonical penalty was removal from the benefice. The curia would appoint judges-delegate to try the accused. If they found the charges proved, the guilty incumbent would be ejected and the petitioner collated in his place. The precise point at which a somewhat dubious practice becomes radically suspect is when it became usual for the petitioner himself to suggest suitable names for appointment as judges-delegate in the case.

This particular text shows the initiation of the procedure designed to promote the son of Nicholas O Flanagan, O.P., bishop of Elphin (1458–94) to the provostship of Elphin. The son was already a canon of the Elphin chapter.

To the priors of the monasteries of SS Peter and Paul de Innocentia near Athlone and of Kilmore in the diocese of Elphin, and Cornelius Osgyngyn, a canon of Elphin. Mandate, as below. The pope has been informed by Donald Oflannagan alias Maghigan, a canon of Elphin, that Odo Omokan, provost of the church of Elphin, has led the life of a fornicator, has dilapidated the previous movables and the immovables of the said provostship, and when under sentence of excommunication, has ministered in divine offices in contempt of the keys, thereby contracting irregularity. The pope, therefore, hereby orders the above three, if the said Donald (who was lately dispensed by authority of the ordinary on account of illegitimacy, as the son of a bishop, of the Order of Friars Preacher and in priest's orders and a married woman, to be made a clerk and receive and retain a canonry and prebend of the said church, after which he was made a clerk, and obtained by collation of the ordinary such canonry and prebend, yearly value not exceeding 3 marks sterling, which he still holds, but without receiving any fruits therefrom), will accuse the said Odo before them, to summon the latter, and if they find the foregoing to be true, or two of them sufficient for the purpose, to deprive and remove him from the said provostship, and in that event to collate and assign it, a non-major, non-elective dignity with cure, yearly value not exceeding 12 marks, to the said Donald. The pope further specially dispenses him to be promoted to all, even holy orders, and receive and retain it and the said canonry and prebend, notwithstanding the said defect, etc.[4]

It would be imprudent to assume the guilt of Provost Odo Omokan without further evidence, or the guilt of those many others similarly charged with serious crimes by those anxious to obtain their livings and possessed of some influence in the selection of the judges who had the deciding voice. But as Fr Gwynn has observed, 'the general impression left by so many entries of this kind is that the late medieval Irish Church was in a state of lamentable disorder, and that metropolitan and episcopal government no longer sufficed to remedy these grave abuses.' An even stronger impression left by the same sources is that the papacy was not interested in remedying these grave abuses. Indeed its toleration of them, unthinkable by thirteenth-century papal standards, undoubtedly fostered them.

There were other abuses for whose growth the curia must take a large part of the responsibility. Abbot John Troy's complaint was all too justified: highly unsuitable persons were irresponsibly promoted to headships of Cistercian monasteries. Augustinian priories suffered similarly. A further indefensible facet of papal policy was its frequent promotion of English clergy to Irish sees with scant regard for the good of the diocese concerned, for these bishops had no intention of residing in their dioceses but intended to make a career as a suffragan bishop in an English or Welsh see. The classical example of this abuse occurred in Dromore. An English Benedictine, John Chourles, was promoted to the see in 1410. He acted as suffragan in Canterbury until his death in 1433. By 1431–33, he had been joined as bishop of Dromore by three more absentee English religious, all appointed by the papacy: a Franciscan who worked in York diocese, a Carmelite in St David's diocese and an Augustinian friar in Durham diocese.

The Friars and Reform

Indiscipline was rife throughout the religious orders in fifteenth-century Ireland. That, however, is far from being the whole story. For the fifteenth century was also a period when the mendicant orders underwent significant expansion and reform. It would perhaps be going too far to claim that this forward movement was comparable to the flowering of Cistercian and Augustinian monasticism in the twelfth century or of the friars in the thirteenth. Nevertheless it was certainly a marked contrast to the fourteenth-century position, when very few new houses were founded and men were, apparently, powerless to halt the slide in observance from the mediocre to the scandalous. A simple statistical table[5] reveals at a glance the new foundations in each of the four mendicant orders, as also their geographical distribution by ecclesiastical province. The period covered is from 1400 to 1508:

	New Houses	Tuam	Armagh	Cashel	Dublin
Franciscan					
Conventual	14	5	1	7	1
Observant	10	2	2	4	2
Third Order	43	16	22	5	0
Dominican	10	8	1	1	0
Augustinian	9	8	0	0	1
Carmelite	4	1	2	1	0
Totals	90	40	28	18	4

Perhaps the most striking feature of the movement which this table shows is that the new houses were founded predominantly in the Gaelic areas, in Connacht and Ulster in particular. These were parts of the country where houses of friars had not previously been numerous. We may perhaps attribute this spread to two factors. One was that search for solitude which is a perennial ingredient of the monastic vocation. It was well expressed by the Dominicans who established themselves at Portumna in 1427: 'certain brethren had chosen this spot as a place remote from the noise and turmoil of the world, in order that they might serve the Most High in a life of regular observance'. The other is attributable to the freshly-awakened enthusiasm of numerous Irish princes who were the patrons of the movement: a religious manifestation of the increasing self-confidence of Gaelic culture which showed itself in many ways in later medieval Ireland. To its founder, a monastery was, so to say, a major spiritual investment: the bequest itself might be an expiation of sin; the community guaranteed continuous prayer both for his intentions in life and for his soul in death and would afford him a place of refuge in his declining years where he might even himself take the habit or where at least, in the conventional words of the Annals obituaries, he might achieve his 'victory of unction and penance' (i.e. receive the Last Sacraments). In a certain way, too, a monastery was a status symbol, the family tombs testifying to the importance of his dynasty. Not infrequently it provided also a public service in the form of competent pastoral care, for this was a time when the parochial clergy might well be of indifferent quality. It was not necessary to be very wealthy to establish a house of friars. They were in search of a life of poverty, often considering that the generosity of patrons in the past had corrupted them. As Philip Bocht O Huiginn (d.1487) the bardic poet who became a Franciscan, put it: 'Chastity and obedience were the inheritance [Francis's] folk got; but the harm it incurred from being helped by alms resulted in its poverty not flourishing'.

It was not only the sheer number of new foundations which gave this movement its importance. The Franciscans, Dominicans and Augustinians were also undergoing a major reform process with the development of the Observant movement.

The term 'Observant' is very simply explained. It referred to *observantia*, observance of the Rule. The Observants wanted a stricter observance, for in their view contemporary practices had departed too far from the way of life which the Rule laid down as proper for friars. The movement grew up spontaneously and independently in the different orders and the different countries. All forms of it were characterised by leadership of unusual spiritual power and when channelled into the appropriate common forms of organisation constituted one of the most influential religious movements of the middle ages. It was to be the great strength of the Irish Observant congregations that they were able to maintain real contact with the movement as a whole.

Observants generally wished both to be autonomous in government but to remain within the body of their own Order. These aims were not always easily reconcilable and there were constitutional problems. In the case of the Franciscans these proved insoluble and in 1517 they were divided into two quite separate Orders of Minors, Conventual and Observant.

Besides running into constitutional difficulties, the Irish friars had a problem peculiarly their own: that of integrating friars from two cultures in the one Order. In origin all the provinces of the friars were English and the houses were predominantly in Anglo-Irish towns. But each in its early history had attracted a substantial Irish element which had grown in importance as the English colony declined. With the most recent wave of new foundations the Irish element became the more numerous and the more important. In this new situation, would it prove possible to achieve a spirit of religious peace and to devise a constitutional framework to maintain it? Could Conventuals and Observants avoid conflict? Would national animosities continue on the old dreary pattern to compound antagonisms generated in ecclesiastical rivalries?

These are important questions with which to test the spiritual depth of the new movement. It is, however, far easier to ask them than to answer them, because of the fragmentary nature of our sources. The attempt to do so will bring out the salient features of Irish Observant history.

Of the nine new Augustinian foundations of the fifteenth century, seven were native Irish: three in the diocese of Killala and four in Tuam diocese. Two of these were founded for Observants: Banada (1423) and Murrisk (1456). The remaining two were both Anglo-Irish: Callan (1468–9) and Galway (1500). A constitutional position of some complexity developed in the second half of the century. In 1457 a special superior for the Connacht (Irish) houses was appointed. He enjoyed the same authority as a vicar provincial, but the vicar provincial and his definitors (Anglo-Irish?) selected him. The Observants formed a separate congregation within the province which remained technically the Irish 'limit' of the English province. The English provincial was forbidden to intervene in the affairs of this congregation though he continued to have a say in the appointment of the vicar provincial of the Conventuals. The Observants had their own annual chapter and the right to elect their own superior.

The Observants made progress, though it was to be rather in the Anglo-Irish towns than in Connacht. Adare, Callan and Cork (but only temporarily) became Observant in 1472. Callan became the head house of the congregation. The two remaining Observant conversions from the

Conventuals were Dublin and Drogheda in 1517. The Observants were independent of the English provincial and name evidence makes it abundantly clear that in the Observant houses of Callan and Dublin and in some of the Conventual houses too, the communities were of mixed nationality. There is no report of mutual hostility. To all seeming, the Order had solved its constitutional and racial problems and enjoyed a high degree of public esteem, particularly for learning.

As with the Augustinians, tensions within the Dominican body betrayed themselves in a certain constitutional complexity. But here too there was a successful resolution of those tensions. In 1509 there were three men calling themselves vicar provincial in Dominican Ireland: one had been appointed by the Master-General over the whole province, another to the same post by the English provincial and a third had charge of the Observant congregation. There was a history of successive attempts to sever the connexion between the English and Irish provinces but it was not successful until 1536. It is, however, symptomatic of the persistence of the English link that the first provincial of the autonomous province was an Englishman, David Brown.

This appointment does not imply, however, that the province was restricted to the Anglo-Irish. Of the ten new houses established in the fifteenth century, nine had native Irish founders. It is known that the communities in the convents situated in the Anglo-Irish towns were generally mixed.

There is mention of a Dominican Observant reform as early as 1390 in connexion with the Drogheda house. But this does not seem to have taken root. Longford (1400) and Portumna (before 1414) were founded as Observant houses. But the Dominican Observant movement was the least prolific of the three. By the beginning of the sixteenth century there were apparently only three houses in the congregation: Drogheda, Youghal and Kilkenny. These were mixed communities and their first vicar came from the congregation of Holland. The Dominicans in general kept up their contacts abroad – with the universities of Oxford and Paris and with the central authority of the Order, as the registers of the Masters General show.

One outstanding Dominican leader of the period was Maurice O Mochain Moral (d.1502). Though his career can be known to us only in the barest outline, he exemplifies that transcendence of the barriers between Gaelic and English traditions which was the characteristic strength of the Observant movement as a whole. His family were erenaghs of Killaraght. He received his training in England, being ordained deacon in Salisbury Cathedral in 1461 and priest the following year while he was a member of the Worcester Dominican community. He obtained an Oxford theology degree in 1474. From 1488 he was frequently provincial of the Irish Dominicans, working assiduously for reform. In 1496 he was vicar of the Observant congregation. The symbol of his harmonious relationship with the Anglo-Irish was the bequest of Thomas de Bermingham and his wife for the upkeep of a chapel in the Dominican church at Athenry, 'in honour of the blessed virgins. Catherine the Virgin and Catherine of Sienna and for the soul of master Maurice Morall, doctor of sacred theology and vicar of Ireland, founder of the chapel'.

It was, however, the Franciscans who, of the reformers, made the biggest impact. The number of new foundations was considerable. The Observant reform made such progress that, after 1517, when the Order finally divided into two, most of the Irish houses became Observant. Nor, this time, was the Order bedevilled with racial strife. This newly reconstituted Franciscan body in Ireland was to be especially singled out by Henry VIII's government for repression because of its determined opposition to the Henrician ecclesiastical changes. Nevertheless it survived to form what was perhaps the major spearhead of the forces of the Irish Counter-reformation.

The rapid spread through Connacht and Ulster of the 'Third Order Regular' or 'Third Order of Penance' was certainly a major event in the history of religion in Ireland. There was no comparable development in Britain and not much similar on the Continent. It was almost a uniquely Irish movement. Unfortunately, as with so much that happened in Gaelic Ireland, it is virtually undocumented and hence beyond the historian's grasp.

The Third Order Regular must be distinguished from the Third Order Secular. This latter which goes back to the early days of the Order used a version of the Rule which could be followed by the laity who continued to live in the world. In the later fourteenth century there was a tendency for small groups of Tertiaries to come together to live a community life. The growth of this movement, particularly in Italy, led to regulation by the papacy. By the end of the fifteenth century, Tertiaries living a 'regular' life had achieved the status of a religious congregation with its own proper organisation.

Whether the Irish brand of this Tertiary claustration was at all influenced by Continental example cannot be decided. It seems very likely that it was a purely spontaneous local development. There is evidence of its possible existence in 1385. But it is more probable that it was the 1420s which saw its beginnings. Originally there were women members as well but this association does not seem to have continued. There is a strong indication that some parochial clergy of western dioceses were attracted to the new congregation. Killeenbrenan (co. Mayo) founded 1426–8 was its centre. One of the most reliable of the Franciscan historians of the early seventeenth century, Fr Donagh Mooney thought that its function had been (it had disappeared by his day) to assist the diocesan clergy and to educate boys.

More important even than the Tertiaries Regular and

certainly better documented were the Franciscan Observants. The Irish Franciscan archivists of the seventeenth century took it that the Observant movement of their order and country began in 1460. Fr Mooney said explicitly that 1460 'is held to be the first year of our reformation'. Nevertheless it was acknowledged that it had begun earlier albeit 'timidly'. The first firm date is 1433 when Eugenius IV conceded a petition of Mac Con Mac Namara that an Observant friary be established at Quin. In 1449 Nicholas V licensed the establishment of two more such, one of which was established by the O Driscolls on Inissherkin. In 1458, however, Nehemias O Donaghue was sent by the Observants to the General Chapter at Rome on a mission which led in 1460 to approval by Pius II of the autonomy of the Irish Observants and the appointment of Nehemias as their first Vicar Provincial. The *Ordo et Series* of vicars and ministers begins in 1460: the names are predominantly native Irish.

By this date the Observants had divided for geographical reasons into two 'families', Cisalpine and Ultramontane, each with its own Vicar General and General Chapter. The new Irish province had the assistance in establishing itself of visitors appointed by the supreme authority. Franciscan necrology recorded the death in Cologne in 1484 of a Frenchman, Michael de Lira, 'three times vicar provincial of Cologne and first vicar and *plantator* (literally: one who plants) of the Observance in the three provinces of Scotland, Ireland and Denmark'. The link with the General Chapter remained close: canonical visitation took place at regular intervals and representatives travelled from Ireland to the triennial Chapters held at different places on the Continent. This link replaced that with the English province. The Observance was a latecomer to England and was never a particularly strong movement. In Ireland the Observants gradually won over the majority of Franciscan houses. The Anglo-Irish houses (which were in any case of mixed communities) became Observant in a sudden spurt on the eve of the Reformation: Kildare (1520), Dublin, Drogheda and Waterford (1521), Trim (1525), Limerick (1534: at the petition of the mayor and citizens), Clonmel (1536), Cashel (1539).

From a Franciscan Observant source, there comes to us a document unique in Irish medieval ecclesiastical history: the catalogue of a monastic library.[6] It comes from Youghal and its two main parts are dated 1491 and 1523. The manuscript reveals that Youghal in 1491 was the residence of the vicar provincial and that it had a mixed community under an Irish guardian.

The Youghal library was a small one: some 130 volumes altogether. The catalogue falls into three main divisions: the contents of the library in 1491, the bulk of the library; a small collection of liturgical, devotional and sermon books reserved for Maurice O Hanlon without indication as to why he had this personal privilege and a list of additions to the library compiled in 1523, not very tidily set out. The first of these divisions itself has three sub-divisions. The first, of some fifty-nine volumes, is a miscellany of liturgical books, (missals, breviaries, psalters and so on) the Bible and exegetical works, some theology and a little philosophy, some of the standard reference books, some books of devotion. The second subdivision was made up of books of sermons, while the third comprised books of canon law. The subdivisions overlapped: canonist works for example, are listed in the first two sections despite the existence of a separate law section.

The overriding impression given by the catalogue is of a library fashioned for the needs of men following an active pastoral life. It is certainly not a library for advanced learning. But it is strong on preaching literature and penitential theology and there is clear evidence that the community was in touch with recent Italian work in these fields. The possession of the sermons of the near-contemporary preachers Leonardo of Udino O.P. and Roberto Caracciolo O.M. as well as the *Summa de casibus consciencie* of the Franciscan Angelus Carletus de Clavasio, is evidence of this. Recent work of another kind is also to be found in the 1491 section: the commentary of St Bonaventure on Peter Lombard's *Sentences*, with the text, is described as being 'impressa in papiro'. This must be the earliest reference to a printed book in Ireland. There is, too, mention under the same date of a collection of devotional treatises, not readily identifiable, as being 'de impressione in papiro'. In the 1523 section a printed Bible is listed.

The Laity

Ecclesiastical historians commonly have much to say about bishops and their clergy and about the religious orders. The laity, numerically of course by far the largest *ordo* in the people of God, is often passed over in a merely incidental way. The result is more a history of churchmen than of the Church. Sometimes this omission occurs despite the best endeavours of historians on whom the nature of the sources themselves imposes silence. For the layman generally cuts no more individual a figure in medieval ecclesiastical records than does the private soldier in military history.

In one important area the sources are not silent about the role of the laity. Medieval churchmen had a deep-rooted distrust of lay intervention in ecclesiastical affairs. Boniface VIII gave classical expression to this feeling in the dictum which he brought out of obscurity to open his celebrated *Clericis laicos*: 'Antiquity teaches that the laity was ever very hostile to the clergy and present experience proves the lesson'. But at the same time as laymen were distrusted, they were very much needed to lend assistance as the secular arm (*brachium seculare*): 'Whom sacerdotal admonition is not able to correct, should be corrected by the secular power'. What churchmen expected, then, of laymen was twofold – negatively, they were expected to keep out of ecclesiastical business; positively, they should co-operate with the clergy. Either way, they were expected to obey without question. Of course performance rarely matched expectations. But churchmen continued to command lay rulers to desist and to implement, not always unsuccessfully. In practical affairs, however, it was the lay power which tended to call the tune.

An example of this has been seen in an earlier chapter when examining the relationship of Archbishop Mac Maol Iosa of Armagh and the Dublin administration. Examples characteristic of the period a century and a half later show the boot on the other foot: English and Anglo-Irish arch-bishops of Armagh coping with Irish princes. It is the so-called 'Armagh registers' – a seven-volume manuscript collection of miscellaneous Armagh documents, still under-exploited by historians because of the lack of modern editions – which offer a glimpse of this relationship.

It is well known that the characteristic feature of the Armagh diocese in the later middle ages was its division into two parts: one *inter Hibernicos*, the northern area with Armagh itself as its centre, the other *inter Anglicos*, approximating to the area of the modern county Louth, with Drogheda, Ardee and Dundalk as its strongholds. This cultural division of the diocese existed on the provincial level, too. Meath and Down and Connor (united in 1453) formed the province *inter Anglicos* and the remaining seven sees, *inter Hibernicos*. The division made for an unusual arrangement in diocesan and provincial jurisdiction. The part *inter Anglicos* the archbishops ruled directly in the ordinary way. Their jurisdiction was not ignored *inter Hibernicos*. They ordained Irish priests, held provincial councils attended by Irish bishops, heard cases from the Irish areas in their courts. But in other matters, particularly visitation, collection of revenue, exercise of jurisdiction during vacancies in the suffragan sees, they exercised their jurisdiction, so to say, at one remove, indirectly through intermediaries rather than by personal action.

This state of affairs left the archbishops particularly dependent on the goodwill of the Irish rulers, particularly of the O Neills. For it was only with their co-operation that the archbishop's commissaries in visitation, exploitation of church lands and enforcement of ecclesiastical sanctions could be effective. Conflict of interest between the O Neills and the archbishops was endemic but not different in kind from the common European experience of this sort of tension. Concord was generally reached ultimately, enforceable under pledges and fines of cows. But ecclesiastical reprisals were frequent. In November 1454, for example, Archbishop John Mey excommunicated Owen O Neill, his wife, sons and kinsmen for usurpation of the lands of the Church, injuries done to ecclesiastical officials and tenants and hindrance of the archbishop's exercise of his jurisdictional and visitational powers. The diocese of Armagh *inter Hibernicos* was put under interdict and, in the true spirit of medieval hierocracy, the subjects of O Neill and his eldest son Henry were released from their allegiance. No doubt material interest often overcame fear of ecclesiastical sanctions:

> Bell, book and candle shall not drive me back
> When gold and silver becks me to come on.[7]

But not always. In 1529, Charles O Reilly was absolved by Archbishop George Cromer from the excommunication he had incurred for offences against church property and tenants in Julianstown. After agreeing on oath to make restitution and to refrain from similar offences in the future, he submitted to the following penance: payment of two cows towards the upkeep of Armagh cathedral; making of a pilgrimage either to St Patrick's Purgatory or to the statue of Our Lady of Trim; a money payment to the poor; recitation of the Office of the Blessed Virgin fifteen times within a stated period.

The safety of the soul was, however, not the only inducement to falling in with the archbishop's wishes. There could be an economic advantage, particularly when acting as the secular arm in legal process against errant clergy. In 1455, in fact not very many months after his excommunication, Henry O Neill was commissioned by Archbishop Mey to take action against priests' concubines. Their property was to be seized and the value of half of it was to be devoted to the repair of Armagh cathedral and the other half O Neill might keep for himself. In the Anglo-Irish areas of the country the same inducement might take a somewhat different form. Thus a statute in force in Waterford after 1430:

> . . . by commene assente, it was ordayned that no preste sholde have no wif or concubyne within the citie, and if they may be founde, the fynders shal have al ther clothes and thar bodies to the jayle of the saide citie unto tyme thei shal mak a fyn.[8]

Other examples of Archbishop Mey calling on the Ulster rulers for help are of interest in revealing the continuation of Irish customs and institutions of long standing. In November 1455 he recalled to all the clergy and laity of the province that the archbishop of Armagh, as successors of St Patrick, had a right to an annual cattle impost, the *primogenita pecudum* or right to the first-born of beasts. It had been challenged by two traditional Armagh dignitaries, the hereditary keepers of St Patrick's Book and of St Patrick's Bell who thought the right was attached to their own Patrician heritage. Henry O Neill and others were to see to it that the archbishop was not cheated of his tribute. Another of Mey's instructions takes us into the still living world of old Irish law. John Mcgeerun, an Armagh *culdee* had killed Niall Mcgillacrai a layman who had been defending the lands and crops of the church of Armagh. In accordance with ancient custom, an *eiríc* or honour price was now due and those who inhabited two deaneries were responsible for paying it. The Armagh cathedral chapter and especially the official of the city were responsible for seeing that it was paid. The archbishop offered an indulgence to those who did pay.

There were times when the O Neills and other princes needed the archbishops. One request, to Archbishop Cromer from Nelan O Neill in 1530, has a distinctively Irish sound. Nelan complained that certain ecclesiastics were 'fasting' and 'ringing bells' against him. The Archbishop was to call off this spiritual blackmail. The theory, which has a long history in Irish hagiography, was that if the person fasted against ate whilst the ecclesiastics did not, he was at the mercy of the revenge of the saint who had been offended in the persons of the accusers and judges who were now fasting in his name. The tolling bells were likewise liable to bring about an act of saintly vengeance.

Much the most important service in demand, however, at least on the evidence of the Registers, concerned matrimonial jurisdiction. It is the measure of the change ecclesiastical reform had wrought in Irish society since the twelfth century that so many instances are recorded of native Irishmen seeking to regularise their sexual relationships according to the universal norms of the Church set out in canon law. The commonest type of case was a request for dispensation in cases of consanguinity and affinity. Sometimes, as with Murtagh Roe O Neill in the years 1449–51, it was a question of the archbishop ordering the ruler to cease living in adultery and to take back his lawful wife who had brought the matter to the archbishop's notice.

Not the least interesting feature of the Armagh Registers, which are essentially collections of the working papers of lawyers, is that they are a unique source for the record of the practical working of an ecclesiastical court in Ireland. The Register attributed to Archbishop George

Cromer (1521–43), for example, begins with an act book of the archbishop's court covering the period 1518–22. The court sat usually at either St Peter's, Drogheda or Termonfeckin church. At this time the archbishop, John Kite (1513–21) was rarely resident in his diocese and the vicar-general presided – up to 1520 it was Alexander Plunket (a distant ancestor of Blessed Oliver), thereafter it was Hugh Inge, then bishop of Meath, until his translation to Dublin.

Almost without exception the cases heard by the judges came from that part of the diocese which now forms county Louth, the area *inter Anglicos*. But it would be a serious misrepresentation of the distribution of the two peoples in this region to think that only Anglo-Irish appeared before the court. The records make it seem most likely that the bulk of the country people of Louth were Irish and that there were significant numbers of Irish living in the towns like Drogheda as cobblers, glovers and other skilled tradesmen. Further, it is clear that there had been and was, very much intermarriage between the peoples. In that part of Armagh described as lying *inter Anglicos* there prevailed a considerable degree of cultural assimilation.

Testamentary and matrimonial cases occupied much of the court's time. The latter included cases concerning decrees of nullity, validity of marriage, separation *a mensa et thoro* (from board and bed), bigamy. That Irish as well as Anglo-Irish were involved in these cases should warn us that generalisations about marriage in Gaelic Ireland remaining a purely secular concern should be treated with caution. Nevertheless, a striking feature of this court record is the large number of cases of 'lay marriage' i.e. marriages not contracted *in facie ecclesiae* (i.e. not in the presence of a priest), which came before the ecclesiastical judge for authentification as valid marriages. This evidence suggests that in Ireland, as in certain other parts of Europe, local matrimonial usages yielded but slowly to the claims of canon law.

Cases concerning diocesan and parochial revenues and possessions were common. Chastisement for assaults on the clergy were duly meted out. Sexual sins were punished, but they do not appear very often in the records. But cases of breach of faith, perjury and especially slander (meaning here malicious gossip or abusive language) were common.

Punishments inflicted for these ecclesiastical offences were private and public penance, and money fines. One found guilty of perjury was ordered to walk round the cemetery of Termonfeckin church clothed in white linens on six different Sundays, to fast on bread and water for three days, to pay 12d. for the expenses of the court and give 3d. to the poor. A parish priest found guilty of solemnising a marriage when his church was under interdict was ordered to provide candles in honour of the patron of his church and to fast. The unlucky couple had also to provide candles and also to observe a separation *a thoro* for a stated period. Two men who had quarrelled in church were each ordered to provide candles in honour of the patron saint of the church and to walk round the graveyard dressed in penitential linen on two different feast days. The more culpable of the two was ordered to give 3d. to the poor, pay 3d. expenses to his parish priest and 12d. to the court.

So far the analysis has been confined to the laity in relationship with their bishop. But of its nature this was an exceptional thing. The ordinary priest–people relationship, the one making most impact on the ordinary routine of life, took place within the parish. What can be gleaned from the sources about religious life at parish level?

We might begin by drawing attention to the historical importance of the creation of a parochial structure. The parish arrived at a relatively late date in the history of Irish

Christianity. It could not precede the formation of a territorial diocesan structure which, as has been seen, was a major part of the twelfth-century reform. Its corollary, the territorial parochial structure then followed. But before it had properly begun the Invasion had taken place and development went differently in the Irish and colonial regions.

Parishes are made for people and thus, reflecting settlement patterns, their size and organisation were determined by both social and physical factors. In the Irish areas, they were probably usually coterminous with the lands of ancient family groups and were to preserve a familial nature which is their distinctive stamp. In the more heavily settled Anglo-Irish areas, the pattern was generally one of small compact parishes, often matching the parcelling-out of land according to feudal tenures. Either way, laymen played an important part in the establishment and maintenance of parishes. In Gaelic Ireland the integration of ancient monastic termons in the parishes allowed the hereditary coarbs and erenaghs of those lands to continue to play a decisive part in the choice of priests and the economic structure of dioceses as well as the parishes themselves. In colonial Ireland the new landowners who had established parishes on their manors retained 'proprietary' right, expressed in retaining the right of advowson or right of choosing the incumbent, subject to the bishop's approval of his choice. Throughout Ireland, the parish was deeply embedded in the social structure with laity playing a very important role.

The spiritual bond of priest and people was beautifully defined by an anonymous versifying preacher in the language of south-east colonial Ireland:

Me to spek and you to lere
That hit be worship, lord, to thee
Me to teche and you to here
That helplich to ure sowles be.

Direct evidence of what the people learned and heard in their parish churches is very scanty. The virtual disappearance of sermon literature, common elsewhere, is a great loss in this respect. A small group of sermons, written for delivery in verse, has survived from Anglo-Ireland. Their context, in doctrine, moral teaching, spiritual exhortation, is the perennial matter of popular sermons. The preacher on the transitoriness of life illustrates that combination of familiar teaching and contemporary idiom characteristic of these sermons:

Man is lif nis bot a schade
Nov he is and nov he nis.[9]

The essential continuity of medieval and modern Catholicism is brought out forcefully in a detailed scheme of instruction designed for use in parish churches. In Armagh diocese in the late middle ages, every priest with care of souls was obliged to possess and use a document known after its opening words as *Ignorantia sacerdotum*. The opening sentence in fact read 'The ignorance of priests casts the people into the pit of error' and the purpose of the document was to equip priests with an outline of the faith and morals expected of every Christian, with the injunction that it should be expounded simply and comprehensively in the vernacular to the faithful under their charge once a quarter.

Ignorantia sacerdotum was already by this date of respectable antiquity. In origin it was a constitution promulgated by the Franciscan archbishop of Canterbury John Pecham (1279–92) at a provincial council held at Lambeth in 1281.[10] It had become a standard work in England and it was probably used more extensively in Ireland than the single reference to its adoption in Armagh might suggest. It is readily recognisable as a far-distant ancestor of the modern Catechism of Christian Doctrine.

It began with a brief exposition of the 'Apostle's Creed',

explaining the chief mysteries of the Faith, concerning the Unity and Trinity of God and the birth, death and resurrection of Christ. It stressed that the Church with the Sacraments and laws conveyed to it by the Holy Spirit had means enough to win salvation for every man no matter how great a sinner he might have been. Next there followed a short consideration of the commandments. A third section treated of the two Gospel precepts of Charity: he is said to love God who follows his commandments for love rather than for fear of punishment, while love of one's neighbour demanded that one should care more for the salvation of his soul than for one's own temporal life or affluence. The seven corporal works of mercy, the seven capital sins and the seven virtues (three theological, four cardinal) then follow: the terminology and thought behind it has passed into the ordinary vocabulary of instruction. The schedule concluded with a section on the seven sacraments.

Still familiar to a modern is the part played by relics, miracles and pilgrimages in popular devotion, though many medieval beliefs and emphases in this context would be found unacceptable. Medieval men were too quick to read the miraculous in everyday life (many examples are to be found in the Annals), were too credulous about relics (as the provincial constitutions prove), and indeed about such places of pilgrimages as St Patrick's Purgatory, which enjoyed an international reputation as a place where a man might literally catch a glimpse of Heaven and Hell. If the relics and shrines venerated in medieval Ireland have virtually disappeared, some centres of pilgrimage such as Croagh Patrick and Lough Derg have kept their places in Irish religious devotion.

Sermons, statues, pilgrimages – the oral, visual and the physical – inevitably played a larger part in devotion than books. There were, however, literate laymen and there was a vernacular literature to cater for their needs. Fr

Canice Mooney has researched deeply into the religious literature in Irish. It is, though, not always easy to relate it to the actualities of popular religion. One treatise is especially worthy of mention as being the most widely circulated devotional work discovered. The *Meditationes vitae Christi*, written by a Tuscan Franciscan in the early fourteenth century and incorporating work of St Bonaventure, to whom authorship was attributed, was an extremely popular book throughout Europe. Its translation into Irish (*Smaointe beatha Chríost*), is a demonstration of Ireland's link with the mainstream of medieval spiritual teaching and its first principle, as expressed by the author, that 'of all spiritual exercises the most profitable and most capable of lifting the soul to its highest degree of perfection is frequent and habitual meditation on the life of Christ'.

Perhaps the best insight we are allowed into the Irish religious mind, however, comes from those lay court poets who are unique to Irish medieval culture. The bards were the professional eulogisers of the mighty and any family with any claim to significance had its *duanaire* (anthology) which preserved the verse in which the family's greatness was extolled. The bards, still working within the literary conventions of their craft, often turned to religious themes. There has been preserved a unique genre of religious writing which, throughout the period from the thirteenth to the seventeenth centuries, retained the common general characteristics.

Fr L. McKenna, who has done the most to make this verse available in editions and translations (which are used here), was a severe critic of its merit. He found it artificial in tone, deficient in spiritual content, riddled with untheological conceits and often distasteful in its unsuitable paradoxes and figures of speech. Nevertheless it is impossible not to feel that in this type of writing we are as near as we are likely to get to how the educated laymen of the time actually did think about their religion. All the other sources are instructional, concerned with telling men how they should think about their religion. Because of the position and employment of its authors, this verse must be a fair reflection of the religious sentiment of the ruling classes of Gaelic Ireland and, written expressly for public recitation, must have been very influential in shaping that sentiment.

Different readers will no doubt select different themes as being especially characteristic of this verse. No one will miss the brooding sense of the proximity of death, the sense of conflict between man's spirit and flesh ('let me and my body consort not'), an awareness of the perils of judgement and especially, of Christ's love shown in his Passion, with a strong sense of his physical suffering. But what, above all, distinguishes this verse is surely its great bursts of encomium – these were praise-poets by profession – which read like litanies. Philip Bocht O Huiginn was particularly effective. This is to the Blessed Virgin, a very popular bardic subject:

> O master-stroke of women; O chart of the sea-path home; O fair-tressed sinless lady, O branch over wood, O bright sun.
>
> O spring unfailing, peace-bond of the six hosts, before whom war recoils; O subduer of God's wrath.
>
> O help of the living world, let me not cause thy poverty to have been in vain, O ivy bearing fresh wine, O guardian of God's child.
>
> O banquet of apostles and virgins, O love never too dearly purchased; O unsullied heart; O sister; O clear guide to heaven.
>
> O Mary, queen of all men, and of women too; to thy help must we flee; thou art refuge of all, even of thy foes.

And again, to Our Lord:

> O strength subject to obedience; O author of wisdom;

O severity easy to overcome; O indulgence unchangeable.

O secret no man can tell; O fortress of divinity; O mystery unknown to prophet; O pardon not hard to get.

O spring-tide in strength, rock in firmness, strong help of men, Mary's darling.

O wood sending forth fruit; O ship with rich argosy; O door of the house of health; O bright secret of peaceful joy.

O door unlocked; O torch of six flames; O dear child of Bethlehem, repress thy wrath and save me.

O arm unsurpassed in strength, bind this foolish heart that I may willingly take up my cross after thee.[11]

Who will deny that this comes from the very heart of medieval Gaelic Ireland?

Conclusion

THIS book has been concerned with the fortunes of the Irish Church in the period marked broadly by two great turning-points in Irish history: the Anglo-Norman Invasion in the twelfth century and the Reformation in the sixteenth century. It is now opportune to attempt the difficult task of adding some general reflexions about that epoch of ecclesiastical history.

What, before all else, gave this period its particular character, was the basic duality in Irish society between the two nations or cultures (*nationes* or *linguae* to use medieval language) which was the consequence of the Invasion and of the establishment of an English colony in Ireland. It had been hoped by responsible churchmen both at the papal curia and in Ireland that Henry II's assumption of the Irish lordship would accelerate the progress of a tide of reform already flowing strongly before 1171. Two centuries later, when the parliament of the colony is found to be promulgating legislation designed rigorously to control the circumstances in which Irish priests and religious were to minister in the colonial areas, and even to exclude them altogether, it is clear that these hopes had not been fulfilled. This discriminatory legislation was the culmination of a long period of mutual distrust and tension between the two nations which formed the Church and it was clearly on the increase as the colony went into decline in the fourteenth century. There can be little doubt that documents like the Register of Stephen of Lexington (1228), the chronicle accounts of the Franciscan riot at Cork (1291), the Statute of Kilkenny (1366), to name but three among many records testifying to national antagonisms, must convince the historian that foreign intervention had been severely disruptive of the Church's spiritual mission.

This said, however, we must not reduce the history of the medieval Irish Church to some simplified story of near-chaos brought about by uninterrupted conflict between Irish and English. The reality of the relationship between the nations in both the diocesan Church and in the religious orders is much more complex. There were plenty of occasions in many parts of Ireland and at different times throughout the middle ages, when churchmen of both nations combined harmoniously. It would be quite wrong to envisage some medieval ecclesiastical equivalent of an iron curtain rigidly dividing two quite separate parts of the Church. Despite endemic warfare and national antagonisms, there was much of constructive achievement in these centuries: the completion of a stable and enduring diocesan and parochial system and the numerical strength and perseverance of the friars through three turbulent centuries certainly reflect favourably on the spiritual vitality of the Irish Church and its ability to transcend great social difficulties.

It was the medieval Church which refused Protestantism and remained Catholic at the Reformation. In the long perspective of Irish history, that decision must surely rank as the most important single contribution of the middle ages to the shaping of modern Ireland. Neither the Irish nor the Old English (as at the end of the middle ages we may call them) were disillusioned in any radical way with the papacy, as were so many sectors of the Church elsewhere. Later medieval Ireland did not develop any attitude or atmosphere of anti-papalism or anti-clericalism to form the seed-bed of revolt against Rome. It had developed an organisational and intellectual separatism from England in ecclesiastical matters which kept not merely Gaelic Ireland Catholic, but also the English-speaking towns. From them came the first resistance to the Reformation. In the Franciscan Observants especially, but also in other areas of the Irish Church, it had produced a spearhead of Counter-Reformation.

Glossary

advowson (*advocatio*) : the right of presentation of a priest to a church or benefice. The person who held the right to present was called the patron.

benefit of clergy : exemption from trial in the civil court in certain cases, principally in cases of felony, granted to all in orders, minor as well as major, of clergy and nuns.

chapter : the corporate body responsible for the spiritual and temporal care of a cathedral, acting also as an advisory body to the bishop, and administering the diocese in vacancy. Its chief official was the dean; next in rank was the precentor, who directed the cathedral services.

coarb (*comharba*: 'heir' or 'successor') : the successor of the founder of a church or monastery. By the late middle ages the successor might be a cleric or layman of differing grade and rank. But his essential duty was stewardship of church lands and fulfilment of the duties they imposed, which varied in different parts of the country. See *erenagh*.

court-christian (*curia Christianitatis*) : ecclesiastical as distinct from civil court.

Culdees (*Céli dé*: 'companions or clients of God') : Literally a man who took God for his lord, entering into a contract with him. (Cf. K. Hughes, *The Church in early Irish Society* 173 n.3).

decretals : papal letters issued in response to a question and having the force of law. In the middle ages selections of them were made to build up the *Corpus Iuris Canonici*: see *canon*.

erenagh (airchinneach: 'superior') *:* in early Irish Church usage, an abbot or administrator of monastic properties. As with the coarb, the word and the institution kept its vitality because of the continuing connexion with the administration of Church property. But if similar in function, the erenagh was of lower status than the coarb, as the usage of the term 'chief erenagh' to describe a coarb testifies.

interdict: an ecclesiastical punishment forbidding the administration of the sacraments in a defined region.

legate, papal: a personal representative of the pope, exercising his authority. Three types of representative may be distinguished in medieval Ireland:

1) the office as held for a number of years by the bishop of an Irish see. 2) the office exercised by cardinals sent on major missions for a limited period 3) the *nuntius*, generally a fiscal officer, responsible for the collection of papal taxes.

liberty of the Church (libertas ecclesiae): generally signified specific immunities of ecclesiastical persons and possessions from lay jurisdiction.

metropolitan: the title of a bishop exercising provincial as well as diocesan jurisdiction. Their chief powers were the holding of provincial synods, visitation of dioceses, care of vacant sees in spiritualities, confirmation of bishops-elect, hearing of appeals from lower courts.

pallium: an ecclesiastical vestment symbolising fulness of pontifical office, granted by the pope to archbishops. They were not entitled to exercise jurisdiction until it had been conferred.

prebend, prebendary: a cathedral benefice and its holder. The prebend furnished (*praebere*) a living to its holder.

primate (primas): the title of the occupant of the first see. Originally the term was applied in Ireland exclusively to Armagh but it was later adopted also by Dublin. A compromise between the conflicting claims was reached on the pattern of the Canterbury-York solution, with the adoption of the styles 'Primate of all Ireland' for Armagh and 'Primate of Ireland' for Dublin.

prohibition, writ of : an instruction from the king prohibiting further action in a case being heard in the court-christian on the grounds that it should be heard in the king's court.

provision (provisio) : nomination to an ecclesiastical benefice by the pope or other appropriate authority.

postulation : canon law did not allow one who was already a bishop to be elected by the chapter to another see. But it might petition the pope for translation to be made from one see to another. If this were granted, the appointment was deemed to have been made by postulation. Appointment by papal provision did not have this capitular participation.

rector : one who had charge of a parish Church and was entitled to the whole tithes of the parish. See *tithes: vicar.*

temporalities of bishops (English law) : the revenues, lands etc. which a bishop in his baronial capacity received from the king and which reverted to the king during vacancy of sees. When a new bishop had been elected and confirmed, the king issued a writ for the restoration of temporalities, for which the bishop swore an oath of fealty or fidelity.

termon lands (Lat. *terminus:* Ir. *termann*) : territory of a church or monastery, enjoying certain immunities.

tithes (decimae : 'tenths') : essentially, the dues paid to maintain the clergy. In the middle ages they were assessed in kind – the tenth part of the fruits of the earth and of a man's labour was owed to the clergy. See: *rector, vicar.*

vicar (vicarius : 'substitute') : when the tithes of a parish were appropriated or annexed to a religious house or other institution or person, as became common, the appropriator would find a substitute for the rector, paying him a portion of the tithes. See *tithes: rector.*

Bibliography

Abbreviations

Gwynn Studies: *Medieval studies presented to A. Gwynn,
S.J.* ed. J. A. Watt, J. B. Morrall and F. X. Martin (Dublin
1961)
IER: *Irish Ecclesiastical Record*
PRIA: *Proceedings of the Royal Irish Academy*
PICHC: *Proceedings of the Irish Catholic Historical Committee*
JRSAI:*Journal of the Royal Society of Antiquaries of Ireland*
HIC: *A History of Irish Catholicism*

Fuller bibliographical guidance than this necessarily
brief note may be sought in J. A. Watt, *The Church and
the Two Nations in Medieval Ireland* (Cambridge 1970)
231–40 and especially P. W. A. Asplin, *Medieval Ireland
c.1170–1495. A bibliography of secondary works*, RIA (Dublin
1971) ch. 8.

Further study of the twelfth-century reform should
begin with St Bernard of Clairvaux. *Life of St Malachy of
Armagh*, translated with Introd. by H. J. Lawlor (London
1920) and ch. 8 of J. F. Kenney, *The sources for the early
history of Ireland: an introduction and guide vol. 1. Ecclesiastical*
(New York 1929). It must then continue with the work of
Fr A. Gwynn whose numerous articles are listed in *Gwynn
Studies* 502–7 and have been extensively revised for a forthcoming book, *The Irish Church in the Eleventh and Twelfth
Centuries* (Oxford Univ. Press). He has written a short
synthesis of his work, 'The twelfth-century Reform' in

HIC ed. P. J. Corish 2.i (Dublin 1968). Other general accounts will be found in Kathleen Hughes, *The Church in Early Irish Society* (London 1966) part V and in my *Church and the Two Nations* ch. 1. Some students of hagiography and liturgy promise a contribution to our knowledge of the reform but publication is still awaited. The archaeologists and art historians, however, have added a major new dimension to the subject: L. and M. de Paor, *Early Christian Ireland* (London 1958); L. de Paor, 'Cormac's Chapel: the beginnings of Irish Romanesque', *North Munster Studies. Essays in commemoration of Mgr M. Moloney* (Limerick 1967) 133–47; L. de Paor, 'Excavations at Mellifont Abbey, co. Louth'. PRIA 68 Sect. C. (1969) 109–64; Françoise Henry, *Irish Art in the Romanesque period (1020–1170)* (London 1970).

The ecclesiastical implications of the Anglo-Norman Invasion and the establishment of the English colony in Ireland may be studied in: G. J. Hand, 'The Church and English Law in medieval Ireland' *PICHC* (1959) 10–18; J. A. Watt, 'English Law and the Irish Church: the reign of Edward I' *Gwynn Studies* (1961) 133–67; G. J. Hand, 'The Church in the English Lordship, 1216–1307' *HIC* 2.iii (1968); A. Gwynn, 'Anglo-Irish Church Life: Fourteenth and Fifteenth Centuries' *ibid.* 2.iv (1968); *Church and the Two Nations passim*.

The Church in Gaelic Ireland has been less systematically studied and indeed is not susceptible of quite the same depth of analysis as the Church in the colonial areas because of the more restricted range of source material. John Barry in *IER* 88–94 (1957–60) has given a lucid account of coarbs and erenaghs. See also K. Nicholls, 'Gaelic and Gaelicised Ireland in the Middle Ages' (*The Gill History of Ireland* 4) ch. 5. The most important work on the Church *inter Hibernicos* is that of Canice Mooney, a courageous 'warts and all' portrait by an experienced Gaelic scholar: 'The Church in Gaelic Ireland' *HIC* 2. v (1970).

There is need for a monograph on the relations of Ireland and the papacy in the middle ages. Among many articles on the *Laudabiliter* issue the following are outstanding: Kate Norgate, 'The bull *Laudabiliter*' *English Hist. Review*. 8 (1893) 18–52; J. F. O'Doherty, 'Rome and the Anglo-Norman Invasion of Ireland' *IER* 42 (1933) 131–45; M. P. Sheehy, 'The bull *Laudabiliter*: a problem in medieval *diplomatique* and history' *Galway Arch. Hist. Jn.* 29 (1961) 45–70. P. J. Dunning has made Innocent III and Ireland his especial preserve without as yet presenting his topic in synthetic form. Among his articles may be noted especially: 'Pope Innocent III and the Irish kings' *Jn. Eccles. History* 8 (1957) 17–32; 'Irish Representatives and Irish Ecclesiastical Affairs at the Fourth Lateran Council' *Gwynn Studies* 90–113. Some aspects of thirteenth and fourteenth-century Hiberno-papal relations are in my '*Laudabiliter* in medieval diplomacy and propaganda' *IER* 87 (1957) 420–32 and 'Negotiations between Edward II and John XXII concerning Ireland' *Irish Hist. Studies* 10 (1956–7) 1–20. Work on the fifteenth century has been largely confined to the question of provisions to benefices: U. G. Flanagan, 'Papal letters of the fifteenth century as a source for Irish history' *PICHC* (1958) 11–15; 'Papal Provisions in Ireland, 1305–78' *Hist. Studies* 3(1961) 92–103; R. D. Edwards, 'Conflict of papal and royal jurisdictions in fifteenth-century Ireland' *PICHC* (1960) 3–9; 'The kings of England and papal provisions in fifteenth-century Ireland' *Gwynn Studies* 265–80.

For the history of the episcopate in medieval Ireland, J. Ware- W. Harris, *The whole works . . .* vol. 1 *The history of the bishops . . .* (Dublin 1764) remains useful. Of Fr Gwynn's episcopal portraits, two are of especial distinction: 'Nicholas Mac Maol Iosa, archbishop of Armagh, 1272–1303' *Féilsgríbhinn E. Mhic Neill* (1940) 394–405; 'Richard Fitz Ralph, archbishop of Armagh' *Studies* 22–25 (1933–36). The development of the Irish diocesan system is succinctly described by Fr Gwynn, *Handbook of British Chronology* (ed. F. M. Powicke and E. B. Fryde, 2nd ed. (London 1961) 302–6. The chapter on Cathedrals in A. Gwynn and N. Hadcock, *Medieval Religious Houses: Ireland* (London 1970) should not be overlooked. Diocesan administration is examined in A. Gwynn and D. Gleeson, *A History of the Diocese of Killaloe* (Dublin 1962) and A. Gwynn, *The medieval province of Armagh, 1470–1545* (Dundalk 1946). But here, W. G. H. Quigley and E. F. D. Roberts, *Registrum Iohannis Mey* (1972) is a major advance. More studies of the type of A. J. Otway-Ruthven, 'The medieval church lands of co. Dublin' *Gwynn Studies* 54–73 are needed.

G. J. Hand has written important analyses of cathedral chapters: 'The medieval chapter of St Patrick's Cathedral, Dublin.1. The early period *c.*1219–*c.*1279' *Reportorium Novum* 3 (1961–4) 229–48; 'The rivalry of the cathedral chapters in medieval Dublin' *JRSAI* 92 (1962) 193–206; 'The medieval chapter of St Mary's, Limerick' *Gwynn Studies* 74–89. The basis for further study of parochial organisation has been supplied by D. F. Gleeson, 'The coarbs of Killaloe diocese' *JRSAI* 79 (1949) 160–9; A. J. Otway-Ruthven, 'Parochial development in the rural deanery of Skreen', *JRSAI* 94 (1964) 111–22; K. W. Nicholls, 'Rectory, vicarage and parish in the western Irish dioceses' *JRSAI* 101 (1970) 53–84.

The essential book for the history of the religious orders is A. Gwynn and R. N. Hadcock, *Medieval Religious Houses: Ireland* (London 1970), a mine of information, concisely and lucidly presented and including a most valuable map of monastic Ireland. Fr Colmcille Conway has written authoritatively, comprehensively and objectively about the medieval Cistercians: *The Story of Mellifont* (Dublin 1958); 'Sources for the history of the Irish Cistercians, 1142–1540' *PICHC* (1958) 16–23; 'Decline and attempted reform of the Irish Cistercians,

1445–1531' *Collectanea Ordinis Cisterciensium Reformatorum* 18 (1956) 290–305; 19 (1957) 146–62, 371–84. B. W. O'Dwyer, 'The conspiracy of Mellifont, 1216–1231' (Dublin Historical Association Pamphlet 1970) approaches this subject somewhat differently from *Church and the Two Nations* ch. 4. Fr B. O'Sullivan's articles on the Dominicans in *Irish Rosary* 52–62 (1948–53) merit publication in a more accessible form. E. B. Fitzmaurice and A. G. Little, *Materials for the history of the Franciscan province of Ireland, 1230–1450* (Manchester 1920) is fundamental. There is much of interest in C. Mooney, 'Franciscan architecture in pre-Reformation Ireland' *JRSAI* 85–87 (1955–57). F. X. Martin, 'The Augustinian friaries in pre-Reformation Ireland' *Augustiniana* 6 (1956) 346–84 is a model analysis. P. O'Dwyer, 'The Carmelite Order in pre-Reformation Ireland' *PICHC* (1968) 49–64 completes the coverage for the four orders of friars. The Canons have been less well served, though P. J. Dunning, 'The Arroasian Order in medieval Ireland' *Irish Hist. Studies* 4 (1944–5) 297–315 is important.

The standard architectural histories are: A. C. Champneys, *Irish Ecclesiastical Architecture* (reprint with introduction by L. de Paor, London 1970) and H. G. Leask, *Irish Churches and Monastic Buildings* 3 vols (Dundalk 1955–60). But these books merely whet the appetite and emphasise how much more remains to be done in Irish medieval ecclesiastical archaeology. A. Gwynn and D. F. Gleeson, *A History of the Diocese of Killaloe* (Dublin 1962) demonstrates what a major contribution the local historian has still to make to our understanding of the medieval Church in Ireland. See now also, E. Bolster, *A History of the Diocese of Cork* (Shannon 1972).

References

Chapter One

[1]K. Hughes, *The Church in early Irish society* (1966) ch. 24. This is a very important book.

[2]Original texts and discussion in my *Church and the Two Nations*, Appendix 1. (Cambridge 1970).

[3]Migne, *Patrologia Latina* 150, 536–7. The translation given here differs in some respects from that of A. Gwynn, 'Lanfranc and the Irish Church' *IER* 58 (1941) 11–13, on which, however, it is based.

[4]The original text has been published by S. H. O'Grady, *Irish Texts Society* 26, 174–5, with translation 27.185. Fr Gwynn's translation is in *IER* 66 (1945) 81–92; 67 (1946) 109–22.

[5]Cf. P. J. Dunning, 'The Arroasian Order in Medieval Ireland' *Irish Hist. Studies* 4 (1944–5) 297–315.

[6]Françoise Henry, *Irish Art in the Romanesque period* (1020–1170) (London 1970).

Chapter Two

[1]P. F. Moran 'Bull of Adrian IV' *IER* 9 (1872) 56.

[2]L. Weckman, *Las bulas Alejandrinas de 1493 y la teoría política del papado medieval. Estudio de la supremacía papal sobre islas, 1091–1493* (Mexico City, 1949) 37.

[3]*Historical Works* ed. W. Stubbs (Rolls Series 1879–80) 1.235.

[4]Text in Sheehy *Pontificia Hibernica* 1 no. 6. The translation is mine.

[5](Giraldus Cambrensis) *Expugnatio Hibernica* 2.19 RS *Opera* 5. 345–6.

Chapter Three

[1]R. W. Southern, *Western Society and the Church in the Middle Ages* (1970) 244.

[2]The translation is that of A. Gwynn and R. N. Hadcock, *Medieval Religious Houses: Ireland* (1970) 206.

[3]Translation by Colmcille Conway, *The Story of Mellifont* (Dublin 1958) 10.

[4]*Registrum epistolarum Stephani de Lexington* ed. B. Griesser, *Analecta s.o. Cisterciencis* 2 (1946) 95, 52. Cf. *Church and the Two Nations*, 101–3, 106.

[5]*Regestum Monasterii fratrum praedicatorum de Athenry* ed. A. Coleman, *Archiv. Hib.* 1 (1912) 201–21.

[6]Sheehy, *Pont. Hib.* 2. 421. My translation.

[7] Translation by B. O'Sullivan, 'Medieval Irish Dominican Studies' *Irish Rosary* 53 (1949) 156.

[8]The Eccleston translations are by L. Sherley-Price, *The coming of the Franciscans: Thomas of Eccleston. De adventu Fratrum Minorum in Anglia* (London 1964).

[9]*Liber exemplorum ad usum praedicantium* ed. A. G. Little (*Brit. Soc. Francisc. Stud.* reprint 1966) pp. 85–6.

[10]Fitzmaurice-Little, *Franciscan Materials* 63–4. My translation.

[11]*Calendar of Ormond Deeds* vol. 1, ed. E. Curtis (Dublin 1932) n. 575. My translation.

Chapter Four

[1]*Cal. doc. Ire.* 1 no. 364 (5 Dec. 1207). My translation is from the full text in *Rot. litt. claus. 1204–27* ed. T. D. Hardy (Rec. Comm. 1835) 97.

[2]Translated texts in *Cal. patent rolls. 1216–25*, 22–3, 27.

[3]Sheehy, *Pont. Hib.* 1. 140. My translation.

[4]Text with translation, C. R. Cheney and W. H. Semple, *Selected Letters of Pope Innocent III concerning England, 1198–1216* (1953) no. 76 at p. 200.

[5]G. J. Hand, 'The Church in the English Lordship 1216–1307 *HIC* 2. iii (1968) 39.

[6]Sheehy, *Pont. Hib.* 1 p. 172.

[7]*The Fasti of St Patrick's, Dublin* (Dundalk 1930) 1.

[8]*The 'Dignitas Decani' of St Patrick's Cathedral, Dublin* ed. N.B. White (1957) p. 82.

Chapter Five

[1]There is a translation of the Remonstrance by C. McNeill in Curtis and McDowell, *Irish Historical Documents* (1943) 38–46.

²A. Theiner, *Vetera monumenta . . .* ep. 433.

³I owe much of the information in the following paragraphs to the generosity of Mr A. P. Wells (Hull University) whose edition of the Sapiti registers is almost completed.

⁴E. Perroy, *L'Angleterre et le grand schisme d'Occident* (Paris 1933) 399, 403.

⁵*De rebus a se gestis, Opera* 1 (Rolls Series 1861) 65–72.

⁶Text in A. Gwynn, *Archiv. Hib.* 11 (1944) 42. My translation.

⁷*Vita S. Patricii. Acta sancta sanctorum* (March t. 2) § 154 pp. 572–3.

⁸Cf. C. R. Cheney, 'A group of related synodal statutes of the thirteenth century' *Gwynn Studies* 114–32.

⁹A. Gwynn, 'The Black Death in Ireland' *Studies* 24 (1935) 31.

¹⁰A. Gwynn, 'Richard Fitzralph, archbishop of Armagh'. *Studies* 25 (1936) 94–5.

Chapter Six

¹Cf. G. V. Jourdan, *Hist. Church Ire.* ed. W. A. Phillips, 177–86.

²Genealogies, somewhat different in detail, in C. Mooney, 'Church in Gaelic Ireland' *HIC* 57–60 and K. W. Nicholls, *Gaelic and Gaelicised Ireland* 93–5.

³*Cal. papal reg.* 14 (1484–92) 60–1.

⁴*Ibid.* 215–6.

⁵Based primarily on Gwynn-Hadcock, *Med. rel. houses Ire.* Inevitably there are some uncertainties about the dates and circumstances of many of these foundations.

⁶Very imperfectly edited by W. M. Brady, *Clerical and Parochial records of Cork, Cloyne and Ross* vol. 3 (1864) 319–23 and J. Coleman, *Bibliographical Society of Ireland* 2 (1925) 111–20.

⁷Shakespeare, *King John* 3, 3.

⁸'Archives of the Municipal Corporation of Waterford' ed. J. T. Gilbert *Hist. MSS. Comm.* 10th Rpt. Appendix pt 5 (1885) 293; see also p. 330 for the case of a citizen who gave them lodging going to prison.

⁹W. Heuser, *Die Kildare-Gedichte* (Bonn 1904) pp. 106, 93.

¹⁰The text of the *Ignorantia sacerdotum* has been reedited by C. R. Cheney in *Councils and synods with other documents relating to the English Church.* II. pt. II 1265–1313 (Oxford 1964) 900–05.

¹¹L. McKenna, *Dáta Philip Bhoicht O Huiginn* (Dublin 1931) pp. 169, 192. Fr McKenna's *Dán Dé. The poems of Donnchadh Mór Ó Dálaigh and the religious poems in the Duanaire of the Yellow Book of Lecan* (Dublin n.d.) should also be consulted for an analysis of the content of this poetry. For a more sympathetic interpretation, cf. J. E. Murphy, 'The religious mind of the Irish bards', *Féilsgríbhinn E. Mhic Néill* (1940) 82–6.

Index

acceptio personarum 104–5
Achonry, diocese of 135, 146–7
advowson 209, 218
Amalarius of Metz 12
Annaghdown, diocese of 46, 146–7
Annals 13, 43, 66, 78–9, 94, 97, 133, 134, 185, 186, 211
Anselm, St 4, 5, 7, 8, 9, 10, 90
Ardagh, diocese of 24, 96, 108, 133
Ardfert, diocese of 65, 103, 109, 112, 122
Armagh, diocese and province of 9, 10, 11, 13, 14, 15, 16, 20, 23, 24, 65, 66, 79, 87, 94, 95–6, 97, 98, 99, 100, 101–2, 106, 108, 109, 113, 133, 141, 145, 150, 161–71, 176–80, 182, 185, 193, 203–7
Arrouaise 21–2, 46, 49, 50, 122
Augustinian Canons 16, 21–3, 43, 45–49, 186–7, 193
Augustinian Friars 60, 71, 86, 195–7

Barry, Philip de 62
bards and religious poetry 212–4
Bede, St 4, 13
Benedictines 41, 42, 46, 47, 115, 122
benefit of clergy 8, 173–4, 218
Bermingham family 62, 198
Bernard, St 15–18, 20, 21–3, 42, 43, 45, 49, 52
Bible 201–2
Bruce, Edward 80, 139, 140
Burgh family 48, 50

Cambrensis, Giraldus 30, 32–3, 35–6, 152–4
canon law 8, 27, 29, 131–3
Canterbury 1, 2, 3, 4, 5, 8, 10, 15, 29–30, 108, 158, 170, 193
Canterbury, Gervase of 34
Carmelite Order 60, 71, 85–86, 193
Cashel, diocese and province of 12, 13, 15, 16, 20, 23, 24, 62, 65, 87, 98, 99, 100, 104, 108, 109, 110, 111, 112–16, 134, 141, 145, 169, 170, 193

Cashel, Rock of 8, 18, 26, 115
Chapters, cathedral 100–1, 106–7, 107, 110–11, 123–7, 218
Chedworth, Thomas of 124
Cistercian Order 17, 20–1, 41–59, 62, 114, 115, 187–8, 193
Clare, Richard de 34
Clarendon, Constitutions of 90–1, 105
Clogher, diocese of 13, 24, 96, 108, 179, 185–6
Clonard, monastery and diocesan centre 11, 22, 24, 46, 94, 98, 134
Clonfert, diocese of 13, 27, 46, 48, 76, 108, 135, 189–90
Clonmacnois, diocese of 11, 13, 15, 46, 48, 73, 76, 96, 108
Cloyne, diocese of 65, 104, 109, 114, 142, 145
coarbs 9, 15, 16, 19, 87, 209
Columban monasticism 19
Concordia discordantium canonum 131
Cong 11, 14, 46, 97
Connacht 13, 14, 15, 46, 49, 64, 76, 85, 86, 91, 94, 96, 97, 137, 194
Connor, diocese of 13, 16, 24, 92, 94, 109, 203
Cork, diocese of 13, 84, 99, 109, 113, 122, 142, 145
Cotton, Bartholomew of 78
councils, diocesan and provincial:
    Armagh (1170) 35
    Athlone (1202) 95, 97, 133
    Cashel I (1101) 1, 7, 8–9, 12, 29
    Cashel II (1171–72) 33, 35, 89, 100, 105, 122, 132, 152, 172
    Clonfert (1172?) 97
    Drogheda (1411) 162–4, 166
    Dublin (1084) 7
    Dublin (1186) 152–7
    Dublin (1192) 157
    Dublin (1202) 94, 133
    Dublin (1217) 157
    Dublin (c.1320) 160
    Dublin (1352) 160
    Inis Pádraig (1148) 23

Kells-Mellifont (1152) 24–26, 29–30, 87, 112, 122
Kilkenny (1366) 160–1
Lambeth (1281) 210
Mellifont (Drogheda 1157) 43
Mullingar (1205?) 96
Rathbreasail (1111) 10–12, 14, 18, 29
Trim (1291) 178
Waterford (1173–4) 30, 33
councils, general:
Lateran III, 132
Lateran IV 120–1, 132, 150, 163
Lyons I 135
Lyons II 66–7
Vienne 141
Courcy, John de 47, 92, 94, 122, 154
courts, ecclesiastical 171–5, 204–8
Croagh Patrick 211
Culdees 205, 219

Dair-Inis 24
Declaration of Arbroath 80–1
De pauperie Salvatoris 167
De statu ecclesiae 11–12
Decretales 96, 131, 132–3, 151, 219
Defensorium curatorum 168
Derry 11, 19, 24, 41, 65, 66, 108, 109
Desmond 15, 18
Dominican Order 47, 60–68, 71, 73, 86, 193, 197–8
Drogheda 60, 62, 95, 162, 168, 207
Dromiskin 176
Down 13, 16, 19, 22, 24, 47, 79, 87, 92, 109, 122, 203
Dromore, diocese of 24, 108, 109, 192–3
Dublin, diocese and province of 1, 2, 8, 14, 40, 87, 92, 94, 109, 110, 112, 114, 116–29, 141, 145, 152, 193
Dublin, Holy Trinity cathedral 22, 122–3, 128, 152
St Mary's abbey 21, 42, 51, 52, 62, 97, 112, 188
St Patrick's cathedral 122–5, 128, 129, 135, 171
Duleek 24
Dungarvan 99
Dunkeld 127

Eadmer 4
Eccleston, Thomas of 69–70, 73–4
eiríc 205
Elphin, diocese of 15, 191–2
Emly, diocese of 11, 13, 103, 109, 115, 175

English law and the Irish Church 91–3, 105–6, 172–8, 183. See Kilkenny, Statute of
English law, request of the Irish for 115–6
erenaghs 9, 209, 219
excommunication 159, 160, 161, 162, 164, 168, 170, 171, 178, 180, 204

Ferns, diocese of 13, 26, 99, 112
Fratres Cruciferi, see Holy Cross, order of
Francis, St 69, 78
Franciscan Order 47, 60, 63, 69–84, 85, 169–70, 193, 195, 200–2, 217
Third Order of Penance 193, 199–200
freedom (liberty) of the Church 8, 35, 156, 159, 162, 180, 220
Furness, Jocelin of 154–5

Gilbert of Limerick 10–12, 18, 29
Glendaloch 11, 24, 26, 41, 120–1, 161
Gratian 131
Great Schism 149–50

Havering, John and Richard of 124, 127
Holy Cross, Order of 47
Holy Land 74, 135
Howden, Roger of 92

Ibracense, 18
Ignorantia sacerdotum, 210–11
interdict 168, 219

Kells, monastery and diocesan centre 11, 24, 96
Kells, John of 177
Kildare, diocese of 73, 78, 124, 145
Kilfenora, diocese of 109
Kilkenny, statute of 84, 116, 149, 183, 216
parliament at (1310) 79, 116, 160
Killala, diocese of 13, 65, 135
Killaloe, diocese of 13, 99, 100, 101, 102, 103–4, 108, 109, 115, 132
Kilmainham 49
Kilmacduagh, diocese of 64, 146
Kilmore, diocese of 24, 108, 109
Kings of England:
Edward I 79, 108, 109, 110, 118, 124, 148, 176, 178
Edward II 81, 127, 128, 140, 141, 143, 148
Edward III 128, 143, 146
Henry I 90

Henry II 28, 29, 30, 31, 34–39, 48, 90, 91, 92, 99, 117, 120, 215
Henry III 70, 100, 107, 113, 114, 118, 124, 135
Henry VI 184
Henry VIII 181
John 33, 62, 92, 94, 95, 96, 98, 99–100, 105, 112, 113, 126, 137
Richard II 148
Knights Hospitallers 48, 49
Knights Templars 49

laity 153, 156, 159–60, 163, 202–14
Lanfranc 1, 2, 3, 4, 5, 7, 8, 9, 10
Leighlin, diocese of 13, 26, 92, 94, 112
lex marchie 165, 166
Lexington, Stephen of 54–59, 83, 114, 115, 215
Liber Niger 125
Libri exemplorum 75, 77–8
Limerick, diocese of 3, 10, 13, 62, 65, 87, 92, 98–9, 103, 107, 109, 114, 122, 175
Lismore, monastery and diocese of 11, 13, 16, 18, 65, 98, 109, 132, 142
Lough Derg 186, 187, 211

Mac Carthy family 15, 18, 42
Mac Dunlevy, Niall 16, 46
Mac Flynn, Florence 64, 138
Mc Gallogly, Art 64
Mac Guiness, Niallan 164
Mac Mahon, Brian 179
Mac Namara, Mac Con 200
Maghera 24
Magna Carta 105
Malachy, St 15–26, 29, 45–6, 52, 87, 95, 155
marriage law 6, 7, 8, 9, 24, 27, 38, 153, 156, 159–60, 206–8
Marsh, Geoffrey 102–3, 106, 117
Marshal, William 47, 94, 100–2, 106, 113, 117; William the Younger 62
Mayo 97, 133
Meath, diocese of 24, 65, 73, 87, 92, 95, 98, 109, 122, 134, 145, 177–8, 182–3, 203
Meath, kingdom of 14; lordship of 94
Meditationes vitae Christi 212
Meelick 48
Mellifont 20–2, 43–5, 52–9, 95, 115, 188

New Ross 47
Norris, Philip 171
Nottingham, William of 74
nuns 22, 46, 47, 199

Observant movement (Friars) 193–9
O Brien family 1, 5, 7, 8, 12, 13, 15, 62, 110
O Carroll, Donal 19, 20, 43–4, 46
O Connor family 14, 18, 46, 64, 91, 97, 132
O Donnell, Donal 65
O Duffy, Donal Mac Flannacan 15
O Hagan, Imar 15, 29
O Heyne, Eugenius 64
O Kelly, Cornelius 64
O Loughlin Connor family 18, 43, 46
Oriel 19, 46, 179
O Neill family 79, 80, 165, 179, 204, 205, 206
O Toole, St Laurence 22, 29, 42, 46, 87, 92, 122, 126, 132
Ossory, diocese of 92, 94, 124

papacy, relationship with Ireland 1, 8, 24, 27, 28–40, 103–6, 130–50, 188–3
papal legates 8, 10, 23, 24, 29, 39, 40, 43, 103–4, 112, 113, 117, 120–1, 132–5, 219
names:
Christian O Conarchy 20, 29, 34, 42–3
James 104, 113, 132, 134
Limerick, Gilbert of 10–12, 18, 29
London, Henry of 62, 99, 101–4, 113, 117, 123, 126
Malachy, St *see* Malachy
O Doonan, Maol Muire 8, 10, 12
O Heney, Matthew 110–11, 112, 132
O Toole, Laurence, St *see* O Toole
Paparo, Cardinal John 24, 120, 132
Salerno, Cardinal John of 94–6, 120, 132
Vivian, Cardinal 39, 132
papal letters:
Celebri fama, 37
Clericis laicos, 179, 202
Exiit qui seminat 75
Laudabiliter 30–4, 37, 139–40
Omnis utriusque sexus 163, 166, 169, 170
Ordinem vestrum 74
Quoniam ea 33
Regnans in excelsis 171
Super cathedram 167, 169
Vas electionis 169, 170
papal *nuntii* 134–5, 219

parishes 208–9, 218
Patrick, St 9, 15, 19, 28, 125, 205
pilgrimage 204, 211
Popes:
    Adrian IV 28, 29, 30, 33, 139
    Alexander II 4
    Alexander III 30, 33, 36–39, 111
    Alexander IV 65–6, 86
    Alexander V 171
    Alexander VI 189
    Boniface VIII 75, 127, 131, 135, 179, 202
    Calixtus III 171
    Clement III 132
    Clement V 74, 127, 131, 138, 143
    Clement VI 164, 182
    Clement VII 149, 150
    Eugenius IV 171, 185, 200
    Gregory I 13, 150
    Gregory VII 1, 29
    Gregory IX 54, 98, 131
    Gregory XI 138, 170
    Honorius III 8, 98, 103–4, 107, 110, 113, 117, 121
    Innocent II 20, 23
    Innocent III 8, 26, 33, 40, 50, 91, 92, 95, 97, 98, 105, 112, 113, 120–1, 126, 132–3, 134, 136, 137
    Innocent IV 74, 86, 111, 113, 114, 135
    Innocent VI 168
    Innocent VIII 189
    John XXII 81, 131, 139, 140, 141, 142, 143, 148, 166, 169, 170
    Lucius III 39, 92
    Nicholas III 75, 118, 126
    Nicholas IV 75
    Nicholas V 200
    Pius II 200
    Sixtus IV 190
    Urban II 33
    Urban III 152
    Urban VI 148, 149
Pouilly, John of 169, 170, 171
Premonstratensian canons 47, 48, 49, 50–2
primacy of Ireland 2–5, 128, 220
primogenita pecudum 205

Raphoe, diocese of 24, 65, 66, 108, 109
Remonstrance of the Irish Princes 79, 80–1, 139–40, 166
Roscommon 15, 46, 64, 65
Ross, diocese of 73, 109, 112, 122
Rudyard, William de 82–4, 124

sacraments 7, 8, 16, 17, 35, 152–3, 159, 162–3, 166, 211
St Patrick's Purgatory 204, 211
St Thomas of Acon, Order of 48, 49
Salisbury 123, 125, 198
Salisbury, John of 24, 28, 32–3
Sapiti, Andrew 143–6
Sarum rite 125
Savigny 16, 19, 21, 42, 46, 49
Scot, Michael 113
Scotland 67, 73, 133, 149
Sentences, of Peter Lombard 202
Simony 6, 7, 8, 24
Sitric 2
Somercote, Laurence 135
Stock, St Simon 85
Strongbow 34, 126
Summa de casibus conscientie 202

termon lands 209, 220
Termonfeckin 46, 176, 208
Thomond, 15, 62
Tickhill, Humphrey of 95
Tiron 16
tithe 24, 35, 159, 220
Torigny, Robert of 30
Trim 24, 94, 98, 122, 134, 178
Trinitarians 49
Troy, John 187–8, 192
Tuam, diocese and province of 13, 27, 91, 95, 96, 97–8, 108, 122, 133, 137, 141, 145, 146–7, 182, 185, 193

Ui Sinaich 9, 15, 18, 19, 95, 97
Universities:
    Bologna 131
    Cambridge 68
    Dublin 127–9, 131
    Oxford 54, 58, 62, 68, 128, 129, 171, 184, 186
    Paris 54, 58, 68, 75, 118, 131, 171

Venenum Malachie 76

Waterford, diocese and town of 3, 8, 16, 62, 87, 91, 92, 98, 99, 103, 104, 109, 134, 142, 177, 178, 184, 205
Wexford 48
Winchester 3, 16, 29
Windsor, council of 91
Worcester 3
Wulfstan, St 3

York 4, 45, 158, 193, 220